Bar|

MW01061981

From working-class dreamer on the cobbled streets of Yorkshire to one of the world's most successful authors on the sweeping avenues of Manhattan, the rise of Barbara Taylor Bradford is by any standard extraordinary.

In this incredible story of suffering, loss and triumph over adversity, fact and fiction proceed side by side in a unique collaboration, the first time that Taylor Bradford has participated in a memoir of any kind, and one that has turned out to be as much a revelation to her as it will certainly be to her readers.

'Astonishing… A fascinating and obsessively close look at one of the great rags-to-riches stories of our time.' *Sunday Express*

'A woman of Real substance: the amazing story of how Barbara Taylor Bradford discovered she was the secret grandchild of a philandering aristocrat.' *The Mail on Sunday*

'Enthralling – a story no less gripping than any of her blockbusters.' *You Magazine*

'Dudgeon is a fine writer with a dogged determination to find out what makes his subject tick.' *The Glasgow Herald*

About the Author

Piers Dudgeon is a publisher and the author of more than thirty books of non-fiction. He worked for ten years as an editor in London before starting his own company, publishing authors as diverse as Daphne du Maurier, John Fowles, Peter Ackroyd, Ted Hughes, Giovanni Guareschi, Angus Stewart and Susan Hill, and writing a number of books celebrating the spirit of place, including *Dickens' London: An Imaginative Vision, The Spirit of Britain: A Guide to Literary Britain and The Country Child: Intimations of Immortality.*

In 1993 he left London for Yorkshire, where he wrote biographies of Catherine Cookson, Maeve Binchy, Barbara Taylor Bradford, J M Barrie and the Du Maurier family, the lateral thinker Edward de Bono and the composer Sir John Tavener, as well as a series of oral histories of Glasgow, Liverpool and London's East End, and the annual Virgin Alternative Guide to British Universities.

In 2020, the American rights in his 2005 biography of Barbara Taylor Bradford (originally entitled *Barbara Taylor Bradford: The Woman of Substance)* fell free and he took the opportunity to revise and reissue the paperback edition and, for the first time, make it available as an e-book throughout the world.

BARBARA TAYLOR BRADFORD

The Biography

PIERS DUDGEON

PILOT PRODUCTIONS

Published by Pilot Productions in 2020
Grove Farm Sawdon, North Yorkshire YO13 9DY

A catalogue record for this book is available
from the British Library

Paperback ISBN 9781900064538

Typesetting and E-book conversion
by www.epubknowhow.co.uk

Cover design by BerniStevensdesign.com

Cover photograph of Barbara Taylor Bradford by Cris Alexander,
by kind permission of Ralph Crocker, Saratoga County, NY 12833, USA

Contents

Photographs

Numbers inserted in the main text, as [1] etc, indicate picture subjects.

1   St Mary's Hospital, sometime Workhouse where Barbara was born
2   Armley's rows of terraced housing where her father's family lived
3   Barbara, 'ironed from top to toe' at 3
4   Her parents, Winston and Freda Taylor
5   Tower Lane where as a little girl Barbara's imagination took flight
6   Christ Church School, which she attended with Alan Bennett
7   Christ Church itself where Barbara worshipped every Sunday
8   The Towers, where Emma Harte would live, seemed to a child's eye to reach to the sky
9   No. 38, the end house of three, the humble home where Barbara first lived
10 The moor she felt sure led to the Top of the World
11 Winston's local, where he was when he wasn't where he should be
12 Top Withens, Barbara's introduction to the Brontës
13 Ripon Minster defined the city's role to provide for the poor
14 The Market Place, hub of life for rich and poor these thousand years
15 The roofless halls and ghostly chambers of Middleham Castle
16 Water Skellgate as Edith knew it in 1904
17 Studley Royal Hall, where Edith dreamt her destiny lay

PART I
CHAPTER ONE
The Party

'The ambience in the dining room was decidedly romantic, had an almost fairytale quality... The flickering candlelight, the women beautiful in their elegant gowns and glittering jewels, the men handsome in their dinner jackets, the conversation brisk, sparkling, entertaining...'

Voice of the Heart

In November 2002, the Bradfords generously arranged a dinner party for me at their elegant fourteen-room apartment, which occupies the sixth floor of a 1930s landmark building overlooking Manhattan's East River. It was an opportunity to meet some of their friends and enjoy Barbara's legendary hospitality, the fruits of her success.

The approach to the apartment by means of a grand ground-floor entrance lobby is classical in style, with massive wall-recessed urns, red-silk *chaise longues* and busy uniformed porters gliding over black marble floors.

A mahogany-lined lift delivers the visitor directly to the front door of the apartment, which, on the evening of the party, lay open, leaving me suddenly surprised by the gaze of the already gathered.

I am met by the Bradfords' butler, Mohammed, aptly named spiriter away of material effects – coats, hats, and in my case a gift, a jar of heather honey, worked by my bees on Barbara's Yorkshire moor.

My hostess arrives and we move swiftly through a cocktail bar to the drawing room, positioned centrally between dining room and library, an enfilade offering a magnificent view over the huge breadth of the East River, where a full moon casts its silvery light over a clear night sky and adds a touch of mystery to a ruined asylum on an island directly opposite.

Within, the immediate impression is one of splendour – spacious rooms, picture windows, high ceilings and crystal chandeliers. Oak-wood floors bestrewn with antique carpets, silk draperied chairs and, as readers of Barbara's novels would expect, a European mix of Biedermeier and Art Deco furniture meet tall silk-upholstered walls hung with Venetian mirrors and Impressionist paintings.

It was here that Allison Pearson came to interview Barbara in 1999, and, swept up in the glamour of so privileged a vantage point, took the tack that it is 'easy to forget that there is a world down there, a world full of pain and ugliness', while at the same time wanting some of what Barbara has: 'Any journalist going to see Barbara Taylor Bradford in New York,' she wrote, 'will find herself asking the question I asked myself, craning my neck and staring up at the north face of the author's mighty apartment building. What has this one-time cub reporter on the *Yorkshire Evening Post* got that I haven't?' Allison's answer: 'Well, about $600 million,' kept the burden of her question at bay.

Champagne and cocktails are made available. People know one another and are immediately welcoming. It is a fluid scene, people swim in and out of view. I slip away and notice a woman alone on the far side of the library looking out through a side window, apparently at an adjacent apartment block, more severe – stark even – than this one.

'I used to live there,' she explains her interest. 'My neighbour was Greta Garbo ... until she died.'

'And now?' I venture, digesting the information that this was where the greatest of all screen goddesses finally found it possible *to be alone*, or might have done had it not been for her friend.

'In Switzerland and the South of France,' she replies. 'New York only for the winter months.'

There then follows the *faux pas* of the evening: 'What on earth do you do?'

With perfect timing Barbara swoops to rescue the lady and makes a full introduction. Garbo's friend turns out to be Rex Harrison's widow, Mercia. She does not *do*. But no matter, it seems that I have opened up the library; people follow Barbara in. I find myself being introduced to the comedienne the late Joan Rivers and fashion designer Arnold Scaasi, whose history Barbara peppers with names such as Liz Taylor, Natalie Wood, Joan Crawford, Candice Bergen, Barbra Streisand, Joan Rivers of course, and, as of now, Laura Bush, wife of the President.[1]

It is November 2002 and talk turns naturally to Bob Woodward's just published *Bush at War*, which I am told will help establish George Bush as the greatest president of all time.[2] I am asked my opinion. I know they are Republicans and have already caught sight of a photograph of Barbara and Bob with the President on the campaign trail. I limit myself to saying that I can empathise with the shock and hurt of 'September 11' – I knew an English girl, daughter of friends of my father, who died in the disaster, but war seems old-fashioned, so primitive a solution, I mutter. Barbara recues me again, confessing that she makes it a rule never to talk politics with her close friend Diahn McGrath, a lawyer and staunch Democrat, to whom she at once directs me.

Barbara is the perfect host, this pre-dinner hour the complete introduction that will allow me to relax at the dinner table, even to contribute a little. There's a former publisher, one Parker Ladd, with the demeanour of a Somerset Maugham, or possibly a Noel Coward (Barbara's Champagne is good), who tells me he is a friend of Ralph Fields, the first person to give me rein in book publishing, and who turns out – to my amazement – still to be alive. So, even in the midst of this Manhattan scene I find myself comfortable anchorage not only in contact through Barbara with our home county of Yorkshire, but in fond memories of the publishing scene. It was not at all what I had expected to find.

---

[1] Barbara was a friend of Laura Bush, wife of President George W Bush. She and her husband Bob Bradford were regular visitors to the White House.

[2] *Bush at War* (2002) concerns President Bush's response to the 9/11 attacks on America in September 2001 and the subsequent war in Afghanistan.

I am led in to dinner by a woman introduced to me as Edwina Kaplan, a sculptor and painter whose husband is an architect, but who talks heatedly (and at the time quite inexplicably) about tapes she has discovered of Winston Churchill's war-time speeches. Would people be interested? she wonders. Later I would see a couple of her works on Barbara's walls, but for some reason nobody thought it pertinent until the following day to explain that Edwina was Sir Winston's granddaughter, Edwina Sandys. Churchill, of course, is one of Barbara's heroes; in her childhood she contributed to his wife Clementine's 'Aid to Russia' fund and still has one of her letters, now framed in the library.

The table, set for fourteen, is exquisite, its furniture dancing to the light of a generously decked antique crystal chandelier. The theme is red, from the walls to the central floral display through floral napkin rings to what seems to be a colourful china zoo occupying the few spaces left by the flower-bowls, crystal tableware and place settings. Beautifully crafted porcelain elephants and giraffes peek out from between silver water receptacles and cut-glass goblets of every conceivable size and design.

There are named place cards and I begin to hunt for mine. I am last to find one and settle down. As soon as I do, Barbara erupts – she had specially chosen a white rose for my napkin ring – the White Rose of Yorkshire – which is lying on the plate of my neighbour to the right. Someone has switched my placement card! Immediately I wonder whether the culprit has made the switch to be near me or to avoid me, but as I settle, and the white rose is restored, my neighbour to the left leaves me in no doubt that I am particularly welcome. She tells me that she is a divorce lawyer, a role of no small importance in the marital chess games of the Manhattan wealthy. How many around this table might she have served?

I reach for the neat vodka that had caught my eye in the smallest stem of my glass cluster, turning our conversation to Barbara and her husband, the film maker Bob Bradford, soon realising that here, around this table, among their friends, are the answers to so many questions I have for my subject's Manhattan years. I set to work, both on my left and to my right, where I find Nancy Evans, Barbara's former publisher at the mighty Doubleday in the mid-1980s.

By this time we have progressed from the caviar and smoked salmon to the couscous and lamb, and Barbara deems it time to widen our perspectives. It would be the first of two calls to order, a party game to introduce everyone to everyone. Hardly a necessity, I think, except in my case. Thumbnail sketches of each participant, edged devilishly with in-group barb, court ripostes and laughter, but it was only when she came around the table and settled on me, mentioning the words 'guest of honour' that I realised for the first time that I was to be the star turn. I needn't have worried; there was at least one other special guest in Joan Rivers and she more than made up for my sadly unimaginative response.

Barbara tells me that Joan is very 'in' with Prince Charles: 'She greets me with, "I've just come back from a painting trip ... with Prince Charles." A friend of hers, Robert Higdon, runs the Prince's Trust. Joan is very involved with that, giving them money. So she was there with Charles and Camilla and the Forbses at some château somewhere. She always says, "Prince Charles likes me a lot; he always laughs at my jokes." But Joan is actually a very ladylike creature when she is off the stage, where she can be a bit edgy sometimes. In real life she is very sweet and she loves me and Bob.'

Now Joan is deftly egging Arnold Scaasi on as he heaps compliments on Barbara loudly from the far end of the table. At the very height of his paean of praise, the comedienne rejoins that Arnold's regard for his hostess is clearly so great that he will no doubt wish to make one of his new creations a gift to her. The designer's face is a picture as he realises he has walked straight into a game at his expense, one in which the very ethos of celebrity Manhattan is at stake. The table applauds his generosity, while Arnold begins an interminable descent into get-out: …he does not have the multifarious talents of Joan, alas, to allow such generosity; he cannot eat publicity, etc, etc.

I felt I was being drawn in to Bob and Barbara's private world. When we first met I had said to her that I would need to be so, and she began the process that night. After cheese and dessert, coffee and liqueurs are served in the drawing room and one after another of her guests offer themselves for interview.

The evening reminded me of the glittering birthday party in the Bavarian ski resort of Konigsee in Barbara's novel, *Voice of the Heart*. The table setting was remarkably similar – the candlelight and bowls of flowers that 'march down the centre of the table', interspersed with 'Meissen porcelain birds in the most radiant of colours', the table itself 'set with the finest china, crystal and silver... The flickering candlelight, the women beautiful in their elegant gowns and glittering jewels, the men handsome in their dinner jackets...', and the conversation 'brisk, sparkling, entertaining...' I will never forget the evening, not least because it gave scale to the nature of Barbara's incredible rise in the world.

CHAPTER TWO
Barbara

"'Go back to your fancy woman!" I heard those words as a child. That happened when I was little. I remembered it and I did ask Grandma Taylor, "What's a fancy woman?"'

Barbara was born on 10th May 1933 to Winston and Freda Taylor in what is today St Mary's Hospital, a short walk from her first home at 38 Tower Lane, Upper Armley, a suburb of Leeds. A map dated the year of Barbara's birth still carries the hospital's original name, 'Bramley Union Workhouse', Bramley being the next 'village' to the west of Armley. The Local Government Act of 1929 had empowered all local authorities to convert workhouse infirmaries to general hospitals. [1]

As the crow flies, Armley is little more than a mile and a half west of the centre of Leeds, which is the capital of the North of England. Straddling the River Aire, which, with the Aire & Calder Navigation (the Leeds canal), helped sustain its once great manufacturing past, Leeds is positioned at the north end of the M1, Britain's first motorway, and is roughly equidistant between London and Edinburgh.

The Manor of Armley, and that of Wortley on the south side of Tong Road, appear in the *Domesday Book* of 1086 as Ermelai and Ristone. Together they were valued at ten shillings, which was half what they had been worth before the Normans had devastated the North in 1069. In William the Conqueror's great survey of England, Armley is described as comprising six *carucates* of taxable land for ploughing[3], six acres of meadow and a wood roughly one mile by three quarters of a mile in area. The second syllable of its name, '-ley', holds the secret of its rural beginnings. It means 'open place in a wood'. Armley was once but a clearing in forest land. Barbara recalls: 'Even in the 1930s this was the edge of Leeds. There were a lot of open spaces … little moors (so called), fields, playing fields for football, as well as parks, such as Gott's Park and Armley Park.' There is still a fair today on Armley Moor, close to where she first went to school: 'Every September the fair or "feast" came, with carousels, stalls, candy floss, etc. We all went there when we were children.'

The village came into its own in the 18th century thanks to one Benjamin Gott, who was *the* outstanding figure among the Leeds woollen textile manufacturers of the Industrial Revolution. Gott was born in 1762, a few miles to the west in Woodall. At eighteen, he was apprenticed to the leading Leeds cloth merchant, Wormald and Fountaine. By 1800 the Fountaine family had bowed out and in 1816 the Wormald family sold up too. Just how far all this was down to manoeuvring on the part of the acquisitive Gott does not come down to us. What is clear is that long before the firm was re-named Benjamin Gott & Sons it was his energy that made it the most successful woollen textile firm in England.

Gott's mills – Bean Ing on the bank of the Aire and a second one in Armley itself – brought railway terminals, factories and rows of terraced houses for the workers, so that Armley was already an important industrial force by the mid-nineteenth century and the whole area was covered in a pall of smoke, not the bucolic idyll that Barbara often likes to suppose. [2] So bad was the pollution in Armley that as early as 1823 Gott was taken to court over it. However, at his trial, the judge concluded that 'in such a place as Leeds, which flourishes in consequence of these nuisances, some inconveniences are to be expected.'

---

[3] One carucate equated to the amount of land eight oxen could till in a season, and was named after the heavy carucate (or carrucate) plough introduced by the Vikings in the 9th century.

Encouragements such as this made Gott a rich man. He bought Armley lock, stock and smoky barrel, built himself a big house there and hung it with his European art collection. Like many Victorian entrepreneurs, he was a philanthropist – he built a school and almshouses, organised worker pensions and gave to the Church's pastoral work in the area. After he died in 1840, two sons carried on the business, made some improvements to the mill, but refused to compromise the quality of their high-grade cloths and take advantage of the ready-made clothing industry, which burgeoned after 1850, preferring instead to exercise their main interest as art and rare-book collectors. Inevitably their markets shrank. When one of the next generation of Gotts left for the priesthood, parts of Bean Ing were leased and by 1897 the entire building was rented out.

William Ewart Gott, the third-generation son who stayed in Armley, is lambasted by David Kallinski in Barbara's first novel, *A Woman of Substance* (1979[4]), for having built statues and fountains rather than helping the poor, although in fact he provided the land for the foundation in 1872 of Christ Church, Armley, where Barbara was christened, received her first Communion and attended service every Sunday, going to Sunday School there as well. Gott gave towards the building of it and appointed its first vicar, the Reverend J. Thompson, who served a longer term (thirteen years) than any vicar since.

Barbara likes to say that she was 'born to ordinary parents in an ordinary part of Leeds and had a similarly ordinary childhood.' But ordinary life was hard in 1933. The industrial revolution had finally ground to a halt. The economy of the nation was in crisis. A similar crisis led in Germany to Adolf Hitler being elected Chancellor in 1933, and inexorably to world war six years after that. Those who lived through the hungry thirties will tell you that the economic slump began in 1928 in the North of England, but it only became world news following the Wall Street crash on the New York Stock Exchange in October 1929. Between 1930 and 1933, following

---

[4] Publication in America came first, in 1979; the book came out in the UK the following year.

President Hoover's decision to raise tariff barriers, world trade fell by two-thirds.

Unemployment in America rose to twelve million (it had been but two million in 1920); while in Germany in 1931 nearly six million people were out of work. In Britain, in January of the year of Barbara's birth unemployment reached an all-time peak of 2,979,000. In the same year Walter Greenwood's classic novel of life in a northern town, *Love on the Dole*, was published. This was real austerity, not the sort that we complain about today. The Great Depression was on. Barbara was born into a failing working-class community at its height.

She told me that her father was unemployed 'for most of my childhood', and was once reduced to shovelling snow, getting paid sixpence for his work, later telling his daughter: 'At that time, Barbara, there was a blight on the land.' Memory of it went into her third novel, *Act Of Will*, and she was furious when her American editor cut out the 'blight on the land' line.

Yet, inexplicably, the Taylors seem not to have had any great difficulty in making ends meet. 'My mother worked,' said Barbara by way of explanation. 'She worked at nursing and she did all sorts of things. She was a housekeeper for a woman for a while.' A day's work might bring Freda in five shillings, perhaps eighteen shillings a week cash in hand (worth about £35 today). The dole, or unemployment benefit, was £1 a week in 1930, thirty shillings for man, woman and child, but it was limited to a few months after job loss. Her father may also have received a small disability allowance, as he was invalided out of the Navy in 1924 with a serious infection which led to his having one of his legs amputated.

In 1930, best butter cost a shilling a pound, bacon threepence for flank, fourpence-halfpenny for side, fivepence or sixpence for ham, two dozen eggs (small) were a shilling, margarine was fourpence a pound, and one pound of steak and rabbit was a shilling. Theoretically, it was just possible to live on the Taylor income, but one cannot help but be struck by the contrast between the lack of income and her memories of how everyone in the family looked at this time: 'I was the kind of little girl who always looked ironed from top to toe, in ankle socks, patent leather shoes and starched dresses. [3]

My parents were well dressed, too,' she says. 'My father in particular was always very well dressed and very well groomed, and even today I can't stand un-groomed men. Any man that I ever went out with before I knew my husband was always good-looking, always well dressed and well groomed. I loved my father. He would have charmed you.' [4]

A photograph does indeed show Barbara as 'ironed from top to toe', it is true, although I know from the late Tyneside writer Catherine Cookson, whose family never knew where the next penny was coming from, that such photographs were commonly engineered to show the family at its imagined finest and I would soon become aware that Barbara lived her childhood through a golden glow of fantasy, which was encouraged by her mother and provided her with self-confidence and, later, significant inspiration for her novels. Nevertheless, I know Barbara well enough to be certain that she wasn't making it up when she said to me that all her clothes, other than hats and coats and shoes, had to be professionally handmade, that she was given shoetrees as a child and hangers for her clothes, which she noticed other children didn't have. There was even money for her father Winston's beer, his gambling on the horses and for family holidays taken at the east coast seaside resort of Bridlington. I am aware of the characteristic Yorkshire care with money, which Barbara still has to this day, and that women in those days were adept at 'making do'. Also, the Taylors did have a large extended family nearby who may have helped out. Nonetheless, here was an apparent anachronism and one to which we will return.

Tower Lane, where Barbara first lived with her parents is today a pretty, leafy little enclave of modest stone cottages, hidden away from the redbrick workers' terraces off Town Street to the east, in which the rest of the Taylor family lived. The lane is set just below Hill Top, the posh end of Armley, where the houses are bigger and were owned by the professional classes. [5]

The whole area seemed a magical resort to Barbara as a child, and she remembered everything as she had seen it as a child when, from her Manhattan apartment, she came to write about it in *A Woman of Substance* as 'especially pretty in summer when the trees and flowers are blooming'. In winter the snow-laden houses remind the heroine of the novel, Emma Harte, of a scene from a fairytale. Barbara selected Armley's Town Street as the spot where Emma first leases a shop and learns the art of retail, setting herself on the road to millions, but when it came to the film, the location for Harte's Emporium was moved to the more pictureque Yorkshire Dales market town of Middleham.

Charging Barbara's childhood love for Armley was its community spirit. According to the local headmistress Judy Blanchland, inhabitants today still feel part of a tradition with sturdy roots in the past and share Barbara's pride in the place. There is continuity in generations of the same families attending Christ Church School, for instance, which, with the church opposite, lies very much at the heart of the local community. [6] [7]

Barbara enrolled at the school (known as Armley National School in her day) on 31st August 1937 along with eleven other infants. Her school number was 364 and when she was elevated to Junior status in 1941, it became 891. Celebrated playwright Alan Bennett, whose father had a butcher's shop in nearby Tong Road, and who was born on 9th May one year after Barbara, joined on 5th September 1938, from his home at 12 Halliday Place. The families didn't know one another. 'My mother used to send me miles to a butcher that she decided she liked. It was all the way down the hill, almost on Stanningley Road.'

Bennett became a household name from the moment in 1960 that he starred in and co-wrote the ground-breaking satirical review *Beyond the Fringe* with Dudley Moore, Peter Cooke and Jonathan Miller at the Edinburgh Arts Festival. Later, the show played to packed audiences in London's West End and in New York. He was on an academic fast-track even at Christ Church School, passing out a year early, bound for West Leeds High School, according to the school log. From there he won a place at Oxford University. After leaving Christ Church, the two forgot they had known one another until the day, fifty years later, when they were both honoured by Leeds University with Doctor of Letters *Honoris Causa* degrees.

Barbara and I walked the area of her childhood together in the summer of 2003, she mourning the fact that generally little seems to have been done to retain the nineteenth-century stone buildings of her birthplace. It was the first time since childhood that Barbara had set foot in Tower Lane, where she lived until she was nine or ten.

She has a mental picture of herself 'at the age of three, sitting under a parasol outside the house, near a rose bush. It *is* a lane, you know,' she promises emphatically, 'and it was a tiny little cottage where we lived. Do you think it is still there? We got off the tram here, Whingate Junction…'

She points to a small triangular strip of grass between Whingate and Town Street, which must have been a talking point if only on account of its extravagant name – Charley Cake Park. An otherwise totally insignificant strip of green, Barbara mentions it in both *A Woman of Substance* and *Act of Will* as a place where a man called Charley hawked cakes. I begin to see how she extends the smallest of childhood memories into everything she writes. 'Then we'd walk across the road and up Tower Lane,' she continues. 'And we will see a very tall wall, and behind that wall were … sort of mansions: they were called The Towers. I had Emma Harte live there…'

She stops and looks towards a cluster of streets called the Moorfields: 'That used to be where the doctor I went to practised – Doctor Stalker was his name. One of those streets went down to the shop where I got the vinegar. Did I tell you about the vinegar? Boyes, a corner shop, that's where I used to get it. I wonder if that's still there?'

The vinegar turns my mind to her famous penchant for fish and chips, mushy peas, and lashings of vinegar. Nothing unusual about a Yorkshire woman eating a traditional Yorkshire meal, but she has been known to demand a bottle of Sarson's to season a rather more delicately serving prepared at the Dorchester Grill in London, and it is the favoured dish of her posh cosmopolitan characters in the novels too.

'My mother used to send me to get the household vinegar from Mr Boyes,' she continues, 'and she sent me with a bottle because it was distilled from a keg, and when I returned with it she'd always look at the bottle and say, "Look at this, he's cheating me!" Until one day she went in herself with the bottle and she said to Mr Boyes, "You're cheating me. I *never* get a full bottle," and Mr Boyes replied, "Eeh, ah knows. Tha' Barbara's drinking it." And it was true, I did drink a bit of it on the way home. Even today I like vinegar on everything, but especially on *cabbage*...

'There's Gisburne's Garage!'

As we pass a garage on our right at the mouth of Tower Lane, she points out an old house, pebble-dashed since she was a girl. 'This was where Mrs Gisburne lived and it had a beautiful garden in the back.' But the gardens have been built on and 'where this is green there used to be a pavement, surely ... but maybe it wasn't, perhaps I am seeing...' Not for the first time, as we continue our trip down memory lane, I hear the chorus of Maurice Chevalier's mournful, ironic song about uncertain childhood memories. Barbara looks for the 'tall wall', boundary-wall to The Towers. There is a wall, but it is not tall. 'That wall used to seem *so* high when I was a child,' she says in amazement. 'Anyway, the building is called The Towers and this is where Emma Harte had a house and they were considered to be very posh. It was all trees here...'

The Towers stretched many floors above us and must have seemed to a child's eye to reach to the sky. [8] The castellated construction in West Riding stone, blackened by industry, gives the mansion a powerful gothic feel, and it was surely this that captured Barbara's wonder when she was growing up here. Her eyes must have fallen upon the building virtually every day, whenever she emerged from the garden of the house opposite.

But where is No. 38 Tower Lane, supposedly situated opposite the tall wall of The Towers? There is Number 42 and Number 44... But no Number 38.

'We *were* 38,' Barbara insists as we move through a gate into a front garden, and sure enough, set back from the lane we see what might have once been the row of three tiny, terraced stone cottages where she had been brought up, 'the small cul-de-sac of cottages,' as she described them in *A Woman of Substance*.

'This seems very narrow,' she says as we make our way gingerly down the flagged path. 'They've knocked it all down, I think, and turned it into this. All right, well, *I'll find it*! There was a house across the bottom,' she murmurs to herself. 'This, the first of the line [of cottages] was No. 38. You went down some steps. Here it was a sort of garden bit, and where the trees are… There were three cottages along here and then a house at the bottom. It has gone. Wait a minute, are there three cottages or only two? Have they torn our house down? Well, this is the site of it anyway.' Her voice breaks. 'There *were* three houses there. There was our cottage, the people in the corner and the lady at the bottom. There *were* three houses.' [9]

Barbara was right, the house she spent the first years of her life, magical No. 38, was the 'first of the line of cottages' up from the 'house' across the bottom of the lane, the 'tiniest little cottage', but it was the most dilapidated of all of them, as a contemporary photograph shows. No. 38 Tower Lane had a front door, a small window on the ground floor and another on the upper floor and is no more. Since she lived there with Winston and Freda, it either fell down, was taken down or converted to increase living space in the cottages that remain. There is no postcode for it today, while the steel ties in the line of cottages attest to their age and fragility.

Barbara then turns my attention to the site of the wartime air-raid shelter where she and her mother would sit when the sirens sounded during the early years of the war. In the whole of the war only a handful of bombs actually fell on Leeds, but the preparations were thorough, the windows of trams and shops covered with netting to prevent glass shattering all over the place from bomb blast, entrances to precincts and markets sandbagged against explosions.

'There were three shelters in a row,' Barbara recalls, 'but they were awful. There were seats to sit on, but no radio because you couldn't plug it in, could you? Yes, you put bottles of water and some things in there and a Thermos flask Mummy would fill. We had candles and my mother always took a book, because she was a reader. She didn't knit like my Auntie Olive.'

'Did you take a book as well?'

'I can't remember, but I know that I listened for that unique, very particular step. It was like a missed step – because of his artificial leg. There was a lot of worry about my father. It's funny, isn't it… I used to worry about him being out when the sirens began to shrill. He always went out, not every night, but some nights a week he'd go down to the local for a pint. Usually he was down at the pub, locked in during the raid, and then later we'd hear his step down the garden. And I'd be so relieved I thought I would cry...

'I went to school with a gas mask, I remember,' Barbara continues. 'We all had them in a canvas bag on our shoulders and there used to be a funny picture of me with these thin little legs with the stockings twisted and a coat and the gas mask and fringe. My mother was cutting her rose bushes and I was playing with my dolls pram the day in 1940 when a doodlebug, a flying bomb, came over. And she just dropped everything and dragged me into the air-raid shelter. I vaguely remember her saying to my father later – he was out somewhere – "Oh, I never thought I'd see that happen over England."'

As we walked the area, Barbara had been absorbed by how things were in her mind as a child and are no more. Now, leaving her disappointments behind, we explore a steep track leading off Tower Lane to the right, which Barbara refers to as 'the ginnel'. I would discover that it is in fact an ancient weavers' track. 'They'd bring up the wool to the looms from the barges on the canal there,' Doreen Armitage, who also grew up in the area, told me later. The old canal system facilitated the city's industrialisation, a highly efficient transport system, taking textiles directly to the docks at Liverpool on the west coast for distribution all over the world.

Barbara changes her mood remembering the fun she had as a little girl skipping up the lane towards Hill Top Road and the moor where she'd play after school. Passing the main gate of The Towers we emerge from a tunnel of trees into a wide-open space, flanked on our left by an estate of modern houses, which has replaced the old stone houses of Barbara's time. Off to the right, we come to what was always referred to as 'the moor', but is no more than half an acre of open ground where we see a few strongly built carthorses are grazing. On the far side is a wall and some trees. Barbara at once exclaims: '*That's* the wall! When you climbed over that wall, you were in something called the Baptist Field – I don't know why it was called that, but ... we used to play in that field, some other children and I, we used to make little villages, little fairylands in the roots of the trees that were all gnarled with bits of moss and stones and bits of broken glass, garnered from that field, and flowers.' [10]

Memories of the field had been magical enough also to earn it a place in *A Woman of Substance* all of forty years later. In the novel it leads to the Crags above Ramsden Ghyll – Brimham Rocks in the film, near Pateley Bridge – not Hill Top, but 'the Top of the World, where the air was cool and bracing and filled with pale lavender tints and misty pinks and greys … and innumerable memories assailed her, dragging her back into the past.' Here, Emma Harte, servant of Fairley Hall, is seduced by Edwin Fairley, who is to the manor born.

There is nothing unusual about a writer being inspired by facets and feelings from their childhood. Look at Dickens, at Hardy, at the Brontë sisters. Indeed, Sir Kenneth Clark, who produced the landmark BBC Television series *Civilisation* in 1969, went further, seeing childhood as the most significant inspiration in all forms of art: 'It is questionable if there is *any* central image in an artist's work which did not come to him as a moment of vision in childhood.'

Thank goodness for an imagination free enough to raise Armley of the 1930s from the more mundane reality, I am thinking, as Barbara breaks the silence between us: 'My father used to walk up here sometimes and go for a drink at the Traveller's Rest.' I had already noted the pub on Hill Top Road. Walking as far as we could up Tower Lane would bring us to it. Barbara said she used to sit there with Winston: 'We were probably waiting for the pub to open, I should think! I used to come here with my father, and we would sit outside… He liked to go out for his pint, you know, and have his bet on the horses… Ripon, York, Doncaster races…' [11]

Barbara's father, Winston Taylor, was born on 13th June 1900 at 6 Wilton Place, Armley, the third son of Alfred and Esther Taylor. 'Daddy was called after Winston Churchill, who had just escaped from the Boer War.' Winston is the model for Vincent Crowther in *Act of Will*, the firstborn of Alfred and Eliza Crowther. He is also Emma Harte's brother Winston in *A Woman of Substance*: 'The fictional Winston Harte looks like him, thinks like him, and has many of his characteristics,' Barbara says.

I also learn that she based Emma Harte's father, 'Big Jack Harte', on Winston's father, Alfred Taylor. 'I loved my grandfather. He was in my mind when I created Jack Harte. He had a moustache, all lovely and furry white, and white hair. He was big … a big man, big moustache. He used to take me on his knee, give me peppermints and tell me stories about when he was a Sergeant Major in the Seaforth Highlanders. He loved me and I loved my grandfather.'

The real-life Alfred Taylor is described as 'a forgeman' (blacksmith) on his son Winston's birth certificate and as 'a cartman' (transporter of goods or people by horse and cart) on Winston and Freda's marriage certificate. Barbara remembers him as the latter, as the Co-op drayman – the man who looked after the horses and drove the cart carrying stores for the Armley link in Britain's first supermarket chain.

Initially, the senior Taylors lived five minutes away from Tower Lane, in Edinburgh Grove, off Town Street. 'The house was a Victorian terraced house with a series of front steps, but also a set of side steps leading down to the cellar kitchen. It was a through-house[5], but I can't remember if there were doors on both sides. They then moved to 5 St Ives Mount, also a Victorian terraced house with front steps down to the cellar kitchen, where you'd always see my grandmother baking. Both were tall houses, as I recall.

'I liked my grandmother, Esther Taylor, too. Her maiden name was Spence. She was very sweet and not quite Alfred Crowther's wife in *Act of Will*. Eliza Crowther is always the voice of doom, saying, "Happiness, that's for them that can afford it." My real grandmother was full of other sayings like, "A stitch in time saves nine", "You'd better watch your p's and q's", though I do remember her baking like Mrs Crowther – bacon-and-egg pies, also apple pie, and sheep's-head broth and lamb stews. On Saturday morning I used to go for her to the Co-op, but we didn't call it the Co-op, it was called the *Cworp* – Armley dialect, I suppose. You could buy everything at the Cworp. It had a meat department, vegetables, groceries, cleaning products... She loved me. I think I was her favourite.'

---

[5] Two buildings back-to-back facing onto two parallel streets, with no stretch of garden between.

All was as Barbara remembered of her grandparents' houses when we found them, and she went on to tell me about the rest of the Taylor brood.

'Winston had a sister called Laura, who lived in Farsley, was married and had a child. She was my favourite aunt. She died of lung cancer during the war, when I was about seven; she died at home and it was a horrible death. I remember going to see her. She was a very heavy smoker. After Laura died, her husband went with their little boy to live with his family, but died not long after. Laura Spencer in *A Woman of Substance* was based on my Aunt Laura, except our family were not Catholic. She was sweet and gentle and so good.

'Then there was Olive, married to Harry Ogle. He had a motorbike and sidecar. He was in the RAF during the war. They never had children. And Aunt Margery, always called Madge … she was beautiful.' Aunt Margery, I was to learn, had the 'uncommon widow's peak above the proud brow' that was Emma Harte's and granddaughter Paula's in *A Woman of Substance*, and Vincent's in *Act of Will*.

'Madge lived in Lower Wortley. She was married, but didn't have children either. I remember I was her bridesmaid when I was six. Olive was another favourite aunt. Everybody loved Olive. She managed a confectioner's shop, Jowett's at Hyde Park Corner – the one in Leeds, not London! – and I used to go and see her there. She used to let me serve a customer now and then. She lived in this house at 21 Cecil Grove, just the other side of the Stanningley Road, by Armley Park.

'We would go on picnics together. She always took her knitting. On one occasion, so the story goes, I nearly drowned. Olive suddenly looked up and said to Uncle Harry, "Where's Barbara?" They couldn't see me. Then, far out in the river, they saw my dress caught on a dead branch, they saw me actually bob up and go under the water again and I was flailing around because I couldn't swim. But the branch had hooked into my dress and was holding me up. Today I have a terrible fear of the sea where I can't put my feet on the bottom. I panic, which I think must go back to that. They got me out in the end, soaked and crying, and dried the dress in the sun, but you know the English sun! They took me home to their house and Auntie

Olive ironed the dress and got me back home looking like the
starched child that I was.

'So, Daddy had three sisters, and because two of them didn't
have children they spoiled me to death, of course. Their brothers
were Jack, Bill, Winston – my father – and Don, the youngest,
who sadly died just recently. He and his wife, Jean, my one
surviving aunt, had a daughter, Vivienne, my only cousin.

'Jack and Bill Taylor lived at home with my grandmother and
never married. I didn't know them very well. Jack was in the
army during the war, I think, and Bill was in minesweepers off
the coast of Russia and places like that. Afterwards they came
home and lived with my grandma, and then when she died they
continued to live in that house – two bachelors, very straight,
but very *dour*. I used to go and see my grandmother, and they
would be sitting in their chairs and nobody spoke. I hated it.
I wasn't scared of them, I paid not a blind bit of notice because
my focus was somewhere else.'

Barbara tells me that she owes her good looks to her father,
and that 'he was very good-looking, dark-haired, green-eyed.'
Barbara describes him in fact and fiction as a natural star,
charismatic, one who drew others (especially women) to him by
force of personality, dashing looks and more than his fair share
of beguiling charm … plus he had 'the gift of the gab'.

Family legend had it that at fourteen Winston ran away to sea
and signed up in the Royal Navy, forging his father's signature
on the application form. Barbara uses the story in *A Woman of
Substance*, applying it to his namesake, Emma Harte's brother.
The real Winston did indeed join the Navy, but as the National
Archive at Kew shows, not until shortly before his sixteenth
birthday. His naval record reads that he signed on as Boy (Class
II) on 20th May, 1916. Previously he had worked as a factory
lad. He was in fact quite small for a 16-year-old – height 5 ft
1 in, chest 31.5 ins.

His first attachment was to *HMS Ganges*, a second-rate,
2,284 ton, 84-gun ship with a ships company of 800, built
of teak one hundred years earlier at the Bombay Dockyard
under master shipbuilder Jamsetjee Bomanjee Wadia. By
the time Winston joined her, *Ganges* was a shore-bound
training establishment for boys at Shotley Gate in Suffolk. He

remained in the Navy until 16th July 1924, when he was invalided out with a serious infection which could have led to septicaemia.

Winston was admitted to Chapel Allerton in Leeds. There is still a specialist limb unit there. Barbara recalls that when he was lying in hospital, 'He said to his mother, "I don't want to have my leg off because I won't be able to dance." His mother said, "Winston, forget dancing. If you don't have the leg off, you won't live." Gangrene was travelling so rapidly that it had reached the knee. That was why it was taken off very high up. And so he couldn't dance, but he did go swimming. You can swim with one leg and two arms. He went swimming in Armley Baths.'

One can only speculate on the impact the loss would have had on one so sociable as he, although Barbara marks him out as pragmatic: 'I think I take after my father in that way. He didn't really give a damn what people thought.'

The specialist at Chapel Allerton told me that the artificial leg Winston was given would have been the best available at the time and made of holed aluminium, which would have been light and possibly easy enough to manoeuvre to allow him to engage in his favourite pastime, though perhaps not the jitterbug from America, the dance that was sweeping the country in the years leading up to the war.

Barbara's parents married on 14th August 1929. Winston was living at nearby Wortley, at the time, and described himself on their marriage certificate as a general labourer, while Freda, of 1 Winker Green, Armley, described herself as a domestic servant.

'I don't actually know where they met,' admitted Barbara. 'Probably at a dance. If my father couldn't really dance any more because of the leg, perhaps he went just to listen to the music. I actually do think he met her at a dance; they used to have church dances and church-hall dances.'

Although Barbara adored both her parents, when she was a child there was little love openly expressed by her father. 'He didn't verbalise it perhaps in the way that Mummy did.' The depth of Barbara's feelings for him were expressed in a touching scene one day, which had to do with his artificial leg.

It had been snowing and Barbara was walking with Winston in Tower Lane when he fell and couldn't get up because of the slippery snow. 'He was down on his back, and there was nobody around, and he told me what to do. He said, "Go and find some stones and pile them up in the snow, near my foot." He was able to wedge his artificial leg against the stones in order to lever himself up. I got him sitting up, I couldn't lift him. I was six or seven years old. But he managed to heave himself to his feet eventually.'

But at least she had helped him, as she had always longed to do, and now he realised what a practical, efficient *doer* of a little girl he had fathered. The leg stirred her feelings for her father again when he died in 1981. 'My mother said, "Your father wanted his leg taken back to the hospital." So my Uncle Don drove me there with it, and three spare legs, and when I handed them over I just broke down in floods of tears. It was like giving away part of him and myself. I was very close to Mummy, but I was close to my father in a different way.'

Being an only child set Barbara apart. In the single-child home the emphasis is on child-parent relationships rather than sibling friendships and rivalries, which may affect a child's ability to relate to contemporaries at school; although when things are going well between child and parents at home it can make family life extra-special.

'There were plenty of times,' she says, 'when I just knew that we were special, the three of us. I think when you are an only child you are a unit more. I always adored them. Yes, rather like Christina does in *Act of Will*.[6]'

Barbara's happiness at home was never more clearly shown than in the only time she spent away from it as a six-year-old war-time evacuee. The school log reads: '*1st September 1939, the school was evacuated to Lincoln this morning. Time of assembly 8.30, departure from school, 9, to Wortley Station, departure of train, 9.43.*'

---

[6] *Act of Will* provides many literal biographical parallels to Barbara's life. Audra and Vincent are modelled on her own parents, and their daughter Christina's life reflects much of Barbara's own.

The school stayed closed until 15th January 1940: '*Reopened this morning, three temporary teachers have been appointed to replace my staff, which are still scattered in the evacuation areas. Miss Laithwaite is at Sawbey, Miss Maitland at Ripon, Miss Musgrave at Lincoln and Miss Bolton is assisting at Mainwood Road. The cellars have been converted into air-raid shelters for the Infants. Accommodation in the shelters, 100. Only children over 6 can be admitted for the present.*'

'I was sent to Lincoln with Miss Musgrave,' remembers Barbara, 'but I only stayed three weeks. It was so stupid to send us to Lincolnshire. I remember having a label on me, a luggage label, and my mother weeping as the school put us on a train. I was little. I wasn't very happy, that I know, I missed my parents terribly. I was very spoiled, I was a very adored child. My mother sent me some Wellington boots, so it must have been in winter. She'd managed to get some oranges and she'd put them in a boot with some other things, but the woman had never looked inside. So, when my father came to get me the oranges were still there and had gone bad. My mother was furious about that.

'Daddy came to get me. He'd gone to the house and they said, "She'll be coming home from school any moment." He said, "Which way is it? I'll go to meet her." And I saw him coming down the road and I was with the little girl who was at the house also. I remember it very well because I started to run – he was there on the road with his stick, walking towards me … and I'm screaming, "Daddy, Daddy, Daddy!" He said, "Come on, our Barbara, we're going home." We stood all the way on the train. I was so happy, because I missed my parents so much it was terrible. I was crying all the time – not all the time, but I cried a lot, I didn't like it. I didn't like being away from them. I loved them so much.'

There were also times, however, when the Taylor family unit was not quite as special as she remembers. On BBC Radio's *Desert Island Discs* Barbara admitted not only that husband and wife Vincent and Audra Crowther in *Act of Will* are modelled on her parents, but that she hadn't been able to write the novel until after her parents had died because of 'this very tumultuous marriage that my parents had. They were either in each other's arms or at each other's throats.' When I asked her to elaborate, she said: 'I think Winston had a bit of an eye for the ladies, but that doesn't mean that he did much about it. Listen, the more I write, the more I read of other people's lives, the more I realise how terribly flawed we all are...'

In the novel, arguments erupt over his drinking and a fancy woman, and this is a particularly real memory for Barbara: '"Go back to your fancy woman!" I heard those words as a child. That happened when I was little. I remembered it and I did ask Grandma Taylor, "What's a fancy woman?" And I know that my mother rejected Winston constantly. No, she didn't talk about it, but I knew about it somehow when I was in my teens. How do children know things? She neglected my father,' and later Freda 'shut the bedroom door' on him.

Barbara alludes to this in *Everything to Gain,* another novel that looks deeply into relationships within the 'special family unit' where the parents have separate bedrooms. Barbara has Mallory Keswick say of her flighty father, Edward: 'He was a human being after all, not a God, even if he had seemed like one to me when I was growing up. He had been all golden and shining and beautiful, the most handsome, the most dashing, the most brilliant man in the world. And the most perfect... Yes, he had been all those things to me as a child.'

Being the only child, Barbara will have needed to perform a balancing act between mother and father when relations between her parents soured, which can't have been easy. She would have had to stand alone under the burden of any discord in the marriage, and sometimes, clearly, the situation between Freda and Winston did become polarised.

In the electoral records of Upper Armley, there is a period when Winston is not included on the register as an inhabitant of the family home. Freda is the sole occupant of electoral age when, in 1945, they have moved from Tower Lane and are living at Greenock Terrace, one of those Armley terraced houses off Town Street. It is the first record available after the war years (during which no records were kept).

In the fiction, Mallory is suddenly shaken one day 'by the sudden knowledge that all the years I was growing up I had been terrified my father would leave us for ever, my mother and

I, terrified that one day he would never come back.' She and her mother discuss her father. Mallory cannot understand 'why Dad was always away when I was a child growing up. Or why we didn't go with him.' Her mother refuses to be drawn. Mallory is no fool, however. She remembers 'that fourth of July weekend so long ago, when I had been a little girl of five … that awful scene in the kitchen … their terrible quarrel [which] had stayed with me all these years.'

I raised this with Barbara when we were discussing her father's absence from the family home. She would not be drawn and said only that 'the trauma must spring from the war years…,' alluding to the scene already described in the air-raid shelter at the end of the garden, when she would worry about where her father was.

'Your father was very often not there?'

'No, he was out having a drink. That's Daddy.'

The waywardness of Barbara's father was not the only factor at issue in the family unit, however. What led to separate bedrooms was the mother switching her attention away from the husband to the child – to Barbara – and that happened for reasons that cut deeper.

CHAPTER THREE
Freda

'There was a cold implacability in the set of the mouth and the thrust of the jaw, a terrible relentlessness in those extraordinary cornflower-blue eyes...'

Act of Will

Freda was 'a rather retiring, quiet woman', in Barbara's words, 'rather reserved, shy, but with an iron will'. This iron will was something Barbara regarded as very special about her apparently timid mother's 'inner resources', not quite stubbornness but an unusual stamina, mental energy and toughness of mind, an 'inner strength'.

'I was very close to Mummy. She totally and completely believed in me. There wasn't a day of her life that if she spoke to me, even after I'd gone to live in London and then America, when she didn't say, "I love you." There wasn't a time when she didn't tell me that I was the most beautiful and the cleverest and the most talented and the most charming and the most wonderful person. And of course that's not true, we all know that we have faults. But what it did ... it gave me tremendous self-confidence and a self-assurance that I had even when I was fifteen and sixteen. And she instilled in me a desire to excel. Her message was: "There's nothing you can't have if you try hard enough, work hard enough and strive towards a goal. And never, never limit yourself."'

The only child may be a spoiled child, and getting one hundred per cent of her mother's attention and approbation there was a danger of this for Barbara: 'I was very spoiled, I was a very adored child,' she freely admits, but her character was not weakened by Freda's strategy. On the contrary, it empowered her. It made her unstoppable.

Barbara took away from their relationship an absolute conviction that she was capable of anything to which she set her mind. 'When your mother tells you all the time that you are loved and that you are the best at everything you do, you gain tremendous self-confidence.' Inadequacy was never entertained. Billie Figg noted this as her defining characteristic when they first met in her early twenties: 'What she had was enormously high expectations of herself and a lot of assurance.'

In *Act of Will*, the novel based on her parents' marriage, Vincent fears that Audra's motivation to do all this for their daughter is tinged with obsession. He notes a possessiveness about his wife's relationship with their daughter, which seems to exclude him, and comes to frighten him. 'There was a cold implacability in the set of the mouth and the thrust of the jaw, a terrible relentlessness in those extraordinary cornflower-blue eyes...' And Vincent fears, 'She's going to make it a crusade.'

Freda gave Barbara the impression that the reason why 'she focused every bit of love and attention on me' was that before Barbara was born she had given birth to a son, a boy called Vivian. 'He died from meningitis six months after he was born and some time before I was born.' There is, however, no public record of the birth of a boy called Vivian to her mother. In spite of every effort to trace such a birth, I and another researcher commissioned by Barbara, drew a complete blank. There *was* a boy called Vivian who was born into the Taylor family and died tragically young, but, as records show, he was born to Freda's mother-in-law, Esther Taylor.

We know that Esther sounded warnings that Freda's strategy was giving Barbara 'ideas above her station' and would lead only to trouble, for, as surely as the starched look of her clothes and shoes, it set her apart from other children in the working-class community. Etiquette became 'a very important part' of her strategy, Barbara told me – not only table manners and the like, but social mores beyond her class, for example she called her parents Mummy and Daddy, rather than Mam and Dad as

other children did. There was speculation that Freda had come,
or may have had the impression that she had come, from better
stock than her husband, Winston. But however much Freda told
her mother-in-law about this, it seems that Esther didn't believe
a word of it. Winston was her favourite child and Esther did not
take kindly to what Freda was up to.

In the North of England there is a nasty word for girls like
Freda with big ideas – 'upstart'. Barbara recognises this: 'the
lower classes are just as bad as the aristocracy when it comes to
that sort of thing. Snobs, too, in their own way.' And it is this,
in *Act of Will*, that drives a wedge between wife and husband
(leading to separate bedrooms) and between wife and mother-
in-law: *'If the circumstances of her life had been different,'*
Barbara writes (her italics), *'she [Audra, who is Freda] would
never have been permitted to marry him [Winston/Vincent].'*

The tension between Freda and her mother-in-law did indeed
lead to a them-and-us situation. Barbara recalls Winston going
'maybe every day to see his mother' and this really upsetting
Freda. 'Why do I think my mother always used to say, "I know
where you've been, you've been to…"?'

'Did it annoy Freda,' I asked, 'his going to see his mother
every day?'

'Probably. I should imagine it would. Don't you think it
would?'

That Barbara became Freda's single-minded focus there is no
doubt. 'If there was a purpose in my mother's life it was *me*,'
she said, but to be fair to Freda, there was much that gave order
to her programme. First, there was discipline in little things at
home. 'I always made my own bed, was always taught to hang
up clothes and put my clothes away … and from when I was six
or seven had my chores at the weekend. I had to help with the
washing up, scraping the potatoes and taking the eyes out, and
I was allowed to dust the sitting room as long as I was careful
with her ornaments and things. I went on errands, went to the
corner shop and things like that. My most favourite thing was
helping my mother to bake, weighing the fruit, and I always got
a bit of dough which was filthy when it went into the oven and
it came out terrible, as hard as a rock…'

Second, there was a clear educational dimension to Freda's project, unusual as that was in the working-class Armley enclave of the 1930s, for Barbara makes the point that no other mothers of her friends did anything like it for their children.

'She would take me to the Theatre Royal in Leeds to see, yes, the pantomime, but also anything she thought might be suitable. For instance, I remember her taking me to see the Russian Ballet when it came to the Grand Theatre in Leeds. I remember it very well because Svetlana Beriosova was the dancer and I was a young girl, fifteen maybe. I loved the theatre…

Freda also taught Barbara to read when she was very young: 'She was a great reader and force-fed books to me. I went to the Armley library as a child. My mother used to take me and plonk me down somewhere while she got her books.' The Library in Town Street, purpose-built in 1902, is five minutes walk from Tower Lane and even less from Greenock Terrace, to which Barbara and her parents moved. By the time she was twelve she had read the whole of Dickens.

But Freda's project extended far beyond theatre and books. 'My mother exposed me to a lot of things,' Barbara continued. 'She showed me – she *taught* me to look, to appreciate beautiful artefacts and styles of design. I always remember she used to say to me, "Barbara, keep your eyes open and then you will see all the beautiful things in the world."

'She used to take me to stately homes because she loved furniture, she loved the patinas of wood. She often took me to Temple Newsam, [a country house] just outside Leeds, and also to nearby Harewood House, home of the Lascelles family and to Ripley Castle…'

How Freda knew about furniture and the patinas of wood, and what drew her to stately homes in the area, Barbara never questioned. When I asked her why she thought her mother took her to these historic houses with their things of beauty, she said: 'She loved those places – it was seeing beautiful things. She used to say to me, "Barbara, you must always use your eyes, you must always look."'

'She was saying this to you because she wanted you to be a designer, a writer, or to draw or to be a painter or –?'

'No. She wanted me to *reach...*'

Barbara's passion for antique furniture and modern Impressionist paintings was nevertheless born directly of these outings, which led, much later, to her writing a nationwide syndicated column in America about design and interior decor and a number of books on interior design, furniture and art for American publishers. And eventually they informed her novels.

In *A Woman of Substance* the optimum architecture is Georgian, and Emma Harte's soul mate Blackie O'Neill's dream is to have a house with Robert Adams fireplaces, Sheraton and Hepplewhite furniture, 'and maybe a little Chippendale'.

In *Act of Will*, as guests of Christina Newman and her husband Alex in their Sutton Place, Manhattan apartment (modelled on Barbara's), we, like Christina's mother, Audra Crowther, are stung by the beauty of 'the priceless art on the walls, two Cézannes, a Gauguin ... the English antiques with their dark glossy woods ... bronze sculpture by Arp ... the profusion of flowers in tall crystal vases ... all illuminated by silk-shaded lamps of rare and ancient Chinese porcelains.'

In *Angel*, Johnny dwells on the paintings and antiques in his living room – a Sisley landscape, a Rouault, a Cézanne, a couple of early Van Goghs, 'an antique Chinese coffee table of carved mahogany, French bergères from Louis XV period, upholstered in striped cream silk...antique occasional tables...a long sofa table holding a small sculpture by Brancusi and a black basalt urn...' Costume designer Ros Madigan's attention is caught by a pair of dessert stands, 'each one composed of two puttis standing on a raised base on either side of a leopard, their plump young arms upstretched to support a silver bowl with a crystal liner,' the silver made by master silversmith Paul Storr. There are George III candlesticks also by Storr dated 1815.

In *Everything To Gain* Mallory Keswick feasts her eyes on a pair of elegant eighteenth-century French, bronze doré candlesticks, and her mother-in-law Diana buys antiques from the great houses of Europe, specialising in eighteenth- and nineteenth-century French furniture, decorative objects, porcelain and paintings.

All this was grounded in her mother Freda's extraordinary cultural project, and Barbara began to fancy that she could

belong to this world. Indeed, in some strange way, that she
already belonged to it. Talking to me about Temple Newsam,
she said, 'I can't really explain this to you how attracted I was to
the place, my mother and I used to go a lot. It was a tram ride,
you'd go on the tram to Leeds and then take another tram ... or
was it a bus? I loved it there, I always loved to go and I felt very
much at home, like I'd been there before.'

'Déjà vu.' I said.

'Yes, déjà vu. Completely.'

'Can you think why that was?'

'No. I have no idea.'

'Did you say anything about it to your mother at the time?'

'No, she just knew I loved to go.'

I didn't know quite what to make of this at the time, but plainly
Barbara, who is not at all fanciful generally, meant what she said.

Pretty soon Freda was taking Barbara further afield. The county
of Yorkshire is blessed with large tracts of wide-open spaces –
breathtaking views of varied character – so that even if you are
brought up in one of the great industrial cities of the county,
as Barbara was, you are but a bus ride away from magnificent
natural beauty, which, in time, when she was separated from
them by an ocean, would inspire her novels.

Barbara's novels are principally of character, the dominant
traits the emotional light and shade of the landscape of her
birth. When she came to write them, she had no hesitation in
anchoring them there, even though she was, by then, cast miles
away in Manhattan.

The author's sense that landscape is more than mere
topography was first awakened when her mother introduced her
to the wild workshop out of which Emily Brontë's Heathcliff
was hewn. 'She took me to the Brontë parsonage at Haworth,
and over the moors to Top Withens, the old ruined farm that
was supposed to be the setting for *Wuthering Heights*. I loved
the fact that this great work of literature was set right there.
I loved the landscape: those endless, empty, windy moors where
the trees all bend one way. I loved Heathcliff.' [12]

There is scarcely any landscape description as such in
Wuthering Heights, but Emily Brontë was the greatest of all

geniuses when it came to evocation of the spirit of a place. Charlotte, her sister, worried what primitive forces Emily had released from the bleak moorland around Haworth: 'Whether it be right or advisable to create things like Heathcliff, I do not know. I scarcely think it is.' She compared her sister's art to that of a sculptor, Heathcliff hewn out of 'a granite block on a solitary moor', his head, 'savage, swart, sinister', elicited from the crag, 'a form moulded with at least one element of grandeur...power... With time and labour, the crag took human shape; and there it stands colossal, dark, and frowning...terrible and goblin-like...'

There are many allusions to *Wuthering Heights* in Barbara's novels. For example, *Voice of the Heart* tells of the making of a film of Emily's novel. *The Triumph of Katie Byrne* is about an actress whose first big break is to play Emily Brontë in a play-within-the-novel about life in Haworth parsonage. And in *A Woman of Substance* the principal love story between Emma and Edwin Fairley draws on Brontë's idea of Cathy's sublimation of her self in Heathcliff and in the spirit of the moor: 'My love for Heathcliff resembles the eternal rocks beneath...' Brontë wrote. 'Nelly, I AM Heathcliff.'

In Barbara's novel the key scene takes place in a similar moorland place, at Ramsden Ghyll, 'a dell between two hills ... an eerie place, filled with grotesque rock formations and blasted tree stumps'. Edwin Fairley makes love to Emma Harte within 'the eternal rocks beneath' beneath the moor (in a cave) and Emma feels she is slowly 'dissolving under Edwin, becoming part of him. Becoming him. They were one person now. She *was* Edwin.'

Later, when Emma conceives their illegitimate daughter, she names her Edwina to point the finger at the identity of her faithless blue-blooded father, Edwin, setting in motion a succession of events that will realise Emma's fabulous destiny.

However, this wildly romantic area of the Yorkshire moors was not, on Barbara's own account, the most influential of the landscapes to which Freda introduced her daughter. That was farther afield: 'Wensleydale and the Valley of the Ure was the area I came to know best,' she told me.

Where there are peaks and high-lying moorlands there are dales (valleys) to skirt them. Wensleydale is the beautiful upper valley of the River Ure, a rich, wonderful landscape open to two centres of power, Middleham and Bolton castles, and it was to the former that Freda directed Barbara's attention.

Middleham lies some sixty miles north of Leeds. Stepping stone to it for mother and daughter was the tiny city of Ripon, where Freda was born in 1904. 'We'd get the bus to Ripon and then my mother had various "cousins" who drove us from Ripon to Middleham...'

The situation being what it was at home with Winston, the duo, 'joined at the hip', travelled alone, staying with Joe Wray and his wife, Lillie, one of these Ripon cousins.

'My mother *always* wanted to be in Ripon,' Barbara recalled. 'All the time.'

'You mean, some time after you were born, when you were eight, nine or ten?' I wondered.

'No, much younger, I went back as a baby.'

Ripon lies at the confluence of three rivers. The Ure – its Celtic name, Isura, meaning physical and spiritual power – washes past Middleham Castle and is met eighteen miles east of Ripon by the Skell, which flows through the city and is itself met southwest of it by the River Laver.

Barbara refers to Ripon as 'a sleepy old backwater' compared to 'a great big metropolis like Leeds', but the description belies its unique and many-faceted appeal. It is officially a city because it has a cathedral, but in truth it is no larger than a market town. Ripon's population was a mere 7,500 when Freda was growing up there, and today it is little more than double that size, retaining the feel of a small, busy, rural community, but with tremendous reserves of history at its fingertips. The twelfth-century cathedral is known as Ripon Minster. [13] There is a seventeenth-century House of Correction, a nineteenth-century workhouse and debtor's prison, old inns bent and worn by time, and, nearby, twelfth-century monastic ruins – Fountains Abbey, since 1768 part of the magnificent Studley Royal estate.

Bronze-age earthworks and henges to the northeast suggest human habitation thousands of years BC, but Ripon itself can be said to have first drawn breath in 634 AD with the birth of the city's patron saint, Wilfrid, in Allhallowgate, Ripon's oldest street, where the workhouse still stands today, just north of what was in Wilfrid's day a newly established Celtic Christian monastery.

The monks sent Wilfrid, an unusually able boy, to be educated in Lindisfarne (Holy Island) off the Northumberland coast, where St Aidan had founded a monastery in 635. Later, he championed Catholicism over Celtic Christianity as the faith of the Church of England, and was appointed Abbot of the Ripon monastery, then Archbishop of York. The church he built in Ripon became a 'matrix' church of the diocese of York, and his work inspired the building of Ripon Minster (the cathedral) in 1175, as well as the foundation of various hospital chapels, which established the city's definitive role in providing food and shelter for the poor and sick.

St Mary Magdalen's hospital and chapel were built in the twelfth century on the approach to the city from the north, and had a special brief to care for lepers and blind priests. St John the Baptist's chapel, mission room and almshouses lie at the southeast Bondgate and New Bridge approach to the city over the River Skell, which also offers a view of Thorpe Prebend House, rebuilt in 1609 and one of the most historic houses in Ripon. Part of the ancient ecclesiastical estate of Ripon Minster, and one of seven houses used by the canons (or prebendaries) of the cathedral, it hosted, at various time, James I and Mary Queen of Scots, and is situated off High St Agnesgate in a peaceful precinct with another hospital chapel, St Anne's, already a ruin in Edith's time, but founded by the Neville family of Middleham Castle.

Thorpe Prebend holds a special place in Barbara's memory, for Joe and Lillie Wray were its caretakers and Barbara became firm friends with Joe's niece, Margery Clarke. 'I spent a lot of weekends with Margery when I was a young girl,' Barbara recalls, and later as teenagers they would attend dances at the Lawrence Café in Ripon's Market Place, which had a first-floor ballroom famous locally for its sprung dance floor. 'We used to go, she and I, to the Saturday night dance there at fifteen, sixteen...When I reminded her and I recalled that we stood waiting to be asked to dance, her swift retort was, "But not for long!" Apparently we were very popular.'

Here, then, was Barbara's second family, far away from the tensions building at home. Margery pointed out the Lawrence Café in the Market Place and an eye-catching Ripon landmark beside Thorpe Prebend – a series of ancient stepping-stones spanning the considerable width of the Skell – where Freda and Margery's father, who went to school together, used to play. According to Jim Gott (a contemporary of Freda), this was a popular pastime and later I learned that the steps had achieved legendary family status when Margery's father pushed Freda in. 'She was wearing a dress her mother Edith had dyed duck-egg blue and she dripped duck-egg blue all the way home on her white pinafore!' Barbara recalled.

What comes across in Jim Gott's reminiscence of life in the city when Freda was a child is the fun he had and the empathy he enjoyed with the spirit of the place – past and present fusing in its ancient architecture and traditions and the daily round. These were the riches of a life that was in other ways hard for most people. Freda would have shared in these riches too, and, as adult, looked back with a real sense of belonging.

The ancient spirit of Ripon is still celebrated every Thursday in the twelfth-century Market Place, with its covered stalls, self-styled entertainers and livestock pens. [14] It features in Barbara's novel, *Voice of the Heart*. In Freda's day, long before the market bell sounded at 11 a.m. to declare trade open, folk poured in from the surrounding moors and dales, and Ripon awoke to the clatter of vehicles laden with fresh produce and squawking hens, and the drovers' fretting sheep and lowing cattle, as flocks and herds made their way through the city's narrow lanes to the colourful square on the final leg of what was often a two- or three-day journey. All came to an end at 9 p.m., as Gott recorded, when the Wakeman Hornblower blows his horn, announcing the night watch, a tradition that survives in Ripon to this day.

With the settled calm of life and the Wrays of Ripon as their base, Freda set about a more dramatic stage of her project with her daughter. At Middleham, less than a half-hour away Barbara formed a taste for the great history of the county of her birth, and plunged into its imagined past. She owes to their expeditions the sense of drama she shares today with mediaeval historian Paul Murray Kendall from 'this region of wild spaces and fierce loyalties and baronial "menies" of fighting men, with craggy castles and great abbeys scattered over the lonely moors ... a breeding ground of violence and civil strife.'[7]

Within the roofless halls and ghostly chambers of Middleham castle, Freda introduced her daughter to the story of Richard Neville, Earl of Warwick, one of the most dynamic figures in English history. The 'reach' of his ambitions and many of the traits would define her woman of substance, and from 2006 provide historical reference for her series, *The Ravenscar Chronicles*. [15]

'My mother told me all about Richard Neville, "the Kingmaker"... how he put Edward IV on the throne of England, and was one of the last great magnates. He held a fascination for my mother.'

Warwick's tireless constitution was rooted in the hard-bitten culture of the North. When Richard was a boy he lined up next to his father to repel attempts to wrest their lands away from them. At eighteen he won his spurs and was hardened further by action in skirmishes to avenge rustling and looting of villages within family territories. He was instinctively the Yorkshire man, but he was also someone who, like the woman of substance herself, was not bound to his home culture. The vitality of his character awakened him to recognise and seize his moment in the wider world when it occurred during the Wars of the Roses, the struggle (1455–1485) between the houses of York and Lancaster for the throne of England.

'The castle at Middleham is all blown-out walls and windows that no longer exist,' Barbara explained to me before we arrived, 'but Warwick, who was raised there and lived there was devastating as a young man, devastating in the sense that he was very driven and ambitious ... and a great warrior.' It is worth noting that Richard of Gloucester [later Richard III], was from the age of thirteen under the tutelage of Warwick and part of his household at the Castle. Warwick trained him as a knight and Richard probably met his future wife, Warwick's younger daughter, Anne Neville, at the castle.

---

[7] *Warwick the Kingmaker*, Paul Murray Kendall, Allen & Unwin (1957).

Warwick's role in changing the English monarchy affected England for two centuries, but his relevance is for all times. As Kendall records: 'The pilgrimage of mankind is, at bottom, a story of human energy, how it has been used and the ends it has sought to encompass... Warwick's prime meaning is the *reach* of human nature he exemplifies and – type of all human struggle – the combat he waged with the shape of things in his time.'

For Barbara, the spirit is all, and in Warwick, as in Middleham castle itself, it is powerfully Northern. He was a figure whose character and actions attracted heroic levels of adulation and gave him mythic status throughout the land as he rode in triumph through his vast estates; a figure who, like Barbara herself and her charismatic heroines, seems to have been marked with a strong sense of destiny from the start.

There is in Kendall's Warwick the same unifying robustness to which the nation rises when England's rugby team presses its game to the end, seizing the Webb Ellis trophy against a background of fans clad in the livery of St George. What he is identifying is what attracts Barbara to Winston Churchill, the character that won us an Empire and coloured what is understood to be our very Englishness and gave her own father a name.

In the young Warwick, Barbara found the sort of substance for which integrity is implicit. In her novels, power is 'the most potent of weapons' which only corrupts 'when those with power will do anything to hold on to that power. Sometimes,' she says in full accord with the Warwick legend, 'it can even be ennobling.'

The character of Warwick that got through to Barbara encompassed more than soldiery values. The fierce loyalties of those times were, in young Warwick's case, not forged in greed, nor were they all about holding on to, or wresting, power from an opponent for its own sake. Long before he fell out with his protégé Edward and, embittered, took sides against him; long before he 'sold what he was for what he thought he ought to be', as Kendall put it, his purpose was to defend the values which true Englishmen held to be good.

Freda made sure that Barbara picked up on this heroic aspect. From an early age she instilled in her 'a sense of honour, duty and purpose', the need for 'integrity in the face of incredible pressure and opposition' and 'not only an honesty with those people who occupied her life, but with herself'. These noble values arise in her earliest novels, *Act of Will* and *A Woman of Substance*, but they first found their impetus in Freda's expeditions into Wensleydale; they are what Barbara always understood to be the values of the landscape of her birth. The seed took root when Freda led her by the hand up the hill through Middleham into the old castle keep, even if she was unable to articulate and bring it to flower until she sat down many years later to write *A Woman of Substance*, where Paul McGill recognises the woman of substance in Emma with reference to Henry VI – 'O tiger's heart wrapp'd in a woman's hide.'

The values Barbara garnered in her childhood through Freda's influence upon her – the sense of honour, duty and purpose – ensure a strong moral code in the novels. Emma is tireless, obsessive, ruthlessly determined and dispassionate. She has a 'contained and regal' posture, there is an imperiousness about her, but she is also 'fastidious, honest, and quietly reserved'. She wears a characteristically inscrutable expression and cannot abide timidity where it indicates fear of failing, which she says has 'stopped more people achieving their goals than I care to think about.' She is physically strong and has a large capacity for hard work. 'Moderation is a vastly overrated virtue,' she believes, 'particularly when applied to work.' Emma is 'tough and resilient, an indomitable woman', with 'strength of will' and 'nerves of steel'. To her PA, Gaye Sloane, she is 'as indestructible as the coldest steel', but granddaughter Paula admires Emma's 'integrity in the face of incredible pressure and opposition', and while she can be 'austere and somewhat stern of eye' there is a 'canny Yorkshire wariness' about her, and when her guard is down it is 'a vulnerable face, open and fine and full of wisdom.' References to Middleham are legion in the novels – In *Angel*, in *Where You Belong*, in *Voice of the Heart*, and key scenes in the film of *A Woman of Substance* were shot in the village – as Freda's guidance found its way ever deeper into her daughter's soul.

When I drove her to the castle early in my research for this book, Barbara said: 'I have very strange feelings there. I must have been about eight or nine when we first went. I thought ... I know this place. As if I had lived there... I want to come back.'

On arrival, an army of horses clattered down the road from the castle to meet us, descending from the gallops and tipping me straightaway into the pages of *Emma's Secret* and *Hold the Dream*, where Allington Hall is one of the greatest riding stables in all England. Barbara was back in her childhood with Freda, however.

Exploring what remains of the massive two-storey, twelfth-century Castle Keep, with Great Chamber and Great Hall above, 'the chief public space in the castle,' I read out loud to Barbara from a sign: 'The Nevilles held court here. Walls were colourful with hangings and perhaps paintings. Clothes were colourful and included heraldic designs...' But she interrupted me, determined to impress upon me a more personal connection with the place: 'I have always been attracted to Middleham and I have always had an eerie feeling that I was here in another life, hundreds of years ago. I know it; why do I know it all? *How* do I know it all? *Was* I here? I know this place, and it is not known because I came in my childhood...'

From outside came the sound of children larking about. We made our way gingerly up steps a thousand years old, the blue sky our roof now, held in place by tall, howling, windowless walls that support scattered clumps of lichen and epiphytic wild flowers. Barbara brought us to a standstill in the Great Hall, taking it all in with almost religious reverence. Then, inevitably, the children burst in upon us. She turned, silencing them before even she opened her mouth: 'Now, look, you've got to stop making a lot of noise. You're disturbing other people. This is not a place for you to play!'

It was as if they had desecrated a church. We descended to areas which were once kitchens and inspected huge fireplaces, at one time used as roasting hearths, and discovered two wells and a couple of circular stone pits, which a signpost suggested may have been fish tanks.

'It was much taller than this; it has lost a lot...' she sighed, and then asked, 'Would it have been crenellated?'

I thought that likely, adding, 'It is … gothic, dark,' before my eyes fell on the wild flowers. 'Look at the harebells,' I said on a lighter tone, but Barbara was not to be diverted. She had come all the way from Manhattan to be there; she wanted me to grasp a point.

'I don't understand why I have this feeling. I don't understand why it is so meaningful to me.'

'There is a very strong sense of place here,' I agreed.

'For me there is.'

I felt a compulsion to test the subjectivity of Barbara's vision. 'I think *anyone* would find that there is a strong sense of place here,' I said.

She leapt back at me immediately: 'No, no, I *know* this… I have been here, not in this life.

'And then you see,' she said, and I felt guilty that I'd broken the spell, 'you can go down here…' But she could not let it go: 'I had the feeling *as a child…*' she said quietly. 'I thought I *knew* it. I had this really strong pull, and I don't know why. I feel I was here in that time, in the Wars of the Roses. I feel that I lived here in the time of Warwick.'

What was I to make of it all? For sure, her childhood experiences at Temple Newsam and at Middleham had been intense, and the déjà-vu element had arisen out of the intensity very probably orchestrated by Freda. At such an impressionable time in Barbara's life these experiences had had a lasting and inspiring effect. Freda's project gave her daughter not only contextual reference for some of her best novels, but an absolute conviction that she somehow *belonged* to the places to which she took her.

In Barbara's novel *Hold the Dream* past and present find a kind of poetic resolution at Middleham, just as happened for Barbara on the day we went there together. So this was not something she had engineered for my benefit. In the novel, Shane O'Neill believes that he is linked to the history of the castle through an ancestor *on his mother's side*.

The image came to mind of Freda standing hand-in-hand with her young daughter in the Keep at Middleham. Everything seemed to lead back to Freda. Why had she thought it so important to take Barbara to this place, whispering to her its stories, letting the rhythms of the place rise up to make her feel she belonged? Clearly the trips promised more than a history lesson. What was it that she wanted Barbara to know but couldn't tell her?

Barbara's insistent empathy with the spirit of Middleham carries a sense of her having been there 'in another life'. I could either dismiss this as pure fantasy or entertain it as being relevant to what I was about, writing her biography, and that meant I needed to know a good deal more about Freda.

CHAPTER FOUR
Edith

'I think we ought to go to Ripon. We've quite a lot of things to review, and to discuss...'

Meredith Stratton in *Her Own Rules*

All Barbara could tell me about her mother's family was what Freda herself had told her. Her parents had brought her up in Ripon. After her father died, her mother, Edith Walker, 'married a man called Simpson. There were three daughters, Freda, Edith and Mary, and two sons, Frederick and Norman. I don't know, to tell you the honest truth, but as far as I remember there was only one Simpson, Norman Simpson.'

I would discover that this was, at best, a sketchy picture. Certainly, nothing in the family's history as told to Barbara explained Freda's apparent belief that she came from better stock than the working-class Taylors into whose family she had married.

Edith Walker, Freda's mother, was the daughter of John and Mary Walker (née Scaife). John Walker was a slater's apprentice. Edith was born on 4th September 1880, the youngest of six children. The family lived at Primrose Hill, Skipton Road (the Ripon side of Harrogate), close to what is now a roundabout by a pub called The Little Wonder.

It seems that Edith never knew her mother, for John Walker was registered in the 1881 census as a widower. Perhaps Mary Walker died in childbirth. Living in the Primrose Hill house with John and Edith were John's other children: Thomas (sixteen), Elizabeth Ann (twelve), John William (ten), Minnie (five), and Joseph (three).

One cannot help but wonder how Edith's arrival on the scene was received by the rest of the family. Was she regarded as a drain on the meagre resources available to a family of seven, in which the breadwinner was on apprenticeship wages? Was she rejected for being the cause of their mother's death? Or was her advent greeted with great love and pity for the motherless mite, and was she spoiled and fussed over by her eldest sister, Elizabeth Ann, and, indeed, doted on by her father, John, who may even have caught glimpses of his lost wife in her?

Being motherless, even with the care of others in the family, Edith may have suffered from maternal deprivation, a condition believed to be as harmful as poor nourishment. It can have a child yearning throughout its life for the kind of unconditional love that only a mother can give, and which no substitute can hope to assuage. Edith may also have suffered physically, for feeding infants was mainly by mother's breast in those days.

The family does seem to have been a close one. It was largely still intact ten years later, and some members of it remained close for a considerable time into the future. It is indeed tempting to surmise that Edith was the apple of her father's eye. If so, it is all the more tragic that he was unable or, for some reason beyond resolution, unwilling to save Edith from the abyss into which she was to fall.

Typically for a working man of the period, John Walker stayed in one area for his entire lifetime. He was born in 1844 in Burton Leonard, a tiny village midway between Harrogate and Ripon, his parents having moved there from Pateley Bridge, ten miles to the west, where his elder sister Mary was born in 1839. After marrying, he went with his wife to live in Scotton, a village three miles to the south of Burton Leonard. Their first son, Thomas, was born there in 1865. The family then moved to Ripon in or around 1869, where siblings Elizabeth Ann, John William and Minnie were born. Then, around 1877, came the move to the outskirts of Harrogate, where first Joseph and then Edith were born. By 1891 the family had moved back to Ripon.

Home for Edith and her family in 1891 was a small stone cottage just two minutes walk south of the Market Place at No. 8 Water Skellgate, a whisper from where Barbara and Margery would dance the night away half a century later. [16]

By this time, Edith's father, John, was forty-seven and had married again, his second wife, Elizabeth, being four years his junior. Edith herself was ten, going on eleven, and either a pupil at the nearby Minster Girls Primary School, or perhaps more likely at the Industrial School, reserved for children of poorer families, including those from the Workhouse school, which had closed its doors for the last time a few years earlier.

Siblings Elizabeth Ann, John William and Joseph (twenty-two, twenty and thirteen respectively) were still at home, but there is no sign on the register of eldest brother Thomas or of Minnie, who, if she was alive, would have been fifteen, old enough to be living out as a maid. Also sharing the house is a lodger, John Judson, and a 'grandson' (possibly Elizabeth's or even Minnie's child) by name of Gabriel Barker. It must have been a tight squeeze. John Walker may have made the move back to Ripon to get more work, as it had a long history of job opportunity.

The city's position on the western fringe of the Vale of York – good sheep-rearing country – had made it the centre of the mediaeval wool trade, its three rivers diverted into a millrace or water course, which flowed through Water Skellgate and sustained three mills. Ripon's pre-eminence in the wool industry had continued into the late fifteenth century, but then steadily declined and various other industries had come to the fore. In the seventeenth century, Ripon rowels (spurs) had gained a worldwide reputation, so that Ben Jonson could write in his play *The Staple of News* (1626):

> *Why, there's an angel, if my spurs*
> *Be not right Rippon.*

The city was also renowned for its saddletrees, frames of saddles worked from local ash, elm and beech – horse racing has been part of Ripon life since 1664, and fourteen days of flat racing are still staged between April and August at Ripon Races, nicknamed the Garden Racecourse.

Button-making made another important economic contribution and, a century later, out of the French Revolution came a gift of an industry from a band of Ripon-bound French refugees, who were befriended by a French-speaking Yorkshireman called Daniel Williamson. In return for his welcome the immigrants handed Williamson the secret details of a varnish-making process, and the lucky man set up the first varnish-making business in England, becoming so successful that today Ripon manufacturers are still doing business in every major country of the world.

Besides these, an iron foundry made a significant contribution from the nineteenth century, and the city also supported a hive of little industries, such as bone- and rope-millers, tanners, fell-mongers, coachbuilders and chandlers. Finally, as many as nineteen per cent of those in employment in the city at this time were able to find work as unskilled labourers.

Upon arrival, Edith's brother, Joseph, found work as 'a rope twister', while his father, John, took up as a lamplighter. 'One of my earliest memories is of kneeling on a chair by a window waiting for the lamplighter,' wrote a Ripon citizen of those days: 'He was a tall figure, who carried a pole with a light on the end. The street lamps were gaslights and he tipped the arm to release the gas and lit the mantle. Presumably he made a second round to extinguish them.'

The history of Ripon in late Victorian and Edwardian times makes clear the huge divergence of lifestyle of rich and poor, who nevertheless lived on top of one another in so small a place as this. When Beryl Thompson arrived in 1956 she was struck by the accessible wealth of history available, and has spent her life looking into the plight of the poorest citizens ever since. 'I have done this over a period of about thirty or forty years,' she told me, 'and some of the places that children lived in Ripon at this time – if you read the medical inspectors' reports – were not fit to be in. They were no better than pigsties down St Marygate or Priest Lane [this is the oldest part of the city]. If you look at the early maps you will find a lot of courts all over the city – there's Foxton's Court and Thomson's Court and Florentine's Court and so on. I think there were a lot of hovels in these courts and they probably shared lavatories or there'd be a cesspool outside or a midden. They were trying to clean it up at the turn of the century, but the reports still comment on this.'

These courts were a throwback to mediaeval times and a common sight in the nineteenth and early twentieth centuries, not only in Ripon. Charles Dickens, as a boy alone in London, his parents incarcerated in the Marshalsea debtors' prison, was beset by 'wild visions' as he lurked around the entrance to courts and peered into their inky depths around Covent Garden. In Ripon, the city centre retained its mediaeval street plan into the twentieth-first century, and the labouring poor were consigned to cottages in just such dark and dismal courts, set behind the narrow streets (or yards, as they were also called). Very often at the top of a court you'd find workshops – a blacksmith, a bakery or perhaps a slaughterhouse.

There was tremendous movement by the poor from one court to another. In the first decade of the twentieth century, Edith's brother Joseph (Barbara's great uncle) moved at least four times in the space of four years through a maze of them. In 1907 he could be found at 2 York Yard, Skellgarths (a continuation to the east of Water Skellgate), having just moved there from 3 Millgate Yard. By 1910 he had moved to 1 York Yard, then to 4 York Yard. In 1911 he took up residence at 3 Johnson's Court, between 14 and 16 Low Skellgate (continuation to the west of the street), settling there and getting wed. Sadly, he was then almost certainly killed in the First War, for when records resumed in 1918 the sole occupant of 3 Johnson's Court was his widow, Ruth Matilda Walker. Within a year she remarried, her second husband a man called James Draper. And life went on.

These courts were private, often close-knit communities, safe from outsiders because few dared venture into them unless they had business there. Beryl was right that conditions were grim. In 1902, a Ripon sanitary inspector reported 'the really antiquated and disgusting sanitary arrangements now existing in the poorer quarters – where it is not unusual to find numbers of homes crowded round a common midden, which is constructed to hold several months' deposit of closet and vegetable matter, ashes and every sort of household refuse imaginable, and which remains in a festering and decaying condition, poisoning what pure air may reach the narrow courts...'

Another Ripon Council report, dated seven years before Freda was born, records one domicile 'where ten human beings have been herded together in a space scarcely adequate for a self-respecting litter of pigs', and it is recorded in *A Ripon Record 1887–1986* that in 1906, when Freda was two, increasing numbers of children were turning up at school without shoes.

The awful conditions in which unskilled working-class people lived in Edwardian England was so widely appreciated that in the hard winter of 1903, the New York *Independent* could find no more deserving case than England to cover: 'The workhouses have no space left in which to pack the starving crowds who are craving every day and night at their doors for food and shelter. All the charitable institutions have exhausted their means in trying to raise supplies of food for the famishing residents of the garrets and cellars of London lanes and alleys.'

As in London, so in Ripon. These horrors were to be found 'within a stone's throw of our cathedrals and palaces,' as William Booth, founder of the Salvation Army, noted.[8] George R. Sims, a respected journalist writing a year earlier, had conjured up a picture that would not have seemed out of place in Dickens's *A Tale of Two Cities*, of 'underground cellars where the vilest outcasts hide from the light of day … [where] it is dangerous to breathe for some hours at a stretch an atmosphere charged with infection and poisoned with indescribable effluvia.'

At precisely the moment that William Booth published his book about the slums of England being 'within a stone's throw of our cathedrals and palaces', life for the Walkers in Water Skellgate, a stone's throw from Ripon cathedral, will have been hard by our standards today, but because the city is so small it would also have given Edith a keen sense of what life was like on the other side of the wealth divide, and an opportunity perhaps to dream of how to make the transition from one to the other.

When John Walker and his first wife lived in the city in 1869 there would still have been water running openly through

---

8 *In Darkest England and the Way Out* (1890).

Water Skellgate – a section of the millrace already described –
and one imagines that the speedy brook provided a useful
if smelly flush in the days before water sewerage systems. In
1875, however, the foetid stream was covered over, perhaps
after pressure from the more well-to-do who had begun to
frequent the area. For, by the time Edith was living there in
the 1890s, Water Skellgate was a social hub, with its pubs and
a musical hall, a theatre and a dance hall, all of which attracted
a wealthier clientele cheek-by-jowl with an intriguing mix of
small businesses, dismal courts and low-rent accommodation,
as well as various charitable organisations, including the Jepson
Hospital and Bluecoat School, the Girls' Friendly Society
Lodge (run by a Miss Taylor) and a Wesleyan Mission Chapel
to which Edith would attach her allegiance whenever required
to state her religion officially.

The leisure facilities in the vicinity of the Walkers' abode
included the Palace Theatre at the lower end of adjacent
Kirkgate, and in Water Skellgate itself the Victoria Hall, a music
hall and theatre, which later became the Opera House. Next
door was the Constitutional Club (a gentleman's club) and
then the Crown Vaults, a pub owned by a Mr Lavin, who was
also a horse dealer. At one stage, in a yard set back from the
main street, between Numbers 8 and 16 Water Skellgate, there
was even a covered casino, a skating rink, where young skaters
would 'glide away to the strains of the Volunteer Band', and the
delights of a permanent fun fair.

We know that among the wealthier patrons of this downtown
area of Ripon were the Studley Royal party. Studley Royal is a
huge estate set in a secluded valley, watered by the River Skell,
just four miles southwest of the Market Place obelisk in Ripon,
a monument to Studley Royal's sometime owner, one William
Aislabie, and designed in 1781 by the celebrated London
architect Nicholas Hawksmoor.

Studley Royal has been called the Wonder of the North. It
is a World Heritage site and contains over 900 years of history
with a twelfth-century abbey, a mediaeval deer park, a Jacobean
Hall, an eighteenth-century water garden, and a Victorian
Church.

Naturally it was high on Freda's list for investigation with Barbara. Other stately homes close to Ripon that were part of their itinerary included Norton Conyers, less than three miles to the north and borrowed by Charlotte Brontë as a model for Thornfield Hall in *Jane Eyre*. Also Newby Hall to the southeast, which is an eighteenth-century Robert Adam house with a magnificent tapestry room, library, statue gallery and some of Thomas Chippendale's finest furniture, Barbara's love of which will leave her readers in no doubt as to the part played by the Hall in her education at Freda's hands. Both Norton Conyers and Newby Hall preoccupied Freda and Barbara and we will come to them shortly. But neither was as influential as Studley Royal. The Estate was the most pervasive reminder of the influence of power, money and politics on all Ripon's citizens from 1180 and, for reasons that will become apparent, it holds a principal place in my story.

Studley Royal reached into the lives of the people of Ripon as one of the city's biggest employers, and the estate owned many of the properties in which they dwelt, particularly in the area where the Walkers lived. For example, in February 1889 Lord Ripon put up six houses for sale in Water Skellgate – Numbers 18 to 23 – No. 20 including in its lot a blacksmith's shop, a joiner's, a brewhouse, stable buildings and yard. These must have been leasehold sales because Studley Royal tenants are still recorded as paying rent on them through 1991, when records stop.

Studley Royal's influence was so ubiquitous in the city that on High Skellgate there traded a cycle-maker, whose top-end product was 'the famous Studley Royal model'. Almost certainly he was supplier by appointment to the Royal Estate, where visitors – amounting to some 40,000 annually before the First World War – could hire bicycles, 'motors', or a bath chair. Even the front stage cloth at the Victoria Hall carried on it a painting of Fountains Abbey, and Jim Gott writes about this with great reverence. Studley Royal had an unseen hand in everything, it impinged on life in Ripon at every level, as employer, as property owner, as political presence, and the male line of it no doubt also impinged on more than a few young girls' dreams, the Estate's very name seeming to recommend it in the matter of breeding.

The Aislabie family had succeeded to Studley Royal in 1664, when a merchant from York, one George Aislabie, married into the ancient, landed Mallory family. A long history led up to this succession. The estate is called Royal because the manor was originally held directly from Henry II, King of England from 1154 to his death in 1189, its earliest owner being one Richard le Aleman. Succession was often carried by means of daughters from one family to another, the Mallory family getting it through marriage into the Tempest family in 1444.

The Tempests had themselves come into the Estate early in the fourteenth century when Sir Richard Tempest married a member of the Le Gras family who succeeded from the Le Alemans in similar fashion. The Tempests died out in the male line, as did the Mallorys in the seventeenth century, but it is perfectly in line with Barbara's interest in Ripon's history that names of these powerful, knightly Ripon families should live on in some of her fictional heroines. Her readers will recognise Mallory Keswick in *Everything to Gain* and Katharine Tempest in *Voice of the Heart*, for example. The film of *A Woman of Substance* actually began shooting at Broughton Hall, near Skipton, which was once the home of the Tempest family.

Ten years after George Aislabie inherited Studley Royal, he was killed in a duel and the Estate passed to his son, John, who, twenty years later, became Member of Parliament for Ripon and rose to Chancellor of the Exchequer, only to be run out of office in 1721, following the most celebrated financial scandal in English history, the South Sea Bubble, a disastrous scheme for paying off the National Debt in which Aislabie appeared personally to profit. He was arrested and imprisoned in the Tower of London, and although at his trial he was unable to explain his great wealth, he somehow managed to keep Studley Royal, dedicating himself thereafter to improving its house and gardens.

The Tudor house at the heart of the estate, Studley Royal Hall, was partly destroyed by fire in 1716. Aislabie's rebuild was never finished and much of it was said to have rather spoiled what was left of the original architecture, reducing it to a grand architectural mess, a terrible muddle of styles, which Blackie O'Neill comments on in *A Woman of Substance* as being the state of Fairly Hall. This instantly recommended it to me as the model for Fairley Hall, where Emma Harte first works as a kitchen maid and which later, after Edwin Fairley, the father of her illegitimate child, abandons her, *she* takes great delight in arranging for it to be razed to the ground.

Along with Studley Royal Hall, the 400-acre deer park and gardens of the estate provided employment for the locals. [17] In 1726, one hundred men were at work making canals and waterworks there, and it is worth noting that while the formal geometric design with its extraordinary vistas was the brainchild of Aislabie, the works were carried out by local labour under the direction of a man called John Simpson, almost certainly a member of a Ripon family that would one day play a significant role in Edith Walker's story.

In 1742, John Aislabie's son, William, inherited the Estate and in 1768 added the nearby ruined Fountains Abbey and adjacent Fountains Hall to it, unifying them with Studley Royal Hall by landscaping the valley between them. The terraced landscaping of the gardens, sweeping vistas and incorporation of the abbey ruins, make Studley Royal today one of the most romantic places in England. Barbara used the front façade of Fountains Hall as that of Pennistone Royal in the seven-novel Emma Harte series.[9]

By 1901, Edith Walker had left the family home and was working as a domestic servant a few miles from Studley Royal at 10 Skell Bank, which leads off the west end of Water Skellgate.

Her father, John, had moved from 8 Water Skellgate to 9 Bedern Bank, a short walk to the east in the shadow of the minster, a property owned by the Studley Royal Estate. He would live there until 1910, but the house would be leased to

---

[9] There are seven books in the Emma Harte series: *A Woman of Substance; Hold the Dream; To Be The Best; Emma's Secret; Unexpected Blessings; Just Rewards* and *Breaking the Rules.*

the Walker family for years afterwards – except for one short but pertinent period into the 1930s when Barbara was born.

Here, in 1901, John and second wife Elizabeth were living with John's son Joseph (who had not yet set up on his own), grandson Gabriel Barker (aged ten) and various lodgers, including a builder called Leo Walker, a boy of nine called Chris (surname illegible on the electoral roll) and a girl, Rebecca, who was thirteen. Next door, at No. 8, John's eldest son Thomas has reappeared and is following in his father's footsteps as a slater. Thomas's wife, whose name looks like Frances, is with him, along with their son, Jamie, who is fifteen, and three daughters, Lillie, Elizabeth and Minnie, who are five, four and two respectively. Lillie – Freda's cousin – is the future wife of Joe Wray, with whom Barbara and Freda would later stay in the caretaker's quarters at Thorpe Prebend House.

This ancient street of Bedern Bank, once called Betherom Bank, runs down the west side of the Minster Precinct, by the old cathedral graveyard, leading to the Minster's south boundary at High St Agnesgate. The street was part of a localised area for census in Freda's time, which included thirty-two dwellings where lived fifty-one servants. Given that only twenty-three per cent of houses in the city employed any servants at all, and Bedern Bank appears from a map of 1909 to have been made up of quite tiny cottages, except for one early Georgian brick house known as The Hall at the top of the hill by the Minster, it seems likely that the cottages were for servants and other workers administering the area.

At the top of the Bank were '*2 cottages with yards and outbuildings behind*', described as such in a leasehold sale by the Studley Royal Estate held at the Unicorn Hotel on 29th November 1887. At that time these cottages – actually 8 and 9 Bedern Bank (to which John Walker was living by 1901) – were 'in the occupation of William Gott Senior and William Gott Junior,' none other than grandfatherly relations (great-great and great respectively) of our Ripon witness of these times, Jim Gott. Thanks to him we have the following contemporary description of two dwellings owned by Studley Royal and inhabited by members of the Walker family from the start of the twentieth century until (with one short gap) 1935 – cottages that Edith and Freda knew particularly well:

> *On top of Bedern Bank, two low, yellow-washed cottages used to stand. One in particular was of great significant [sic] to me, being the residence of a great, great grandfather of mine – William Gott – who was a jeweller, clock and watchmaker … The style of the establishment was unique itself, especially the front with its low window. The pathway continued the sill, and the gradient of the hill made it seem lower still. In fact, one had to bend down to see into the window. Steep steps led down to the inner doorway. From inside, one got a grand view through the window of feet and legs.*

So, in 1901, for the first time in her life, Edith was living independently of her father. Her employer was thirty-seven-year-old Richard Guy, who hailed from Waterford in Ireland and lived in Skell Bank with his wife, Annie, and their four children. Richard Guy was a tailor; he had his own business and shop. His younger brother George also lived in the house and worked in the business with him.

You did not have to be very rich to afford a servant in those days – they cost little to hire – but as early as 1897 Richard Guy was prosperous enough to pay for an advertisement in the West Riding edition of *Kelly's Trade Directory*, and by 1908 he had moved from Skell Bank to 6 North Street, on the north side of the Market Place, a better address, though nothing special. Jim Gott recalled Richard Guy's shop in North Street, and offers a rather unsettling glimpse of its contents, seeming to carry the dust of ages: 'Day after day, year after year, I have gazed into the window of the clothier's shop [Mr Guy's] where time virtually stands still,' he wrote. 'The same old wax models in the same old place with their sweaty, sickly complexions tanned by the grime and dust of age, fixedly staring with death-like ghostly impressions. There they stand bedecked in the very latest – a la Fauntleroy; or the choicest design – the Norfolk pattern; or the *pièce de résistance* – the ever popular children's sailor outfit complete with wooden whistle. Surrounding these … are the well-known chicken chokers, dicky fronts, straw boaters and

Beau Brummel bows.' Richard Guy was still at 6 North Street in 1936. By 1923 he carried the letter 'J' beside his name, indicating that he was respected enough to serve as a juror.

When I discovered the Guy family from Waterford in Ireland it occurred to me what a coincidence it was that servant-girl Edith Walker will have been surrounded by the same kind of Irish cheer that servant-girl Emma Harte experiences in the close company of Blackie O'Neill at precisely the same period of her life, when she is kitchen maid at Fairley Hall. The Guys' home county even supplies the origins of Blackie's 'spectacular Waterford crystal chandelier', which hangs from the 'soaring ceiling' of his Harrogate mansion after he and Emma Harte become rich.

In the novel, Blackie is Emma Harte's succour. His liveliness and gaiety, his distinctive character, an 'unquenchable spirit and a soul that was joyous and without rancour', transform her. From the start he calls her 'mavourneen', an Irish term of endearment which turns up time and again in the novels.

Blackie and his Irishness are pertinent to Emma's ambition because it is he and his unquenchable spirit which open Emma's eyes to the very idea that she can make a fortune. 'It was the magical word "fortune" that had made the most profound impact on her... Emma's heart was pounding so hard she thought her chest would burst... "Can a girl like me make a fortune?" she asked, breathless in her anticipation of his answer.' It's the word 'fortune' that holds Emma spellbound. When she savours it, Blackie sees in her face 'ambition, raw and inexorable'.

I understand that Blackie O'Neill will be a principal character in the prequel to *A Woman of Substance* on which, as I write in 2020, Barbara is working. It is not fanciful to suppose that Richard Guy was similarly encouraging of Edith in reality as Blackie is of Emma in the novel, or that Edith first considered she might make herself a fortune and lift herself out of the poverty into which she was born, buoyed up by the Irishman's blarney. Certainly Richard Guy was on the 'up' and would have been full of his own ambitions, and for a girl like Edith (as for Emma Harte), dreams of success would have been measured in material terms, in terms of *making a fortune*.

In 1902, when Jack London came to England from America to conduct an investigation into the living conditions of the poor, he commented that they were as materialistic, indeed perhaps more so than the rich, and this is important in charting the lives of Edith, Freda and, later, Barbara – the one life, the seed in the garden of Barbara's fiction, where success means money. In *A Woman of Substance* Emma Harte's whole purpose is money, 'Vast amounts of it. For money was power. She would become so rich and powerful she would be invulnerable to the world.'

Given the conditions of life for Emma, as for Edith and Freda in the real world, and other of Barbara's fictional heroines whose money 'arms them against the world', one can see why.

Barbara never knew the want and vulnerability she describes in the fiction, but, like Emma Harte, her grandmother Edith did. By the end of the novel, however, money no longer had the same significance: 'Once you have these essentials taken care of and go beyond them, money is simply a unit, a tool to work with,' writes Barbara. But at the start, it is making a fortune that motivates Emma.

For maidservants, their only realistic hope was to find a man from a better class to marry and the dream was usually as far as it went. The prospect was fraught with the risk of exploitation and invariably led to complete disaster. Not so for Emma Harte of course, whose exploitation by Edwin Fairley ironically gives her the guts, the fury, to claw herself up by her own efforts.

Edith had a similarly forceful character. Barbara gave me a photograph of her in her mid- to late twenties with her hand set purposefully on hip, wearing her hair in the Edwardian style, a sparkling broach at her neck and a lace-trimmed dress. It was almost certainly taken when she was enjoying a period of uncharacteristic prosperity to which we will come. [18]

During this period, towards the end of 1903, Edith, having just turned twenty-three, became pregnant, and on 3rd June the following year gave birth out of wedlock to a baby girl she named Freda.

The 'when and where' column of Freda's birth certificate reads: 'Third June 1904; 9A Water Skellgate'. Mother and child were living not at the Guys' house, nor at the Bedern Bank cottage with Edith's father, but in that yard of dwellings between Numbers 8 and 16 Water Skellgate already described, set back from the main street, a place of razzmatazz, which had once offered a covered casino, a skating rink, and the delights of a permanent fun fair. [19]

A comment on the 1901 census return suggests that 9A Water Skellgate was something of a hideaway, where anonymity could be assured. Normally an occupier's name is given for each census address, but in the case of 9A Water Skellgate no name was given. Instead, the words 'in occupation' were appended. No name in an occupied property is unheard of even in the case of Ripon's yards or courts, where there was often great occupancy drift. It is not the purpose of a census to establish *whether* a property is occupied, but *who* is in occupation. If a house is known to be occupied, an occupant's name has to be made available to the Authorities. But the name of the occupant of 9A Water Skellgate was withheld. Why? It would have needed sanctioning by someone high up and with the connivance of the freeholder. Like most of the property in this area the freeholder was the Studley Royal Estate, like Bedern Bank, where Edith's family were living. The 1901 census return says that 9A Water Skellgate was leased to the Irish League, a charitable organisation supported by the Estate.

There are more telling questions posed by Freda's birth certificate. The name of her father has been withheld. Lines are drawn through the column headed 'Name and Surname of Father' and 'Occupation of Father'. Again, this is most unusual and indicates a definite decision by Edith or the father or both to keep paternity a secret. In an official Ripon illegitimacy return dated 1857, where eight out of nine single mothers were granted five shillings per week for the first six weeks and one shilling and sixpence until the child was thirteen, there is *in every case* appended the name of a father, whether or not the true father was. It was done even if the mother wasn't sure who the father was, because in those days illegitimacy was regarded as a terrible stigma, a burden no mother would wish to heap upon her illegitimate child. Such a stigma was it that when Freda married Winston and had to fill in their marriage certificate she used her grandfather's name (John Walker) in the column headed 'Father's Name and Surname', thereby falsifying the return rather than admitting that she was what was commonly known as 'a bastard'. My contact at the Harrogate area registry confirmed that it is unheard of on a birth certificate for a name not to be conjured up from somewhere, especially on three consecutive certificates, as was the case for Freda. For, as we shall see, Edith gave birth to three illegitimate children between 1904 and 1910, and in each case no father was named on the birth certificate. Two black diagonal lines were drawn where the father's name and occupation should have been.

We may safely conclude that a definite decision was taken by Edith not to put down any name. Perhaps she wanted to maximise her chances of keeping the father onside. Very likely he was a married man with a position to uphold, a man whose reputation would suffer were his 'indiscretions' made known, someone perhaps Edith hoped to marry and so did not want to compromise his true identity officially by entering a false name.

Not naming the father on three certificates – in 1904, 1907 and 1910 – does suggest continuity, that the father was the same man in each case, that each birth was not a one-time fling. If Edith had been leading a profligate life with different men, there would be no reason *not* to name the children's fathers, or to invent a name, as was the usual way in such cases. The three children are in this sense bound to one father by the very fact of his not being named on all three certificates.

And if one man fathers three children by the same woman out of wedlock over a period of seven years, financial support and possibly even love would have been involved. Being pregnant so often would have made it impossible for Edith to hold down a job. No one would have hired her. I already had it from Barbara that her mother always said that Edith never did work because *she didn't need to*. This, together with the photograph mentioned above of Edith with her hand set purposefully on hip, wearing a lace-trimmed dress with her hair in the Edwardian style and a sparkling broach at her neck, suggest that Edith's support was indeed bound up in the arrangement.

Almost a decade after first publication, this view was by chance corroborated by a telephone call I received from the writer, Shirley Conran, who had read my book and felt that I had missed something significant about the standing of Freda's father. Referring to the photograph of Edith, she began as follows:

'I was an advisor to the Jewellery Association for about eight years, part of my work for the Council for Industrial Design. Anyway, I was very interested in jewellery, and the brooch that Edith is wearing in that picture in particular. It would cost you today – if you were selling it, you'd get about £3,000. If you were buying it, it would definitely be £10,000, maybe up to £20,000. Any jeweller would know what you meant by an Edwardian Star, or a Late Victorian Diamond Star broach.

'Now, if you look up Winston Churchill's mother she quite often wore them in her hair. Firstly you covered your chest with these things, and the more stars you had the more desirable you were. It was a status thing. These stars you could sprinkle over your hair, over your body, down your front, right to the hem. They were a fashion, they were a fashion among very rich people.

'You knew you were safe giving your wife one of these things, so you would roll into Cartier and choose one and while you were at it you would buy one for your girlfriend. It was very much – that was how they bought jewellery for the mistress. It didn't occur to them that it was at all demeaning to give the wife the same bit of jewellery.

'Now, Barbara's grandmother – no way would she have one of those. One of the joys of them was the workmanship that went into the diamonds in the Star, you see. I'm surprised she even wore it in public actually, because it's such a giveaway. It certainly gave away that she had a lover who was rich. A middle-class man couldn't have afforded it. Middle-class men gave their wives trinkets, they gave them seed pearls, they gave them semi-precious stones, amethysts set on gold. They did not give them great big hulking Stars! What I do know is that piece came from a good source, and a good source would not have been in Manchester or Leeds, it would have been in Bond Street.'

All things considered, it is likely that Edith will have seen Freda's birth at the time as anything but a calamity, rather as the first step to realising a dream of great fortune... If only she could persuade the fellow to marry her, for she was clearly vulnerable.

Feeling bound to enquire further as to who Freda's father might be, it seemed that we were looking for a married man, a wealthy, probably local man with whom Edith could conceivably have come into contact, ideally a man with a pretty good reason why marriage was off the agenda for the time being, one good enough to have sustained his affair with Edith for the seven years in which she conceived his three children.

CHAPTER FIVE
The Marquess

'She glanced over at Studley Church, so picturesque in the snow, and at the obelisk nearby. She then directed her gaze to the lake below, glittering in the sunlight... A strange sensation came over her... Déjà vu, the French call it.'

Her Own Rules

Edith's second child was born on 21st July 1907, a boy named Fred – not Frederick, but Fred, as his birth certificate shows. Transparently, his was almost the same name as the one Edith gave her first child – Freda. The local Register of Births told me that it was common practice for a single mother in those days to name her illegitimate child after the father, a desire to out the father's identity often no doubt born of revenge when the father failed to do the right thing; or perhaps for the child's sake, to seal its identity for the future, however clandestinely.

I have already mentioned that Barbara adopted the practice in *A Woman of Substance*, naming Emma Harte's illegitimate daughter Edwina to point the finger at the identity of her blue-blooded father, Edwin Fairley. Barbara did this without knowing anything about her mother's illegitimacy. Indeed, she would register deep shock when she learned it from me in 2004, even though eighteen years earlier, she had made Audra (Freda's alter ego in *Act of Will*) illegitimate, named her mother Edith and described her father as Edith's 'benefactor and protector'.

I toyed with this apparent coincidence for a while and all the references in her novels to the increasingly fascinating

story of her maternal line, about which Barbara claimed to
know nothing. A divergence of interest presented itself –
1. How much did Barbara really know and if nothing, were these
references in the novels merely coincidence? And 2. Who was
Freda's father? The search for the latter won through as being the
more immediate and proved fruitful in more ways than one.

The names of Edith's first two children were both diminutives
of 'Frederick'. I could now be more specific about the man we
were looking for: a wealthy man by name of Frederick, almost
certainly prominent in the local community but someone with
whom Edith could conceivably have come into contact and,
ideally, a man with a pretty good reason why marriage to Edith
was off the agenda, at least for the time being.

One afternoon, as all this unravelled before me, I asked a
local studies archivist, steeped in Ripon's history, whether she
could think of anyone that fitted the description. It turned out
not to be too searching a request. Given the tidy nature of the
city, the wealth of research available, the archivist's knowledge
of it and the fact that one prominent family is well-known even
today for the sheer number of Fredericks in it, she did not pause
for one moment before replying.

Frederick has been the family name of the Robinsons of
Ripon since at least 1746, when one Frederick Robinson
first drew breath. In 1782 a Frederick John was added to the
family, in 1816 a Hobart Frederick and in 1830 a Frederick
William. In 1832, Lady Mary Gertrude Robinson married
into the Vyners of Gautby, Lincolnshire, and soon Fredericks
began to litter their family records too – in 1836 Henry
Frederick Clare Vyner was born and Frederick Grantham
Vyner in 1847. Meanwhile, in 1827, Frederick John Robinson
had a son named George Frederick Samuel. And in 1852
George Frederick's son by his wife and cousin Henrietta Ann
Theodosia Vyner, Frederick Oliver Robinson was born. These
last two Fredericks – George Frederick and Frederick Oliver –
were contemporaries of Edith in Ripon. There couldn't have
been a more visible or, as it turns out, more accessible family of
Fredericks available to her.

The Robinsons of Ripon were prominent in the local
community by virtue of the fact that Studley Royal had passed

into their hands by marriage into the Aislabie family, who you will recall had owned the estate since 1664.[10] After George Frederick Samuel Robinson succeeded to it in 1859 Prime Minister Gladstone conferred on him the title 1st Marquess of Ripon, as a reward for drawing up the Treaty of Washington. With George Frederick's death in 1909, his son, Frederick Oliver succeeded to both the title and the estate to which Freda remembered Edith dragging her constantly when she was a child.

I have kept until now the name of Edith's third illegitimate child, a girl born on 18th February 1910. Again, no father was named. Edith called the child Mary. Frederick Oliver Robinson, 2nd Marquess of Ripon and Master of Studley Royal, had only one sibling, a dear sister who died in infancy. Her name was Mary.

Fredrick Oliver was born on 29th January 1852, and when he fell dead while out grouse shooting in 1923, he was, like Jim Fairley of Fairley Hall in *A Woman of Substance*, the last of the family line, the last legitimate Robinson who could lay claim to Studley Royal. They made way for the Vyners, their cousins. The Robinsons, 'a sturdy and canny race typical Yorkshire',[11] had risen from being merchant adventurers in the sixteen century to rich aristocrats with quite a track record in national politics. Frederick Oliver's grandfather, Frederick John, had actually made it to 10 Downing Street as Prime Minister, succeeding George Canning in the summer of 1827 (a relative of mine, as it happens), but earning the distinction of holding

---

[10] Studley Royal came into the Robinson family as a result of William Robinson marrying Mary Aislabie in 1679. Mary was the daughter of George Aislabie, the estate's owner since 1664. Subsequently, his grandson, William, decreed in his will that should the Aislabie line die out, which it did in 1845, Studley Royal should pass to the next most direct descendent, which turned out to be William Robinson's great-grandson, Thomas Philip Robinson, older brother of Frederick John Robinson, who succeeded to the estate after Thomas died without issue in 1859, when it passed to George Frederick and then to the last of the Robinsons, Frederick Oliver. After his death in 1923, Studley Royal passed to the Vyners, cousins of the Robinsons. A triumph of postremogeniture!

[11] Lucien Wolf's *Life of the First Marquess of Ripon* (1921).

office for so short a time – the autumn and winter of 1827-8 – that he never once addressed the House. Frederick John's son, George Frederick Robinson, was a good deal more successful, entering Parliament as member for Hull in 1852, the House of Lords seven years later, and serving in every Liberal government for the next half-century and rising to Lord Privy Seal.

George Frederick's son, Frederick Oliver, in whose direction my research into Freda's paternity was pointing, was a rather different kettle of fish. Like his forebears he stood for Parliament, but took little interest in the affairs of the House of Commons and spent most of his time in Ripon, shooting game at Studley Royal, which was the principal shoot in all England. A fantastic shot, he made it his career to garner a reputation as one of the best shots in the country (the other was his friend Lord Walsingham). There are countless legendary stories of his skills, for example the speed with which he could change guns is supposed to have led to his accounting for seven birds dead in the air before any hit the ground. In 1905 he took 306 at Studley Royal, and that was small compared to the 576 out of 2,745 partridges at a shoot in Austria. On Dallowgill Moor the best score ever made was 1216 grouse to four guns in 1915. Frederick Oliver personally took 588 of them. He expired while picking up his grouse after a drive on Dallowgill Moor, on 22nd September 1923. A month earlier he had killed 249 birds in one day. He was seventy-three.

We have already seen how Studley Royal reached into the lives of everyone in Ripon as employer and landlord and how their party would come into the area where Edith was living for their entertainment to eat and drink, go to the theatre and so on. Frederick Oliver, who by all accounts pursued his pleasures above his duties, led the way. [20] It was the Victoria Hall in particular that would have given young Edith an opportunity to see how the Marquess and the other half lived. In late Victorian and Edwardian England such places were accessible to rich and poor alike, and full to overflowing. Once again, Jim Gott, Edith's contemporary, takes us into the world she would have known so well, recalling the Victoria Hall as a place that drew the nobility in their droves:

See the carriages sway and whirl to the main entrance. In the long-necked brass candle lamps, the flames flicker and dance as the carriages trundle away.

Intermingling shadows appear and disappear into the Hall, amid the flickering yellow lights. Flashing gems highlight the colourful satins and silks swished by my ladies, echoed by the sheen of their escorts' black velvet toppers. This is their hour – the local nobility – as they vanish within the gas-lit auditorium. Can we forget those Primrose League, Conservative, and Volunteer balls – sparkling and colourful? From a distance we watched these grand spectacles, with the Beckwith orchestra playing music, soothing, simple and haunting.

Edith was living in the thick of it all just a few doors up, in Water Skellgate, and no doubt wanting it all too. Did she have her first thrilling taste of theatre at the Victoria Hall, and later did her daughter Freda come bustling along in her wake and perhaps that of some male escort, the little girl thrilling to the brief suspension of daily care?

'Freda loved opera and she loved all the musical things like Gilbert and Sullivan and all of the things that I mention [that Audra likes] in *Act of Will...*' Barbara told me. It seems very likely that her mother's love of it was sparked at the Victoria Hall in Water Skellgate.

Frederick also called frequently at Water Skellgate to pursue his particular interest as patron of the Ripon Home For Girls. His father and mother had done a huge amount of social and philanthropic work in Ripon and were held in esteem by its inhabitants – Frederick was very much in the shadow of his father in this, but the Ripon Home For Girls was his particular focus of interest.

Water Skellgate also brought Frederick within a few yards of where Edith was living to attend regular meetings of the de Grey & Ripon Lodge (No. 837)[12], which bore his titles as Marquess

---

[12] 'De Grey' because the magnificent de Grey Estate at Wrest Park in Bedfordshire had passed into the Robinson family as a result of another canny marriage, this time between Thomas Robinson (1738-1786) to Lady Mary Grey Yorke, daughter of the 2nd Marchioness Grey. It was thus that the wealth of England was passed around.

and met at the Masonic Temple built by the Robinsons on the corner of High Skellgate and Water Skellgate, directly opposite the Victoria Hall. Its members would meet up afterwards for refreshments at the Unicorn Hotel on the southeast side of the Market Place, another of Studley Royal's properties in this corner of Ripon. The Lodge still meets there today.

Frederick's father, the 1st Marquess of Ripon had been a leading light nationally in the Masonic Craft, holding the position of Provincial Grand Master for thirteen years, and then Grand Master for four years (that's top dog, a most unusual appointment outside of London). But in 1874 he resigned after a sudden conversion to the Roman Catholic faith, which he believed to be incompatible with the Craft due to some outstanding Papal Bulls levelled against it. George Frederick had been received into the Catholic Church at the London Oratory on 4 September 1874. I have it from the secretary of the Masonic Lodge that he did so 'after marrying a Catholic', in other words at the behest of his aforementioned wife, Henrietta Ann Theodosia Vyner.

News of George's conversion was received with astonishment by the British establishment. *The Times* launched a vicious attack, accusing the 1st Marquess of renouncing 'his mental and moral freedom. A statesman who becomes a convert to Roman Catholicism forfeits at once the confidence of the English people.' Such was the anti-Catholic feeling of the time, following the assertion of papal infallibility by the Vatican Council of 1870.

In the Marquess of Ripon's circle, to be a Freemason was to be the quintessential Englishman, a part of the establishment at the height of the British Empire. It would have taken a strong woman to persuade him to become a Catholic and resign from the Craft, and my informant within the de Grey and Ripon Masonic Lodge made it absolutely clear that it was indeed the Marquess's wife, Henrietta, who persuaded him.

This new, deeply-laid Catholic influence within the Robinson family may, ironically, have provided Henrietta's son, who lacked his father's seriousness of purpose, with the best excuse for keeping Edith's wish to marry him in check. For Frederick was already married to another woman and the Roman Catholic

Church did not recognise divorce. A marriage could only end when one partner dies or if there are grounds for an annulment. If Henrietta was powerful enough to persuade her husband to resign from being a Mason, then standing in the way of her son divorcing in order to marry Edith Walker would have been well within her capabilities. For Frederick it would have been the kindest way of disabusing Edith of the notion that he did not love her enough to marry her, while he kept stringing her along.

And this is what we find going on in Barbara's novels. In *A Woman of Substance* and in *Everything to Gain* the Catholic Church's hostile attitude to divorce has a crucial bearing on the plot. In the first, wealthy, dashing Australian Paul McGill, with whom Emma Harte falls deeply in love, cannot break free of his Catholic wife, Constance. It is as a direct result of this that Paul sires Emma's second illegitimate child.

It is as well to consider what in Edith might have appealed to Frederick. In the Prince of Wales's Marlborough House set, in which the 2nd Marquess moved, he was a popular figure and there was something in him that attracted, and was attracted by, women of great vitality and vigour.

On 7 May 1885, some two decades before he would have met Edith, he had married Constance Gladys Lonsdale, widow of the Fourth Earl of Lonsdale. He will have been in no doubt when he married Gladys, as she was known, as to what was in store for him. Gladys Ripon was something of a Lillie Langtry figure. She knew how to have a good time, and had a reputation for living in the fast lane. Edward VII once referred to her as 'a professional beauty'. Her first husband, Lonsdale, himself once an ardent admirer of Lillie Langtry, the actress mistress of Edward VII, died in a brothel in 1882.

As it turned out, however, Gladys was away from the Ripon estate a lot, leaving Frederick to his own devices. She owned the lease of a house – Coombe Court, Kingston Hill in Surrey, on the edge of London, and when she died she breathed her last not at Studley Royal but at 13 Bryanston Square in London.

'Lady Ripon was the uncrowned queen of a smart, artistic, bohemian, and frivolous social set,' Donald Taylor reports in an article entitled 'The Bohemian Mistress of Studley Royal'. The bohemian and artistic elements of her reputation were deserved, even if, a little unkindly, Oscar Wilde dedicated his satirical play on English high society to Gladys and called it *A Woman of No Importance* (1893). She became a close friend of the Russian dancer Nijinsky, and managed him socially during the Russian ballet's first season in Covent Garden in 1911, booking him into the Savoy and advising him on where to go and which invitations to accept. Later she would galvanise support for him when he was detained as a prisoner of war in Hungary.

The party atmosphere Gladys enjoyed was racy but she combined it with a spirited, idealistic reverence for art, which apparently justified anything. As tireless fundraising patron of the arts she once had the puritanical Raymond Asquith, son of the Prime Minister, view 'with a jaundiced eye' her seduction of a millionaire neighbour of his at dinner: 'By the end of dinner she had got £35,000 out of him, and probably had more before she went to bed – or after,' Asquith was reported to have said.

When Gladys was around, you could expect a party, and often a noisy one. Her party-piece was to arrange a surprise smashing of quantities of crockery at dinner, an event which in fact guests looked forward to, and which was, according to the Duchess of Marlborough, originally precipitated by a real incident: 'Once a footman had dropped a tray,' she recounted, 'producing the amusement that the misfortune of others usually creates; since then the incident was repeated, with the china specially bought for making a noise.'

Gladys was as much at home in the company of royals as that of artists. Queen Alexandra, Edward VII's wife, became a close friend, and arranged for her to be on the house-party guest list of all the royal estates, another reason why she was frequently absent from Studley Royal. There was, however, no danger of Gladys sidelining her husband. As a result of her contacts, Edward VII became a shooting companion of Frederick Oliver's, and she brought her party-set lifestyle often enough to the estate for the gardeners to know never to mow the lawns until late in the day when she was in residence, owing to her 'delicate nature'. (Delicate she may have been the morning after, but not so by nature.)

It is, therefore, to Gladys Ripon that we can ascribe an exciting, *laissez faire* attitude within Studley Royal during Frederick's time, which servants and employees clearly enjoyed and which was in line with Gladys dropping her first name, Constance, which spelled steadfast qualities she preferred not to advertise.

As I have suggested, a love of glamour and a natural vitality were defining elements in Edith Walker's character, too. In *Act of Will*, she is 'the beautiful Edith. That was how they always spoke about her hereabouts.' Barbara confirmed this to me and to Billie Figg: 'She was called "the beautiful Edith" by members of the family.' It will have been how people in Ripon spoke of her, too. It is possible that this glittering something which Edith had and which Gladys Ripon clearly had in spades (and which attracted Frederick Oliver to her), was also what attracted Frederick to Edith. And one cannot help but wonder whether during Gladys's many absences from the Estate, the sudden removal of her vivacity left her husband with expectations which he then pursued on his own account with Edith. If so, and Gladys knew about his affairs, she was sufficiently a woman of the world not to object, having earlier come to terms with her first husband meeting his maker in a brothel possibly for similar reasons. As for Edith herself, since Gladys clearly had no intention of giving the Marquess an heir – she and Frederick were a childless couple – perhaps she decided to give Frederick what his wife wouldn't or couldn't.

We have a possible match, access, and on both sides a need. It is of course possible that Edith came to be in the Studley Royal employ. Many from Ripon were. Sadly, there are no records to substantiate this, or to rule it out.

What we know for sure is that Studley Royal had a special allure for Edith, which she passed on to her daughter Freda, and which Freda impressed upon Barbara as a child, sufficient for it to play a central role in the novels.

One crisp winter afternoon I walked in the freezing sunlight from Skellgarths through Water Skellgate, via *High Cleugh*, across the fields into Studley Royal, where the Marquess once dwelt. Barbara's readers will recognise the name 'High Cleugh'. It is Freda's double Audra's 'memory place' in *Act of Will*, the place from which she can look out at the long, low, eighteenth-century manor house where she was brought up and bewail the loss of her station in life. High Cleugh attracts her 'like a magnet', as I learned from Barbara it attracted Freda in real life.

It is in fact a tree-lined green space on the bank of the River Laver, just before it melds with the Skell as you exit the city by means of Mallorie Park Drive and Studley Road. High Cleugh is so close to Studley Royal that when Lord Wemyss set fire to a butt on the Estate one hundred years ago during a shoot and the flames took hold of the dry turf and spread out of control, a workforce was raised in Ripon and the flames were extinguished by means of buckets passed hand-to-hand from the river there. From High Cleugh the only eighteenth-century manor house Freda would be able to look onto, and mourn what might have been hers, was Studley Royal Hall.

It was as crystal clear to me as the air I breathed that High Cleugh had been Freda's memory place, a window onto her past and what-might-have-been, a past that was, for her mother, the reality in which she truly dwelt. My walk there, which retraced the route in Barbara's novel *Her Own Rules* followed by Meredith Stratton, who has come halfway across the world to discover her true identity, took me less than an hour, no distance at all in the days when a pair of legs was the most likely mode of transport.

There is a public footpath between High Cleugh and Studley Royal to ease one's passage. Before you know it, you are walking through the gates of the Estate and passing along the '*stately avenue of lime trees*', the vista which leads up to '*Studley church*', as Barbara writes in the novel. It is in fact the church of St Mary the Virgin, where all the Robinsons I have described lie buried, and which was built by Frederick's mother, Henrietta, from 1871–8, at a cost of £15,000. There is a monument to the Marchioness, a big white marble effigy on a tomb chest dated 1908.

A hundred head of deer crossed my path as I walked the route Edith and Freda (and later Barbara) will have taken so many times. The beasts came thundering past in the crisp light as I gazed in awe at the sublime marriage of the picturesque landscape and wild nature that is Studley Royal. I saw ancient, broken-down trees on which Edith's eyes would have rested when they were saplings. At the top of the rise, like Meredith Stratton in *Her Own Rules*, I 'glanced over at Studley Church, so picturesque in the snow, and at the obelisk nearby', and then directed my gaze to the lake below, glittering in the sunlight. The River Skell flowed beyond it, and there, just a short distance upstream, was the abbey...' Small wonder that here Barbara invoked her own déjà vu experiences of the place:

> *It was just turning nine o'clock on Tuesday morning. Meredith was bundled up in boots and a sheepskin coat, walking through Studley Park. The stately avenue of lime trees down which she hurried led to Studley Church, just visible on top of the hill at the end of the avenue...*
>
> *I'm almost there, Meredith told herself, as she finally reached the top of the hill at the end of the avenue of limes. She glanced over at Studley Church, so picturesque in the snow, and at the obelisk nearby. She then directed her gaze to the lake below, glittering in the sunlight. The River Skell flowed beyond it, and there, just a short distance upstream, was the abbey...*
>
> *A strange sensation came over her. She stood very still, all of her senses alert. Instantly, she knew what it was ... a curious feeling that she had been here before, that she had stood on this very spot, on this very hill, gazing down at those mediaeval ruins... She shivered again. Déjà vu, the French call it, already seen, she reminded herself. But she had not been here before; she had never even been to Yorkshire ...*
>
> *As she looked around, absorbing everything, her heart clenched, and she felt a strange sense of loss. So acute, so strong, so overwhelming was this feeling that tears came into her eyes. Her throat closed with such a rush of emotion she was further startled at herself.*
>
> *Something was taken from me here ... something of immense value to me. I have been here before. I know this ancient place ... somehow it is a part of me. What was it I lost here? ...She closed her eyes, not understanding what was happening to her; it was as though her heart was breaking. Something had been taken from her... The only thing she really knew at this moment was that she was experiencing an immense sense of deprivation ...*
>
> *Pain, she thought. Why do I feel pain and hurt and despair?*[13]

---

[13] *Her Own Rules.*

By this time a common denominator had emerged in my investigations. Prominent among the places to which Freda took Barbara from her base in Ripon and which provoked such empathic déjà vu experiences in the child as this, had a specific connection to the Robinson family.

Studley Royal obviously did, but so did Newby Hall, the 18th-century country house, three miles south-east of Ripon and another popular destination for mother and daughter. It had been in the Robinson family since 1792.

Again, the Robinsons had been associated with Middleham Castle since at least 1627. The castle was administered by Nappa Hall, a high roofed fortified manor house nearby, for centuries owned by the Metcalfe family who held high office as Surveyor of the Castle and Lessor of its estates and who received ranks and honours from the lordship, including from Richard of Gloucester, later Richard III. The Robinsons had come into the picture in 1627, when Frances Metcalfe, daughter of Sir Thomas Metcalfe, the then owner, married Sir William Robinson. Nappa Hall passed into Robinson ownership a century later. Middleham Castle would have been a regular port of call for members of both families during the most exciting period in its history, which Freda described to Barbara and she re-created in her historical novels.

At the end of Chapter Three I noted that in *Hold the Dream*, Shane O'Neill believes he is linked to the history of Middleham Castle through an ancestor *on his mother's side*. I had underlined it in the text because my thoughts were already focusing on Freda. It is 'the one spot on earth where he felt he truly belonged,' Barbara wrote. Freda had made it her business to impress this feeling on Barbara. I was beginning to discover what the whole Middleham experience had been about.

The point about Norton Conyers, another of their favourite destinations from Ripon, is that it is celebrated as the original of Thornfield Hall in Charlotte Brontë's *Jane Eyre*. Visiting the country house was part of Freda's immersion of her daughter in the lives and works of the Brontë sisters, which had begun with their trips to Top Withens, likely inspiration for Heathcliff's Wuthering Heights in Emily Brontë's novel. But now we learn from the Brontë Society that even the Brontës were intertwined with the Robinsons of Ripon. They were 'the only grand family that the Brontës knew'[14]. The connection had come to a tempestuous climax at Thorp Green Hall, eight miles north-west of York, in the period between 1840 and 1845 when Anne Brontë tutored the children of the Reverend Edmund Robinson and Anne's brother Branwell was discovered having an affair with the Reverend's wife. That these Robinsons and those of Newby Hall and Nappa Hall and Studley Royal are one and the same family has only recently been made public. The association was well known in the area, however, and is important because Anne, Charlotte and Emily were at their most productive at this point and the Robinsons were 'a primary source of inspiration for many of the characters, situations and attitudes which the Brontë sisters called upon in their work'[15]. If one book only had found its way into the impoverished home of Edith Walker and into the hands of her little daughter, Freda, who by the time Barbara was born had become a bookworm, it was surely written by a Brontë. How satisfied would Freda have been to know that today her daughter's manuscripts sit next to ones written by Charlotte Brontë among the Collections at the famous Brotherton Library in Leeds.

Barbara's empathic déjà-vu experiences with these engaging and telling sites carry a thrilling suggestion not only that the past is in some way contained in the present for all of us to savour, but that they were part of *her* history, in a very real sense they have been in Barbara's blood for centuries.

As crucially, these déjà-vu experiences are characterised in Barbara's personal experience and in her fiction by a deep sense of loss, of 'immense deprivation', of 'something taken', of 'pain and hurt and despair' which she describes as 'humiliation and despair and more heartache than I ever realised' and which, as ever, bring us back to Freda. For long before I revealed Freda's story to her daughter, Barbara said to me:

---

[14] 'Robinson Reflections Part 1: The Robinsons (of Newby Hall)' by Bob Gamble. Published in 2012 in *Brontë Studies: The Journal of the Brontë Society*, 37:2, 145-158, DOI: 10.1179/174582212X13279217752868.

[15] Abstract, ibid.

'I believe that my mother always had a great sense of loss, in fact I know that she did.'

I considered that all the Emma Harte novels[16] are bound up with what is lost when a character is dispossessed, cheated out of the rights attached to their birth, and *Act of Will*, *Everything to Gain* and *Her Own Rules* – all involve these places as inspiration. I was now ready to look into the nature of this appalling loss which so resounded through the lives of Freda and now her daughter.

---

[16] *A Woman of Substance; Hold the Dream; To Be The Best; Emma's Secret; Unexpected Blessings; Just Rewards* and *Breaking the Rules.*

CHAPTER SIX
The Abyss

'Who are you, Meredith Stratton. And why are you so troubled? Where does that deep well of sadness spring from? Who was it that hurt you so badly they've scarred your soul?'

Her Own Rules

Having an illegitimate child, with no partner to bring in the money, was next to suicide in Edwardian England. Edith would not have been able to go out to work: there was no crèche or other child support mechanism available, no State financial aid. That she managed to keep her head above water financially between 1904 and 1910 must certainly mean that she was receiving support from the father of her children. Her own father, John Walker, was in no position to help. John (by 1910 a man of sixty-six years) had registered as a builder and lived on Bedern Bank in a property owned, you will recall, by the Marquess of Ripon.

Edith was in any case riding high, as the photograph of her, taken during the period of her association with the father of her children, shows. The Diamond Star jewel had a particular significance in 1909, which is very probably the year that Edith was photographed wearing one.

In that year everyone was talking about the imminent appearance of Halley's Comet, probably a once-in-a-lifetime experience, as it only appears every seventy-five or seventy-six years. Never before had the comet been so well publicised or excitedly anticipated, and it was to pass closer to the Earth than had ever been recorded. Indeed the tail of it would actually pass

through the Earth: gas masks and anti-comet pills were sold for
fear of contamination; there were major hoaxes: newspapers
claimed that an Oklahoma religious group called the Sacred
Followers planned to sacrifice a virgin to ward off the impending
disaster of a collision, but had been stopped by the police.

For the writer Mark Twain the event had a particular
significance: 'I came in with Halley's Comet in 1835,' he said.
'It is coming again next year, and I expect to go out with it.'
Twain died on April 21, 1910, one day after the comet emerged
from the far side of the sun.

Such was the excitement surrounding the anticipated
spectacle that from midway through 1909 it fuelled the buying
among the rich of any jewellery with a stellar significance – the
Diamond Star was in particular demand, and crescent shaped
brooches were also popular.

So, that year Barbara's grandmother was in good company.
Her Diamond Star was all the rage. In today's money, as I have
since discovered independently, it would have cost anything
from £2,500 to some £80,000. She couldn't have paid for it.
In the photograph she is wearing it at the neck, centrally placed.
Aristocrats would never have worn it there. Edith was not one
of the very rich. She was the impoverished daughter, youngest
of six children, of a slater's apprentice. She was what was known
as 'dirt poor'. But she was Barbara's grandmother, and she had
plans. From around 1903 she had been seeing a very rich man
indeed. The Diamond Star bore testimony to that.

These years of material and emotional happiness were her
daughter Freda's first six and most impressionable years when, as
she told Barbara, she made frequent visits to Studley Royal. There
would surely have been happiness all around and Barbara certainly
had that impression. 'My mother loved Ripon so much, and she
always spoke happily and lovingly of her childhood,' she said. The
image Barbara created for me was what it was that drew Freda
back to Ripon time and again during her childhood. Freda told
Barbara they were happy times. Of course she did. Her otherwise
childless father, Frederick, no doubt enjoyed her company in
the beautiful surroundings of his estate. He had a real sense of
the spirit of landscape and loved to talk about the beauty of the
birds of the moors in flight (albeit oblivious to the fact that he

killed more of them than anybody else), once writing: 'Maybe a generation will spring up to whom all these things [the beauty of the moors, the colour and characteristic sounds of the birds of the shoot] will be a closed book; but when that day comes England will lose her most attractive and distinctive feature, and one of her most cherished traditions. For the England of whom the poets have sung will have ceased to exist.'

Alas for Edith and Freda and her siblings, it was not to last. On 9th July, 1909, as she was proudly sporting her Diamond Star and preparing for the birth of her third child with her very rich lover, his father died and Frederick found himself with new responsibilities as the newly entitled 2nd Marquess of Ripon.

For a while, Edith disappears off the Ripon map. As Halley's Comet passed, eventually to become a distant memory, Edith and her children vanish from sight. I could find no mention of them anywhere in the city. The electoral rolls even showed 9 Bedern Bank standing empty. Edith's father, John, seems also to have disappeared; yet we know he was still alive until 1912. Had the Studley Royal lease on Bedern Bank been withdrawn by the Marquess? Did Frederick foreclose on Edith? Was he wiping the slate clean, shoring up his public reputation before taking on the onerous responsibilities of Marquess?

A year earlier Frederick's mother, Henrietta, had died. With the removal of the heavy Catholic influence, her son's 'good reason' for not divorcing Gladys and marrying Edith disappeared. Had Edith called in his promises, piled pressure on Frederick to do the right thing and marry her? Had he responded by ridding himself of the bind of his second family by withdrawing his support of Edith and their children?

Losing sight of them in the various city records I decided as a last resort to explore the handwritten records of Ripon Workhouse. Hours later, with a rush of excitement cut with anguish, which any genealogist will recognise, I found the names of Edith, Freda, Fred and Mary listed among official workhouse admissions.

Upon entry, Edith would have been separated from her children. The story of their fall into the abyss is tragic in the extreme and it affected the children for the rest of their lives, as we shall see. For sadly, as Nietzsche wrote, if you gaze long enough into the abyss, the abyss will also gaze into you. [21]

Ripon Workhouse records are contained within half-year periods. They show that in the first half-year of 1910, Edith, Freda, Fred and Mary spent continuously 52, 49, 49 and 41 consecutive days in the workhouse respectively, that the four of them then spent the entire 184 days of the next half-year incarcerated, and fifteen days into the first half-year of 1911 as well.

What this means is that Barbara's mother was not only illegitimate, but was delivered into the care of the workhouse when she was a child of six going on seven, while Mary, her sister, was a babe in arms. This news was met with yet deeper distress than Freda's illegitimacy, when Barbara read the finished manuscript of this book, as one might imagine. She was stunned, and yet it was there on paper. At first she found it difficult to accept the evidence of the workhouse archival records, but the evidence was cast iron, written by hand at the time in the official record books of Ripon Workhouse.

It is perhaps difficult for us to imagine fully what their incarceration in the workhouse meant to Edith, Freda and her tiny children. The Ripon Union Workhouse that Edith, Freda and her siblings knew was built in 1854 at 75 Allhallowgate; as a museum it stands there still today. Twenty years earlier the Poor Law Amendment Act had brought an end to 'outdoor relief' (top-up wages when earnings fell below a certain level). Henceforth, only asylum within the workhouse, in exchange for work, was on offer and all claimants had to prove themselves paupers. If a vagrant possessed even a shilling he would be turned away. The pauper test, along with the conditions of the new residential workhouses – made awful to deter claimants – were the demeaning aspects of the law that caused such a furore.

The declared purpose of the Act was to encourage unemployed, able-bodied men to get a job and all employers to pay at least a subsistence wage; while the asylum aspect would, it was felt, prevent paupers from breeding because once in the workhouse a man would be separated from his wife. Also, as shown in a report on the West Riding of Yorkshire, it was expected that 'the separation of husband and wife would have a beneficial tendency in rousing the indolent to exert themselves.' Records depict firm discipline and terrible sorrow. In reality, the agonies of the receiving wards, where husbands were separated from wives, and children from parents, were devastating.

What had also been overlooked was the effect upon the *needy*, that the unemployed and vagrants were not all shirkers, that unmarried mothers were not all prostitutes, that orphans were not a lower order, and that if you lived into your sixties you could easily become destitute because there were no state pensions in those days. All had effectively been criminalised by the Act. Adding to their burden, workhouses were made to take in 'lunatics', mentally defective children and the physically sick. Guardians displayed their patronising attitude by lumping their charges – 'idiots and lunatics, bastards, venereals, the idle and dissolute' – together. Yet segregation was by gender and age only.

Today, visitors to the Workhouse Museum will approach the same nineteenth-century portico through which Barbara's mother passed in 1910. The entrance to the Grubber, as it was known, is a low, one- and two-storey, brick-built construct with a stone gateway and imposing twelve-foot doors, behind which lie a village-sized collection of buildings within very much higher walls. There were adult wards (into which sane and insane intermingled) and receiving wards, where the separations – male/female, child/adult – took place, and bodies were stripped, disinfected and clothed in workhouse attire before being taken to segregated dormitories, exercise yards or casual ward cells barely big enough for a bed.

If inmates wanted to eat they must work: breaking stone, chopping wood (there was a chopping shed built in 1903), weeding, lifting potatoes (Ripon Workhouse had its own garden), or picking oakum, the loose fibre obtained by unravelling old rope, as in Dickens. Respite was only given after the task was complete. Inmates would dine in gender-segregated areas, sitting on benches at long tables, all facing the same way and eating in silence. Edith's daily diet consisted of less than half a pint of milk, just under a pound of flour (bread was baked on the premises until 1916), a few potatoes (equivalent to four small new potatoes), a little sugar, butter and cheese (about 3 oz a week), a quarter of a pound of meat, and a cup full of oatmeal. Coffee was not introduced until 1917. Bedtime was '*8.30 p.m., rising in summer at 6.15 a.m. and in winter at 6.45 a.m.*'

There were also children's nurseries and at one time a schoolroom, and a hospital block (male and female wards, and a special maternity ward) and mortuary. The maternity or lying-in ward was available to unmarried mothers and others who, in the days before National Health Service hospitals, could not afford hospitalisation. Edith, perhaps because she had had a difficult birth with Freda, availed herself of the facility in 1907 and 1910 for the births of Fred and Mary. She would have been in and out as quickly as possible, for the ward was notably without frills. Mostly, the women in the ward were regarded as of 'low moral character'. Some were youngsters in their teens expecting their first baby, generally frightened and apprehensive, but most were 'regulars' with a lifetime of prostitution behind them. Quarrelling and fighting often broke out and the workhouse staff found these inmates resentful and uncooperative.

Our man on the ground, Jim Gott, was a thirteen-year-old lad living in Allhallowgate at the very moment that the Walkers passed through the workhouse gates for the first time. In his memoir he gives a sense of how children playing in the street outside would be lured towards the workhouse walls in the hope of the odd glimpse of an inmate. How the imagination would take flight when so rewarded – as when Tommy Jackson suddenly bobbed his head above the side gates: 'It was like a nightmare in the daylight. He used to stare with eyes like lemonade glass alleys set in the circular rings of raw liver; and when he laughed it was like the opening of the Mersey Tunnel on a wet day.' Then there was Tommy Coates with his 'one upper molar', and 'Bill Sykes' cap ... perched on his thin, worn head... He always reminded me, when he walked, of those jointed wooden dolls, his every movement stiff and mechanical as though he had to be wound up like a clockwork model.'

One who had not actually witnessed life within the Ripon Workhouse walls assured me that, 'This was a small, rural workhouse. Forget Charles Dickens. There would be gramophone evenings from people in the city, special treats at Christmas, they even went to the theatre.'

It is true, as specialist Anthony Chadwick points out in an excellent booklet on the subject, that 'some Yorkshire workhouses were reprimanded by London for allowing such comforts as tobacco or seaside trips,' and Ripon's own records point to a Magic Lantern Entertainment for aged inmates in 1884, a mayoral tea and concert eight years later, a pint of beer and an ounce of tobacco on the occasion of the marriage of the Duke of York in 1893, and outings to the Victoria Hall (I have a note that in November 1912, inmates were treated to a production of Gilbert and Sullivan's *Pirates of Penzance* there), Studley Royal and Fountains Abbey – what would Edith have made of these! But they were very occasional and anyone who has braved the Ripon Workhouse museum, housed in the old male casual wards, on a chilly autumnal morning, as I did, will beg to differ. The tiny vagrant cells, one complete with restraining chair for rowdies or lunatics, are as cold as stone. The ignominy, the uncertainty and fear, the absence of warmth of any kind, love and comfort, the loneliness, the sheer despair are missing from any equation that delivers a pleasure verdict to a child on such a place as this. And unaccounted for are the authoritarian and patronising attitude of such a system in respect of the poor, and the stigma and humiliating aspect of being in receipt of charity.

As for the view that Ripon Workhouse was an occasional place of entertainment, let Jim Gott give us the benefit of actual experience, for he was once an entertainer there:

> *Years ago, when I was throng in the entertainment world, I appeared at No. 75 Allhallowgate ... and really the memory of the night will always be with me. I remember I sang one of my compositions, 'Down at Fishergreen'. I've often wondered since what were their thoughts as I reminded them of their early days.*
>
> *Many old familiar faces were before me – some that I had thought had passed on. How strange to see them there like a long-forgotten community cut off from the rest of the world. Not that I am decrying the administration of those in charge, but through my eyes, the inmates seemed so lonely with a pitiful hunger for the warmth of their own kith and kin ...*

The stigma and the fear lived on. The stigma of being a workhouse child was burned into its very soul. However solicitous some may have been in lightening the burden, 75 Allhallowgate was the gateway to hell, as the endless lists of those who died there bears terrible testimony.

If Edith had been let down by the 2nd Marquess it would have been very difficult for her to make enough of a rumpus from inside the Grubber to put a stain on his reputation. It would have taken time to make accusations stick or raise much credibility from inside the workhouse. Yet this would have been her only hope, unless…

In Edith's case the facts are that on 15 October 1910 she was taken from the workhouse to Ripon Minster and married to one John Thomas Simpson, a labourer five years her junior. She was then returned to the workhouse. Simpson described himself on their marriage certificate as a labourer, and gave his address as 8 Belle Vue Yard, Somerset Place, where we know his father, Thomas, lived.

John Thomas Simpson was born in 1886 and had three brothers: James, Arthur and Alfred. He was only twenty-four when the wedding took place. His bride's sister-in-law, Ruth Matilda Walker (wife of Edith's brother Joseph), was one of two witnesses to the wedding, which had clearly been a low-profile affair, in spite of its location, although in fact the Minster was simply performing its role as the parish church of the workhouse.

What seems so strange is that Edith returned after the wedding to the workhouse. What kind of marriage was this? Had Simpson, five years younger than she, been pushed forward to rescue her from the abyss and remove her once and for all from any connection with Frederick?

Edith left the workhouse in January 1911, three months after the wedding. On 3 February 1912 she produced her fourth child, Norman, the first with a father on the birth certificate by name of Simpson. He gave his residence as 9 Bondgate, Ripon, while Edith gave hers as 9 Bedern Bank. Why the two addresses if she and Simpson were husband and wife in the normal way? Furthermore, what sort of circumstances could have suddenly made the Bedern Bank address, owned by Studley Royal, available once more to the Walker family?

Increasingly, the whole thing feels like a put-up job, a marriage of convenience and not one that necessarily involved any emotional input on anyone's part. Was he put forward as a safe way forward? Consider the ramifications. Simpson could be guaranteed employment. Edith would be free. As soon as the keys of Bedern Bank were returned to her, she could quit the workhouse and repair to her own home. As far as the Marquess was concerned, she could have her babies where she liked. So long as there was a husband registered on the birth certificate, the Robinson name was nothing to do with it. Edith was an independent married woman, with all the boxes neatly ticked.

It was a solution that appealed to everyone for their own reasons, and it is quite possible for it to have been cooked up in the Workhouse. Records for the period show various Simpsons as inmates. One Elizabeth Ann Simpson had an almost permanent residence there – could this be Edith's elder sister who had also married a Simpson? And there's a Thomas Simpson (born 1845), who is in and out of the Grubber constantly – could this be John Thomas's father? He would be the right age. Also a Joseph Simpson crops up time and again, as does a labourer called James Simpson – could this be John Thomas's brother, James?

Furthermore, just as Edith had contact with the Simpson family through the workhouse, so the Marquess or his people may have had contact with the Simpson family too. At the time, a branch of the family had a gardening business at Kirby Road in Ripon and, among other duties, looked after the cemetery gardens. Edith's husband described himself on his marriage certificate as a labourer, but at the birth of their first child, he was more specific, calling himself a 'grocer's waggoner' on Norman's birth certificate. This commercial gardening role connects J T Simpson to the time-honoured gardening Simpsons of Ripon and, further, to the Studley Royal Estate, one John Simpson heading the gardening workforce there when the main works were done, as I have described. Ripon is a very small city, people did not move around like they do today. The Simpsons of Ripon, whom Edith knew, may well have been of that same family.

Other facts also suggest a connection between J T Simpson and Studley Royal. Records show that on 3rd July 1914, Edith gave birth to a fifth child, named Frances, about whom Barbara had known nothing. Nor was it easy to find out much about Frances. The only Frances Simpson born in 1914, the year recorded as the year of her birth in a later workhouse record, to which I will come, was indeed registered as born to John Thomas Simpson and his wife, Edith (née Walker), but she was born in Millar's Lane, Morpeth, which is in Northumberland, not in Yorkshire at all.

By her own account, when Barbara read this in the original manuscript she was immediately transported to a childhood memory of her mother talking of Morpeth as a feature of her life at this time – this market town some eighty-six miles to the north of Ripon.

Why Morpeth? Had Simpson taken his wife there on holiday? Not likely. Given paucity of funds and general inclination, holidays eighty or so miles away to the north are an unlikely part of the Simpson family agenda. Could it be that work had taken him up there, possibly at the behest of the Studley Royal Estate? I rang the local library at Morpeth and asked a helpful young lady whether she knew of any connection between Studley Royal and any estates in the area.

'Funnily enough,' she said, 'there is a connection. In my village of Swarland, just north of Morpeth, Commander Clare Vyner had an estate there, where workers from the Yorkshire estate could relocate, live in their own house and work a piece of land.' I knew that the Vyners and Robinsons were connected by marriage and that Commander Clare Vyner inherited Studley Royal after Frederick died, his right to the estate passing down through Frederick's mother Henrietta Ann Theodosia Vyner's line.

In fact, the ownership by Studley Royal of land in the area of Morpeth goes back at least to the 16th century and the so-called Swarland Settlement evinces the particular character of the Ripons of Studley Royal: land ownership and social conscience is what engaged them, as is evident at other times and is clearly consistent with the notion of Edith being 'looked after' and kept out of the way up there.

The Studley Royal Estate had land holdings in this area of Northumberland at least as early as 1575 and the specific connection between Morpeth and Ripon goes back to the twelfth century, when Ranulph de Merlay, 2nd Baron of Morpeth, financed the monks of Fountains Abbey to build an exact replica of their domicile, calling it Newminster Abbey, and in a similar position southwest of the town. In Victorian, Edwardian and more modern times there were ever-closer collaborations between Studley Royal and Morpeth. The 2nd Marquess, being one of the two best shots in England, fraternised in the other big grouse and pheasant shooting areas, of which Northumberland was key. And Commander Clare Vyner would seal the connection by marrying into the Northumberland aristocracy. In 1923 he married Lady Doris Gordon Lennox, who was the niece of Helen, Duchess of Northumberland.

As ever, strange echoes of this sound in Barbara's *Act Of Will*. Lady Doris and Helen, Duchess of Northumberland were granddaughter and daughter of the Duke of Richmond and Gordon, and their maiden names were both Gordon Lennox. In *Act of Will*, Matron Lennox is a women's libber of the old school – 'she was of a new breed of woman, very modern in her way of thinking, some said even radical. She was well known in the North of England for her passionate *espousal of reforms in woman and child welfare*, and for her dedication to the advancement of women's rights in general.' Matron Lennox is willing and able to pull strings at a time when work was becoming difficult to find. Was Edith's Northumberland sojourn perhaps a sign that she was a beneficiary of the Lennox family social conscience? Freda would have known all about this.

Was the Marquess's interest in the social welfare of females – as patron of the Ripon Home For Girls – Edith's ticket to Morpeth? Did the Ripon Masons smooth the path to the Edith Simpson 'solution', perhaps? The question is relevant because in Morpeth, at Winton House, was the headquarters of the Freemasons in the North. The Robinsons of Studley Royal were leading lights in the Craft, not only in Ripon but nationally, and will have been hand-in-glove with the Morpeth Masons. That Winton House had previously been the home of the famous suffragette, Emily Davison, may be deemed coincidence even in the light of the Lennox/Robinson interest in women's welfare, but it is perfectly consistent with practice elsewhere at this time that the Masons would have been involved in welfare projects of this sort.

The Morpeth Masons would first and foremost have included in their membership the local landed gentry, the most visible of whom in the town was J R Blackett-Ord. Just as the 2nd Marquess, Frederick Oliver Robinson, owned Fountains Abbey, so Blackett-Ord had the Newminster Abbey Estate, among other significant holdings in Morpeth. He employed an estate manager called John Sadler who looked after Newminster and owned various properties in the town on his own account. We know from an assessment undertaken in 1910, following the Finance Act, which people owned and occupied every property in England and Wales. For a few years afterwards, in localities up and down the country, copies of the assessment were updated as land or properties changed hands and new occupiers moved in. The 1910 names were simply crossed out and new names added. Imagine my surprise to find the name J. Simpson replacing that of the 1910 occupier of a small house in a yard in the same block as Winton House. The humble abode was owned by Blackett-Ord's manager, John Sadler. Was Simpson put to work for Sadler/Blackett-Ord while he, Edith and the children were up there? It seems likely.

If so, this was surely an ongoing protection strategy of Edith of an extraordinary kind, and one that, for the Marquess, happily distanced 'the problem' geographically from Ripon.

The Northumbrian experiment came to an end around 1916, and the couple returned to live not in Bedern Bank, but in Yorkshire Hussar Yard. The Yorkshire Hussars was an inn, marked on the 1909 map of Ripon on the east side of the Market Place, by what is now the archway entrance to the main city car park. There, on 14th August 1917, Edith gave birth to her sixth and last child, a girl, also called Edith, to be referred to as Little Edith.

It is odd that Simpson had not been called up. At the start of the First World War, married men were not required to serve in the forces, but by 1916 the killing fields of France were not so choosy and men avoiding the draft would be shamed with white feathers. From that time it would have been very difficult for Simpson to remain in Morpeth, which was headquarters of C

Squadron of the Northumberland Yeomanry and of A Company of the 7th Battalion of the Northumberland Fusiliers. Perhaps that is why they returned. Ripon was, by Freda's account, also full of soldiers, but the situation may have been more manageable there, where Edith would have felt more at home.

We come now to three key events in our story. The first, which is part of Barbara's memory of what Freda told her, is that in 1918 Edith died. It is on record that in that year, Freda, aged fourteen, took a job at the Ripon Fever Hospital in Stonebridgegate, off Allhallowgate, adjacent to the workhouse. Erected in 1878 and enlarged in 1916, the hospital provided for twenty-five patients. Although it was to one side of the workhouse, it was not part of the Grubber, which had its own hospital. Freda was subjected to endless, gruelling work, scrubbing and cleaning and washing and ironing, terrible drudgery. But with her toughness of mind and inner strength we know that she made it through.

The second key event occurred six years later. We know from the Ripon Workhouse Admissions record that just three days before Christmas 1924, Edith's youngest three children – the three Simpson children – Norman, Frances and Little Edith – were taken by the Authorities from No. 1 Florentine Court in Ripon's Stonebridgegate, where they'd been living with their father, John Thomas Simpson, and delivered to the workhouse by order of the Children's Act 1908. Little Edith was only seven years of age, Norman and Frances twelve and ten respectively. Barbara knows who it was that delivered them up. She wrote about it in *Act of Will*, quite consciously this time.

No. 9 Bedern Bank had by this time been let to a couple called John and Lily Taylor. With people called Taylor suddenly entering upon the scene, it is as if one generation is handing over to the next, although I have no information as to their relationship to Freda's future husband. At this time, one Frances Walker is registered on the electoral roll as living at No. 8 Bedern Bank. Frances Walker was Edith's older brother Thomas Walker's widow, whom Barbara knew as Great-Aunt Frances Walker. She is yet another figure to emerge from the shadows of her past by means of Barbara's fiction, where ironically the truth is so often to be found in our story.

In *Act of Will*, Frances is the mother of 'wicked Aunt Alicia', the person responsible for reporting the children to the Authorities and having them taken into care. Barbara told me that there had indeed been an Aunt Alicia figure in real life, the person who called in the Authorities who admitted Freda's half-siblings (Barbara's uncles and aunts) – Norman, Frances and Little Edith – to the workhouse.

After forty-eight weeks in the Grubber, on the 10th of February 1925, the three children were discharged into the care of the NSPCC 'for removal to Dr Barnardo's Homes', as records show, a few years later to be passed on by Barnardo's to organisations in Canada and Australia and transported singly to these far-off places on their own and at different times – Little Edith was ten when she was despatched to the arid wasteland of Western Australia. As Barbara writes in her novel, the children's 'fiercest protestations and anguished pleadings to stay together had made no impression. They were helpless in the face of their aunt's determination.'

Little Edith was sent to Australia in 1927 (aged ten), Frances in 1929 (aged fifteen). Norman was shipped out of Liverpool to Quebec in Canada in 1926, when he was fourteen, the minimum age for manual labour in that country at the time.

The only one of her siblings that Freda ever saw again was Norman, who, as a serving member of the Canadian army in World War II, came to visit her in Leeds when he was stationed in England.

The official justification for the deportation scheme was that it would relieve Britain's overcrowded cities of orphans and child victims of poverty, illegitimacy or broken homes, while the receiving nation would benefit from the cheapness of labour these children provided.

For seventy years, over fifty British childcare organisations sent 100,000 children aged between four and fifteen to work as indentured farm workers and domestic servants. The scheme to Australia and New Zealand continued until the mid-1960s. Barbara made the often heartless practice of child deportation the wellspring of her novel, *Her Own Rules*, first published in 1996.

I found no mention in the workhouse records of the three Robinson children – Freda, Fred and Mary, and there seems to have been none of the degradation or 'anguished pleadings' in their case. On the contrary, Fred (aged sixteen) set sail for New South Wales in Australia on 26th April 1924, eight months *prior* to the three Simpson children's admission to the workhouse. Freda told Barbara that she herself had considered emigrating to Australia and decided not to go. There appears to have been no coercion involved in Fred's departure – Fred opted to go, Freda to stay – albeit his emigration was brokered by Barnardo's. Later, their sister Mary also emigrated to Australia, arriving in Sydney on 11th February, 1926, one week before her sixteenth birthday. Again this was arranged by Barnardo's.

It's easy to see why, young as they were, they had been impressed enough to take the plunge. Newspaper articles of the period proclaimed only a positive message about the opportunities that the colonies provided: 'Open Door to Canada – free loans to nominated immigrants ... No Exploitation ... cooperative policies of Great Britain and Canada.' In Ripon, the *Gazette* urged locals to rally to an 'Australia Calls' slogan, which heralded the arrival of a certain Mr Stabler of the Australian Immigration Office. At the YMCA Lecture Hall, Stabler waxed lyrical about 'the splendid opportunities afforded to young men of this country desiring to emigrate to the far-distant colony of Australia.' On 12th February 1925, a party of Barnardo's boys was promoting the organisation in the YMCA Lecture Hall in Ripon, as the *Gazette* reported: 'A very delightful entertainment was given by the boys, who exhibited remarkable skill in the manipulation of the different instruments, the playing of the handbells being especially good.'

Now we come to the third key event at this time. Freda told Barbara that the final disintegration of Edith's family occurred on account of her mother Edith's death in 1918. There is, however, no small amount of uncertainty attached to the date Freda gave Barbara for Edith's death. A thorough search of official records for all Edith Simpsons and Edith Walkers who died between 1917 (the year in which our Edith returned from Morpeth and gave birth to Little Edith) and 1942, turned up only one in Ripon, and that was on the 9th of January 1934, a farmer's daughter aged forty-three, so no match there. Our Edith was born on the 4th of September 1880 and would have been fifty-three and was certainly not born to a farmer called Richard Simpson, shown as the father on the death certificate. Beyond Ripon, a number of Edith Walkers and Edith Simpsons died in this period: at Dewsbury (1917), at Goole (1920), at Spilsby in Lincolnshire (1922), Halifax (1927), Barnsley (1929), Birkenhead (1935), Marylebone (1937). But there are no grounds to suggest any of these is our Edith. If she had died in 1918, as Freda told Barbara, there would definitely be a death certificate. And when I interviewed Barbara's close childhood friend Margery Clarke, who lived in Ripon all her life, she remembered Freda's mother being alive and living in Bedern Bank when Barbara was a young girl, i.e. in the 1930s.

The three Simpson children were not in fact taken into the workhouse until December 1924, and during this period of time there was a much more likely reason for the family's downfall than Edith's supposed death six years earlier. On the 23rd of September 1923 Frederick Oliver Robinson, benefactor and protector of Edith and their three children, met his maker. You may recall that thirteen years earlier, in 1910, Freda, Fred and Mary had been admitted to the Grubber after the 1st Marquess had died and Frederick withdrew from his affair with Edith. That Norman, Frances and Little Edith – the Simpson-three – were admitted to the Grubber immediately after the 2nd Marquess died surely constitutes more than random coincidence.

If the family had been living under his protection – and remember, Barbara understood from her mother that Edith had *never* needed to work – then the financial burden of the children would have fallen suddenly upon Edith (assuming she was still alive), and even if Edith had some material inheritance from her affair with the 2nd Marquess she would have found the challenge of five dependent children difficult, if not impossible, to meet.[17]

---

[17] A residue of funds, perhaps from the sale by Edith of the Diamond Star, would help to explain the apparent anachronism of Freda being able to dress Barbara like the perfect middle-class child, with expensive coats and patent-leather shoes, and why Barbara would remember Freda and Winston as always well dressed, when Winston rarely worked. But it was not deployed by 'wicked Aunt Alicia' to save the Simpson-three.

True, the children's father, John Thomas Simpson, was still alive and living at No. 1 Florentine Court, close to the Fever Hospital where Freda was working and the place where the Simpson-three were seized by the Authorities, but according to Barnardo's, Simpson was now 'a labourer who hardly worked, preferring to spend his time in public houses from where he mostly returned home in an intoxicated state'. In 1930, I discovered, he would die a pauper's death in the workhouse, aged forty-four. No use to Edith and her family, then, although I can't help but feel sorry for him, for when Edith took him as her husband in 1910 he was only twenty-four, five years younger than this powerhouse of a woman. Edith's star may have been on the wane but she no doubt still had big plans, in which poor old Simpson was never more than a pawn.

From Christmas 1924, following the committal of the children, the situation for Edith's family was hopeless and one can begin to see how distraught Freda must have been to see all her brothers and sisters thrown to the four winds in successive years. We know that some time after Little Edith was shipped to Australia Freda tried to contact her.

When Freda first wrote to Barnardo's, they replied that '[Little Edith] is extremely happy and getting on nicely out there... [She] had good reports all round.' Freda, they said, was perfectly at liberty to write directly to the child at Fairbridge Farm School, Pinjarra, Western Australia, where she was living.

Fairbridge Farm School was the organisation into which Barnardo's had passed Little Edith after housing her for three years in a holding centre in Essex, called Barkingside Girls Orphanage. The orphanage was constructed on a 'cottage homes' model, with children living in small groups under the supervision of a house-mother.

Freda had written a second time, replying to Barnardo's letter politely, thanking them for their response and the good news that Edith was getting on well. Then she wrote again to ask them to let Little Edith come and live with them at 38 Tower Lane in Armley, where she now lived with Winston. She told them that she and Winston had a 'nice little cottage in the nice part of the city,' and commended the idea further by saying that she could now take good care of Edith and eventually secure her a 'good situation'.

Barnardo's response was blunt and to the point: 'I am afraid we could not bear the expense of bringing Edith back to England, even if it were decided it would be well for her to return.' Repatriation, they said, would cost between £32 and £36. Freda replied expressing surprise that it couldn't be arranged and begged them to 'excuse us for our ignorance in thinking so'. She was clearly very disappointed: 'We were beginning to think we were going to have Edith,' she wrote.

In fact, it wasn't up to Barnardo's to deny Freda, because they had washed their hands of any rights to Little Edith when they'd handed her over to Fairbridge Farm School.

The pathos of Freda's humility and the blunt response with which it was met, is heart rending and there is another telling and touching aspect to the correspondence: Freda's letters were dictated to Winston. Barbara recognised her father's hand immediately: 'As soon as I saw the letter, I recognised my father's copperplate handwriting,' she wrote. 'Dated August 31, 1931, the letter was addressed to Dr Barnardo's and written on my mother's behalf.'

Freda did write to Edith at the farm school in Western Australia, as advised by Barnardo's, but received no reply. Evidence has since been submitted to Public Inquiries into the conduct at the school that letters from concerned relatives were routinely not passed on to the children.

Allegations of abuse and exploitation in the whole transportation system have been rife. In the case of Barnardo's, one of the main vehicles for the emigration of child victims of poverty, illegitimacy or broken homes to Canada, there was an employer agreement with the receiving farmer, which covered the period of 'adoption', stating that the child would be provided with sufficient and proper board, that he or she would attend church and school, and a wage was agreed, which was remitted to Barnardo's in trust. In addition a fee was paid by the Canadian government to Barnardo's for each child that emigrated to Canada. Each child had a trust account with the Bank of Commerce in Canada, but the passbook was sent to Barnardo's office in Toronto and no withdrawal could be

made by a child without Barnardo's permission. At the ages of
eighteen and twenty-one respectively, Barnardo's boys and girls
could withdraw money from their account.

There was also a system of inspection to protect a child
from abuse, but 'rewards for endurance' were given to those
who remained on Canadian farms for long periods of time,
and very few if any children were ever removed for reasons of
abuse or neglect. Meanwhile, many reports reached the ears of
the public, and Barnardo's employees admitted that there were
employers 'who are far from desirable guardians or associates of
young children.'

Whatever the level of treatment, the terrible psychological
effect of enforced removal from one's roots and country
emerges from a film made by Granada TV called, *The Lost
Children of the Empire*, as a lasting problem. Leslie Shaw was
sent to Halifax, Nova Scotia on 23rd March 1927, and a lifetime
later asserts that the problem this set in motion was one of
identity, still needing solution: 'It is important to know *who I
am*,' she said, even at this late stage seeing the TV team as an
opportunity too good to lose. An eighty-year-old grandmother
says that in all the years she has been in her adopted country,
'my mother was never out of my mind'. The migration scheme
was Freda's own sorrow writ large.

Accusations of sexual abuse also fly in the film, as terrible
memories lift the veil on indignity, degradation and suffering.
But beneath it all there is this sense of dispossession, of loss, lost
identity, which can never be made good. 'I love my children,'
says one woman. 'But even they don't completely fill that gap.
I feel as if I was robbed... Even today I am very insecure, deep
down. I feel a nobody.'

Back in 2004 I faced all kinds of problem tracing what had
happened to Barbara's uncles and aunts, but it was the reach
of the book itself and the ITV documentary, *Secrets From The
Workhouse* made on the back of it, which at last produced some
answers. One woman in particular contacted Barbara with news
of Little Edith.

Dr Margaret McBride, an Australian, had received a
telephone call from her sister, who had joined a local genealogy
group in Sydney and been looking into their late mother's

background. All that the sisters, Margaret and Barbara, had known was that she had arrived in Western Australia on a boat named HMS Ballarat. Now, Barbara had managed to pinpoint the ship's only listed arrival and found their mother's name on the passenger list. The document read: 'Edith Simpson, age 10, *Barnardo orphan*.'

They were stunned. Like Freda, Little Edith had told her two daughters nothing about her tragic background. Margaret contacted Barnardo's 'Making Connections' service, which identified her mother as the sixth child of one Edith Simpson.

According to Barnardo's, Edith Simpson had died in January 1920 'at Goole in the East Riding of Yorkshire, aged 38 years', many miles from Ripon and two years after Freda said that Edith had died. What's more, the Edith on Barnardo's 1920 death certificate was married to a 'Farm Cowman' not of Goole but of the tiny little farming village of Airmyn, a few miles away – clearly not the John Thomas Simpson we know. Finally, in January 1920, our Edith, Barbara's grandmother, would have been 39, not 38. There is no doubt at all that the death certificate that Barnardo's produced was not for Barbara's grandmother.

There have been multiple claims of children being taken from parents without their consent when they were not in fact orphans. I have no idea whether that was the case in the transportation of Little Edith, but, as Little Edith was transported at ten years of age, Barnardo's were clearly concerned, as a priority, to establish that her mother had been dead at the time she was taken.

Their letter to Margaret went further. Wholly gratuitously, given their account that Edith was long dead by the time her children were taken into care, and insensitively, given that they were writing to two of Edith Simpson's granddaughters, they went out of their way to denigrate Little Edith's mother and to demolish her father. Why do so, other than to justify Little Edith's transportation, which never was the issue? Simpson they describe as 'drunken and immoral', a labourer who hardly worked, preferring to spend his time in public houses from where he mostly returned home in an intoxicated state. The description of Simpson, the urban Ripon labourer, is no doubt apt, but way beyond their remit and wholly unlikely of the 'farm cowman' of Airmyn, an East Riding agricultural village with a few hundred population in 1920, which they take him to have been.

Dr McBride paid £30 for what Barnardo's describe as a 'summary of information relating to your mother, Edith Simpson', but which is at best insensitive and at worst inaccurate.

Inaccuracies include the date of Edith's marriage to Simpson, when the marriage certificate is publicly available and clearly states that they were wed on the 15th October, 1910. The letter also states that 'all five children' were admitted to Barnardo's on the 10th of February, 1925, after having been 'found to be in a verminous and filthy condition, swarming with lice and clad in little more than rags'. This cannot be true. As they confirm elsewhere in the letter, Little Edith's brother Fred was already in Australia at this time. He had set sail for New South Wales, Australia, eight months before the Simpson-three were admitted to the workhouse. What's more, Norman, Frances and Little Edith were discharged into Barnardo's care *via the NSPCC from Ripon Workhouse*, as workhouse records show. At the workhouse, the Simpson three would have been sanitised and dressed uniformly upon their admission at Christmas 1924.

Had Barnardo's been making a case for the Defence in a legal challenge to the transportation of a ten-year-old girl to the ends of the earth, they could not have tried harder and less effectively to conceal their intent. The letter left Little Edith's daughters cold and upset. However, Margaret then received an email from a genealogist with whom she'd been corresponding, saying that he had come across an article on the internet by the novelist Barbara Taylor Bradford, which he attached. The article was written following the *Secrets from the Workhouse* TV documentary which accompanied first publication of my book. From it, Margaret learned the sad facts of her mother's confinement in Ripon Workhouse.

Snippets of what Margaret read stirred up dim childhood memories of a visit by 'Auntie Frances' (Little Edith's sister) and of her mother mentioning that she had a half-brother, Norman, who lived in Canada. But their incarceration in the workhouse was terrible news and she became determined to find out all she could about the first ten years of her mother's life. She contacted our Barbara, who put her in touch with me. She read my book and went on to research and write a manuscript of her own about her mother's life, which, as I write, awaits publication.

Margaret recognised immediately the brow-beaten aspect of Freda in her own mother Edith's character, the result, as she understood for the first time, of childhood trauma. I would add of repression from bottling up that trauma. Freda and Little Edith had both kept their early life a secret from their children, even unto the end.

'I acknowledge Mum did eventually find love [with her husband and children] and was happy to a certain degree,' writes Margaret in her book. 'But there was always something there that I was unable to pinpoint. I never saw her laugh. I'm sure she never let her guard down. Always waiting for the next blow...'

Margaret conducted a wide-ranging, in-depth review of Fairbridge Farm School, building up a detailed picture of her mother's life, even interviewing a 101-year-old man who had been there at the same time as Little Edith and remembered her. She describes the environment as spartan, regimented and harsh, a dead and sometimes sadistic environment where 'physical labour was the norm from an early age and the psychological and emotional welfare of children who were separated from their roots was never considered'. Some inmates have since benefited from compensation and an apology from the highest political level. There are few survivors today, which makes her record an important document.

In 2015 the Australian authorities paid A$24 million in compensation to victims of abuse at the Fairbridge School after lawyers took a claim against the state and federal governments. According to the *Guardian* newspaper, abuse included sexual abuse and being beaten with hockey sticks, with one child spending three years in hospital when his back was broken at the school.

In 2007, Kevin Rudd, the Australian Prime Minister at the time, made an official apology. The British authorities were aware of serious allegations of maltreatment and abuse at Fairbridge, but at first failed to act until in 2010, Prime Minister Gordon Brown made a formal apology and, in 2019, following an Independent Inquiry into Child Sexual Abuse, the then British Government provided ex-gratia payments of £20,000 each to living British child migrants.

*

At 8 Bedern Bank in Ripon, following the children's dispersal, Barbara's Great-Aunt Frances Walker had been joined by one Elizabeth Walker, possibly her daughter. Frances and her husband, Edith Walker's brother, Thomas, had had three daughters – Lillie (who married Joe Wray, with whom Freda and Barbara would later stay in Ripon), Elizabeth, and Minnie.

But what of 'the beautiful Edith' herself? When I faxed Barbara that her childhood friend from Ripon Margery Clarke told me that she clearly remembered Edith being alive and living in Bedern Bank when Barbara was a young girl, she had returned it with 'NO' written in capital letters in the margin of the fax, 'She's thinking of Great-Aunt Frances.'

I checked back with Margery and she confirmed that she was *not* confusing Edith with Great-Aunt Frances and that Edith had indeed been living there when Barbara was a young girl. Subsequently, I researched the Electoral Register and discovered that in 1933 (the year our Barbara was born), Great-Aunt Frances was no longer living in Bedern Bank.

If Edith Walker had not in fact died in 1918, as Barbara supposed, or in 1920, as Barnardo's supposed, she would only have been forty-four in 1924, when the children were put into care, and fifty-three years of age in the year Barbara was born.

Secrets, there were so many in our family... I never wanted to face those secrets from my childhood. Better to forget them; better still to pretend they did not exist. But they did. My childhood was constructed on secrets layered one on top of the other[18].

---

[18] *Everything to Gain* (1994).

All Edith's children had suffered terribly. Freda, like her siblings, knew what it was to feel robbed, insecure, and fatherless, uncertain deep down of who she was, but she had been the one who got away, and the only one to resolve her problems, which she did through ensuring her daughter's fantastic success. Incredibly, given all that she had faced, Freda remained quietly determined and in control of her life. Control was a fundamental element of her character, which Barbara, when I put it to her, recognised too. If Edith Walker had indeed been alive when Barbara was a young girl and Freda came often to Ripon to visit her, how would the hard core of secrets these women shared have been exercised?

The one major theme in Barbara's novels – steered by Freda – which is absent from our story of Edith and Freda so far, is *retribution*, the very motivation of Emma Harte to get back at the exploitative aristocracy. But the evidence for it in reality is not lacking.

In *A Woman of Substance* the gentry get their comeuppance. Emma Harte, who has been hurt so deeply by Edwin Fairley that she can no longer bear the perfume of roses, which filled the air when he deserted her, takes her revenge. She ruins Edwin Fairley's family and burns Fairley Hall to the ground – 'I do not want one rosebud, one single leaf left growing,' Emma orders those who then do her will. There opportunity for Edith also to wreak her revenge and a precedent.

Pushing further into the history of Studley Royal Hall, I discovered that it, too, had been burned to the ground. Twice. First, as I have said, long before our players entered the theatre of action. In 1716, vengeful arson was actually suspected and the finger pointed at a local Ripon woman, one Anne Gill – 'so divilish a woman that there is no mischief she could invent'. But then, 230 years later, on Saturday, 13th April 1946, when Edith, if still alive, would have been in her mid-sixties and her daughter, Freda, was taking twelve-year-old Barbara regularly from their little home in Leeds to Ripon, the Hall was razed to the ground again, as the *Times* newspaper reported...

Within half an hour of the outbreak the whole length of the two-storey building was ablaze, and the light of the fire could be seen thirty to forty miles away. Firemen from eight areas in the North Riding were called out. Water had to be pumped about three-quarters of a mile from a lake in the grounds and an adjoining reservoir. An eye-witness stated that valuable paintings, tapestries, and furniture were saved by villagers, estate workers, and police, who formed themselves into a chain and passed the articles from hand to hand.

Commander Clare Vyner, who had inherited Studley Royal on Frederick's death, was away at the time it was set alight. I felt a warm feeling of empathy with Freda as to how she might have felt on coming upon the ashes of Studley Royal Hall in 1946 and then, thirty or so years later, reading her daughter's words in *A Woman of Substance*:

In the middle of May, Emma made a second trip to Fairley Hall. She walked along the terrace, which still remained intact, and regarded the great tract of rough, bare ground where the house and stables had formerly stood. Not one brick was left and the rose garden, too, had disappeared. Emma felt an enormous surge of relief and an unexpected sense of liberation. Fairley Hall, that house where she had suffered such humiliation and heartache, might never have existed. It could no longer hurt her with the painful memories it evoked. She had exorcised all the ghosts of her childhood.

She was free at last...

PART II
CHAPTER SEVEN
A New Start

'Yesterday was now.'

A Woman of Substance

Barbara had been able to tell me very little about her mother and grandmother and as my research progressed I realised that she could not possibly have known their astonishing story. If she had known, surely she would have told me. If she had not wanted me to know, why set me loose on her biography? In the end, after I sent her the manuscript, her shock surely confirmed that she had not known.

'It wasn't until I saw the finished manuscript that I realised what he had found,' Barbara told reporters. 'By the time my husband came home from work on the day it arrived I was in a state of shock. He said I was as white as a sheet and there were tears in my eyes...' She found it especially difficult to accept that she had written about these things of which she had no conscious knowledge: 'What's strangest of all is how my books mirror what happened to my family.'

A few weeks and some difficult transatlantic phone calls after reading the book, Barbara summoned me to a meeting at the Plaza Athenée, a plush hotel off the Champs Elysée, her favourite Paris base, to explain myself in person. I struggled into the lobby with my R-kive box and for three hours she combed through its contents, the documentary evidence for all that I had found. It is to her eternal credit that she finally gave my book her blessing, feeling that 'by letting the truth come out, it validated my mother's and grandmother's lives.'

But theirs is barely half the story. In Part II we see their legacy empower Barbara as she rises from working-class Yorkshire lass to a place in the vanguard of the 'new women' who burst upon the Fleet Street scene in London in the 1950s, marries a Hollywood movie producer with apartments in Paris, Los Angeles and New York, and finally returns to her rootedness in the world of her childhood and becomes one of the world's most successful authors.

*

The firing of Fairley Hall set Emma Harte free in Barbara's flagship novel, as was the case with Rochester and Jane when fire destroyed Thornfield Hall in Charlotte Brontë's *Jane Eyre* and as it was with Maxim de Winter when the firing of Manderley freed him and his second wife from the phantom of Rebecca in Daphne du Maurier's classic novel.

But in the case of Studley Royal Hall we are dealing with stone-cold reality. In 1946, when the Hall burned down, Freda will have been determined that a new era should rise phoenix-like from the burned-out ashes, and appropriately, resurrection was the theme of Barbara's own remembrance of her mother's missions to Ripon in those far-off days.

'Easter Sunday. My mother used to *love* to go to Ripon Cathedral on Easter Sunday and she used to take me there.' Good Friday was spent in Armley, and Barbara would busy herself with comforting food. 'Good Friday I always think of hot cross buns, at home with mother and father, for tea. I used to go and get them and I see this long-legged skinny little girl of ten running down to the local baker my mother liked in Town Street.' Then it was off to celebrate Easter, the Feast of the Resurrection, in the very sepulchre of Edith's dreams – Studley Royal: 'I loved to be outdoors all the time and especially when we went to Ripon,' Barbara said. 'We (mother and I) would go for long walks picking flowers in the hedgerows. We would especially go to Studley Royal. But Studley Hall burned down during the war years, some accident … it always fascinated me.'

They would take picnics, home-made sandwiches, and there is even a 'Manderley moment' in Chapter Two of *Act of Will*, where Audra comes upon High Cleugh, not unlike the way du Maurier's heroine comes upon the house of her dreams early in *Rebecca* – 'Last night I dreamt I went to Manderley again...' Audra sits down upon the grass and looks at the big house, symbol of her great loss. The house 'appeared to slumber in the brilliant sunshine as if it were not inhabited'.

> *A peacefulness lay over the motionless gardens. Not a blade of grass, not a single leaf stirred... Audra's gaze became more intense than ever. She saw beyond the exterior walls to the inner core of the house. She closed her eyes, let herself sink down into her imagination, remembering, remembering...*

As in *Rebecca*, Barbara's heroine imagines herself inside the house: 'She closed her eyes, let herself sink down into her imagination, remembering, remembering ...' and there she is. Edith, her mother, is as it were standing before her, while she, a little girl again, is mindful of...

> *...her mother's laughter, the swish of her silk gown, as she joined her by the fire. The Beautiful Edith Kenton. That was how they always spoke of her hereabouts. Sapphires blazed at her throat, on her cool white arms. Blue fire against that translucent skin. Hair the colour of new pennies, an aureole of burnished copper light around the pale heart-shaped face. Warm and loving lips were pressed down to her young cheek. The smell of gardenias and Coty powder enveloped her. A slender, elegant hand took hold of hers, guided her out of the room...*

Had Freda sat Barbara down and shared with her the real story behind her great loss, it could not have made a greater impact upon the little girl. Freda's way – taking her to High Cleugh, Studley Royal, Middleham Castle, all the places connected with the Robinsons or closely associated with the kind of life that was theirs – shrines, all of them, to what-might-have-been – appealed directly to the child's subconscious and there was never a need for her to suspend disbelief. So powerful, so intense was the sense of loss that Freda associated with these spiritually thrilling places that by immersing Barbara in her feelings subliminally, she was connecting with her daughter at a creative level. She alone could do this, because no one was closer to Barbara at this most impressionable time of her life.

And then of course Freda knew that Barbara was genetically susceptible. 'My mother saw in me something she felt had to be cultivated,' Barbara said to me long before she knew the truth of it. And cultivate that 'something' Freda did – in effect nursing Edith's ambition and Frederick's to-the-manor-born self-assurance in her daughter with all the persistence that allied Freda to her own natural grandfather. For the 1st Marquess, Freda's grandfather George Frederick Robinson, was described as 'a rather timid' fellow, 'serious-minded, a voracious reader of books ... noted for his sincerity and moral earnestness ... prosaic, endowed with neither grace nor sparkle ... *Persistence* was Ripon's outstanding quality.'[19] Freda's natural style to a 'T'.

The novelist Muriel Spark once said: 'You can't separate style from the person. You bring that package into the world with you.' Generations of our ancestors shape and colour the human psyches they bequeath to us as surely as they do our muscular and nervous systems. Cells have memory and this memory is durable. Call it style even if we remain unaware of it, our behaviour is affected by inherited patterns of behaviour, inclinations, thoughts and feelings which emerge from our unconscious to help mould who and what we become. In that sense the spirit of Edith and Frederick ran in Barbara's veins and Freda played nurse to what she saw and, we are to believe, recognised in her daughter.

As ever, Barbara's novels explore this as a theme. Time and again we see the mother figure nurture what is already inherent in the daughter. Nor is it insignificant that when we see style inherited in the novels it is the grandchild who inherits more completely than the daughter, as if the qualities skip a generation. For example, in *A Woman of Substance* it is granddaughter Paula who inherits Emma Harte's style, and not Daisy, Emma's second illegitimate daughter and Paula's mother.

In selecting for her daughter's 'education' every aristocratic seat and museum of antiques and *objets d'art* in the

---

[19] M. Bence-Jones in his book, *Viceroys of India* (1982).

neighbourhood to which Barbara might aspire – from Ripley Castle to Middleham, from Temple Newsam to Harewood House, from Newby Hall to Norton Conyers, and in particular Studley Royal, where her identity lay buried – Freda was holding up a mirror image of the life of which Edith and her children had been dispossessed. Freda's mission spoke of her purpose to resurrect the dream that Edith had shared for a few short years with her daughter amongst the rubble of her childhood.

And the point is that it worked, Barbara's déjà vu experiences were living proof that in some strange way her past was indeed already becoming her future.

By the time of the firing of Studley Royal Hall, the Taylors had left 38 Tower Lane, the bucolic sanctuary of Barbara's earliest years, and moved a quarter of a mile east to No. 5 Greenock Terrace – 'One sitting room and kitchen, two bedrooms upstairs and an attic,' said Barbara as we approached the house. 'I remember it very well.' Greenock Terrace is in the thick of the brick-built terraces where Alfred and Esther Taylor dwelt, a stroll away from Christ Church School and the church, and still a long way from the low end of Armley, with its prison and Wortley Cemetery.

When we got there she was astonished that the house had only a few small steps leading up to the front door. 'I used to scour the steps. I had to do a line around the steps,' Barbara explained. [22] Marking the edges of front steps of a house with a donkey stone (light brown chalk) is an ancient ritual dating back to Celtic times to ward off evil spirits, though in the working-class North it is taken to be a token of respectability, hard fought for in the terraced streets of industrial England. How had donkey-stoning two little steps so preoccupied her?

The reality, a rundown terrace unloved, disturbed comfortable childhood memories and was dealt with instantly with the observation that at least No. 5 – her house – was well kept. It was the only one in the street that was.

'There was a fish-and-chip shop in the next street,' she said. 'My mother used to say, "Run around to the fish-and-chip shop." And next door lived another family called Taylor, and one of the girls was called Barbara, no relation!'

I told her that when Graham Greene travelled the world, he was habitually met with the news at hotel receptions that another Graham Greene had just left, as if he were constantly one step behind his *doppelgänger*. The difference here was that Barbara was confronted by hers *every day*; she even attended the same school. 'They called her Barbara "Poppy" Taylor because she was born on Poppy Day. She had a disabled sister in a wheelchair, damaged at birth. She went to Thorsby Girls High School, I remember, got married and moved to some seaside place.

'Oh, but none of it looked like this, because everyone was so proud of their front steps and so on. I'm glad our house looks nice. It was a community then. I'll tell you something, we played in all these streets, and they all had window boxes and they were all pristine. I used to run down this way [via Ridge Road] to my church...'

A couple of years after the move, Barbara left Christ Church School and enrolled at Northcote School on nearby Town Street, a private establishment independent of the State system. We find our way to the site, but look in vain. 'It *was* on Town Street and it was facing Keene's Dairy. What a memory I've got, Keene's Dairy! The school was an old house with a garden behind a wall, a high stone wall, a little like a manor house. There were trees. They must have knocked it down! Is that the Barley Corn? My father used to go there for a drink. These shops didn't look so garish then, they didn't have all the signs outside, they were very old-fashioned, you know. It was *all* more like a village then...'

The absence of the school building was soon forgotten in the search for another. Barbara attended Northcote for three years, leaving in 1948, following which she and her parents moved from Greenock Terrace to a house next door to the school, and Freda cooked meals for the teachers. So now we were looking for No. 148. 'This is the house! My mother used to take those lunches into the back door of the school. You see, a door opened from the school into our backyard. And it didn't look so shabby! Ours was all one house, and I think they have made it into two – 148 and 146. It was all one house, surely, or have they built one on? That was the front room and you entered there where it says 146. That was the sitting room and the dining room, with the kitchen at the back. There were three bedrooms upstairs. It was all brick, not all concreted over like this...'

Not brick but grey pebbledash confronted us. It seemed that from somewhere an apology was in order, but the scene did not bend to her will. Barbara was twelve in 1945. The decision to go to Northcote was all Freda's of course, but had not been taken easily. A private school meant fees, a uniform. When Barbara's grandmother, Esther Taylor, rebuked Freda for suggesting such a thing, telling her it would give Barbara 'big ideas', Freda had retorted: 'Nothing's too good for our Barbara.'

I asked her what the school brought to mind. 'We wore green gymslips, yes, a green gymslip with a white cotton blouse, a green tie with a yellow stripe, and a green coat; and in summer green dresses, cotton, green and white (I don't know, maybe it was striped) and panama hats, cream panama hats with ribbon – green with yellow – and we had green skirts and white cotton shirts, if we wanted with the tie. Oh, I remember things like the little plays, the parties, the church service and the present-exchange we used to have before Christmas when the senior classroom smelled like a perfumery from all the pot pourri and scented presents we used to give each other. Lots of people come up when I'm signing books in Leeds and say: "Hello love, you don't know who I am, do you, but we know who you are." And I'm looking at a woman who used to be at Northcote School with me.'

June Kettlelow sat next to Barbara at Northcote: 'Exelby was my name then. Barbara didn't live next door at that time, she lived at the Greenocks. We were the same age, her birthday was a week before mine. The school took children in from five, but the boys could only stay in the primary department, they left at eleven or something like that. We stayed until we left at fourteen or fifteen. It came in just at that point that you had to stay at school until you were fifteen. The morning was General Studies and then in the afternoon was typing and shorthand, and French. The headmistress was Mrs Harrison. Miss Smith taught the commercial subjects. Our form teacher was Mrs Cox. I didn't go until I was eleven, until I failed my eleven-plus. That's when I went. I think there were three classes from then on, probably fifteen or something in each class.'

Shirley Martin, another contemporary of Barbara at Northcote, told me: 'It was a lovely little school, a very small prep school and commercial college, from five upwards. A particular friend of Barbara, Alma Franks, lived across the road. At eleven, if you were a boy you might go to West Leeds High School or somewhere like that. From eleven or twelve everybody mixed together, all ages. You weren't divided up into grades. You'd do General Studies in the morning and then in the afternoon you'd do commercial, shorthand, typing certificates. In those days it went up to fifteen. Barbara left at fifteen and so did I. You could go on after fifteen, but if by then you already had 100, 120 words a minute shorthand and typing, why bother?'

Shirley, who works for solicitors Irwin Mitchell in Leeds, also remembers the Taylors living next door to the school, because her family lived next door to them. She remembers in particular how proud Barbara's mother was of her. 'I remember our mothers talking in the garden, over the fence, and it sticks in my mind her mother always talking about "*our Barbara*". She was a lovely person, very, very friendly, and it was a lovely school. I cried my eyes out when I left. No shortage of jobs secretarial-wise, but you needed good qualifications.'

Barbara, however, had no intention of becoming a secretary. She is adamant that Freda had only university in mind for her. I saw this as a measure of the dangerous level of fantasy in Freda's plans for her daughter, there being no precedent for a child going to university from Northcote or any school like it. Northcote provided a vocational training, for university you needed the Higher School Certificate, normally taken at 18.

The 1944 Education Act had made secondary education compulsory and available free to all, and there evolved three categories of secondary school. Alongside grammar schools came technical schools (including those biased to commerce – like Northcote – or art) and so-called secondary modern schools (for pupils who had failed the eleven-plus and did not elect to go to one of the technical schools).

The notion of schools with a commercial bias had arisen out of a London-based network of 'central schools' established as early as 1911. When these were transformed into technical schools in 1945, a number of recognised secondary schools (many girls' schools among them) followed suit, offering thirteen- to fifteen-year-olds a two-year course that included shorthand, typewriting, bookkeeping and commercial practice. Northcote was one of these, and the practice never became widespread (Northcote itself would not survive).

Freda's opinion that Barbara would go on to university might have seemed feasible in the general context of change, the chief consequences of which lay in a socio-economic spread of university applications, and a massive increase of state scholarships and local authority awards towards that end. Barbara's school friend, the butcher's son Alan Bennett, benefited from a state scholarship, as he writes in *Telling Tales* (2000). Acceptance by a university meant that 'a boy or girl was automatically awarded a scholarship by the city... My education – elementary school [Christ Church, Armley], secondary school [West Leeds High School], university [Exeter College, Oxford] – cost my parents nothing, their only sacrifice (which they didn't see as a sacrifice) that by staying on at school beyond sixteen, I'm not bringing in a wage.'

Between 1900 and 1909, six new universities – Birmingham, Liverpool, Manchester, Sheffield, Bristol and Leeds – had been created. Three of them, including Leeds, had come out of science colleges, where vocational training (training for jobs) had been uppermost. As early as 1900 Joseph Chamberlain inserted into the charter of Birmingham University (created in that year) a faculty of commerce, and now Leeds, Manchester, Durham, London, Bristol and Southampton all had them.

Nevertheless, none of these was ever on the cards for Barbara. The world was changing, opening up all sorts of opportunities, and Barbara was forming her own ideas. Besides their visits out, sometimes as often as twice a week Freda took her to the Picturedome: '...she wanted to go, and had no one to leave me with. I think I learned a lot from the movies,' Barbara said. 'I know that I thought Nelson Eddy was the greatest thing since sliced bread – wonderful musicals.' Eddy had a hugely successful partnership in musical films in the 1930s with Jeanette MacDonald. By the mid-1940s there were more than fifty cinemas in Leeds, all changing their programmes twice a week. Barbara was 'absolutely blown away' in the cinema, watching people like Cary Grant and Ginger Rogers and Fred Astaire and admitting on BBC Radio's Desert Island Discs, 'I think I fell in love with glamour then, because it was a time when movie stars really were glamorous and elegant and beautiful, and where are they today?' The presenter of the programme, Sue Lawley, was on the right track when she asked her, 'Fell in love with it in the sense that you wanted to write about it, or that you wanted to have it to yourself…?'

Barbara stopped in her tracks and said only, 'I'm not sure…'

Movie glamour was a contemporary extension of the increasingly dated aristocratic world to which Freda was introducing Barbara in Yorkshire's stately homes. Very quickly, moviedom was integrated into her image of self and that of people who mattered to her, especially the main man in her life at this time – her father, Winston Taylor – who may not have had an aristocratic drop of blood in him or indeed have been as well-groomed as she remembers, but in her mind he could play the part as well as his namesake, Robert Taylor – another of Barbara's movie heroes and the idealised measure against which all her boyfriends would later be assessed:

His looks dazzled.

It was his colouring that was so sensational. The gleaming black hair and the black brows were in marked contrast to a light, creamy complexion and cheeks that held a tinge of pink like the bloom on a peach; he had cool green eyes, the colour of light, clear tourmalines, fringed with thick black lashes. His eyes and his skin were the envy of his sisters – and most other women.

Matched to the striking colouring and handsome profile was a superb athletic body. He was exactly five feet nine and a half inches tall, well muscled, firm and taut and without one ounce of fat or flab on him.

Immaculate at all times, Vincent considered himself to be a bit of a dandy, loved clothes, wore them with flair and elegance. He cut quite a swathe wherever he went, especially on the dance floor, where his easy grace and good looks showed to such advantage.

Act of Will

Hollywood took Freda's strategy on, modernising it, giving it roots in a world beyond the aristocratic fantasy bubble she had created for her daughter. 1940s Hollywood was simply a modern extension of Frederick Ripon's aristocratic style, which Freda continued to nurse in Barbara and which was part of her identity long before her contemporaries had begun fashioning theirs. The 1940s and early Fifties became Barbara's period and would remain her period for the rest of her life. In the Sixties she would avoid pop culture like the plague.

Similarly compatible with Freda's mission in her early teens, Barbara read Kathleen Winsor's *Forever Amber*, first published in 1944, in which heroine Amber St Clare is prepared to go to any lengths to get what she wants. 'I remember that I could not put it down,' Barbara wrote in the Foreword to the Penguin edition years later. 'In fact, I read it so quickly that I immediately reread it to be certain I hadn't missed anything important.' What transfixed Barbara as a teenager was that Amber reached for what she wanted, as Freda encouraged Barbara to reach. 'As a teenager, I was determined to get ahead. There was no way I was going to end up slaving in some textile factory, married off and perpetually pregnant like so many Yorkshire girls of my generation.'

What Barbara had in mind for herself was journalism and in her mind's eye she had a strong journalistic image to which she aspired: 'At different times, depending on what movie I'd seen with Mummy at the Picturedome, I thought I was Rosalind Russell in *Front Page* or Jimmy Stewart in *Call Northside 777*, which was a newspaper story. I wanted to be a foreign correspondent or maybe a crime reporter.'

Being a journalist was not her principal ambition, however, more a means to an end. 'What I wanted to do was write books. I remember saying to my mother – whatever the words were – I want to write novels, I want to write books, I want to write stories when I grow up; and she smiled. And that was after I sold my first short story when I was twelve to a children's magazine. I don't think I meant to sell it to them. Mummy sent the story in and they bought it. They paid me seven shillings and sixpence. I bought Daddy some handkerchiefs and Mummy a green vase, and put the rest in my moneybox.

'Daddy was always saying to me, "When I'm rich I'm going to buy you a pony." I don't know why he said it. I didn't want a pony actually, but he was always saying it. Anyway, he was never rich, so I never got the pony. But I wrote the story about a little girl who does get a pony. It was only about three or four pages, and three months later we got a letter and a postal order for seven shillings and sixpence. I said to my mother, I don't care about the money, I want to see my name there. So there was obviously that ambition and ego about writing already in me, wasn't there? I think my destiny was sealed that day. I said to my mother, "I'm going to write books one day." And she said, "Oh, that'll be nice." And then she said something to me that has always remained in my mind. She said, "You have to live life a little before you can write about it." She was right. Where better than in the reporters' room of a newspaper to do that? So the next best thing to writing novels, in my mind, was to become a journalist.'

Barbara loved reading, writing and telling stories – 'I was a big library girl. I had three library cards at one point' – and she had been writing them since she was seven: 'I always told stories – to my mother, to my doll – and wrote a lot of stories and poems and things, which my mother kept and I now have in New York, all yellowed with time.' Then, when she was twelve, her father bought her a second-hand typewriter. 'Now I wrote all sorts of stories and put them in a folder and stitched the folder so that they were held together firmly, then hand-painted the name of whatever book it was. I say "book", I mean just a dozen pages typed very badly.'

Soon, 'from about thirteen to fifteen I was taking out of the library books on journalism and on Fleet Street', the true home of journalism in London. She began writing little bits and pieces for the *Armley & Wortley News*, one of a group of newspapers within the Leeds Guardian Series, which also included the *North Leeds News* and the *Leeds Guardian* itself.

The *Armley & Wortley News* was published south of the river. Its editors seem to have taken a leaf out of Fagin's book, encouraging gangs of city kids – budding reporters all of them – to deliver news on a daily basis, often for free. The papers were at a lower level than the three main Leeds papers, the

Yorkshire Post, the *Yorkshire Evening Post* and the *Yorkshire Evening News*, and, not unlike the freebie papers of today, ran on a shoestring. On the *Leeds Guardian* the editor was also the compositor, wearing an apron and lining the type characters up on the hot metal printing machine, as well as being the main reporter, advertising executive and sub. Editors on these papers were willing to consider for publication any items that their reporters might bring in. When Barbara went to see the editor of the *Armley & Wortley News*, he was non-committal but encouraging to the fourteen-year-old. 'I said, "Can I do some local stories?" and he said, "Well you can, love, but I don't know if I'll use them."' It was enough. Barbara's uncle and aunt, Don and Jean Taylor, remembered taking her to a fair in Armley one time, and her running up to them to ask for change to make a telephone call. She had just witnessed a crash on one of the rides and wanted to file her story to the *Armley & Wortley News*.

Then one day at Northcote, her typing and shorthand teacher, Dorothy Smith, told her that the *Yorkshire Evening Post* was interviewing for staff. 'She was the one who got me the interview, because she knew the woman from the typist pool.' Barbara went home and told Freda that she had an interview on the *Post*, but not what job it was for. This was 1948, and Barbara was turning fifteen. Her mother still had it firmly fixed in her mind that she would get her daughter to university, but this was an interview with the respected *Yorkshire Evening Post* and Barbara played her cards tight to her chest. 'So it was sort of like, "Well if I don't like it – let me go and see if I like it." You know, she wanted to go to the interview *with me*! I said, "You can't! My mother cannot go with me to a job interview!"

'And then of course I got the job. I came back and she said, "I can't believe they've given a fifteen-and-a-half-year-old a job in the reporters' room." I said, "Oh, Mummy, it's in the typist pool." Well that did it, she was furious! To cut a long story short, I don't remember any rows about it. I remember long discussions and me pleading, and me finally convincing her to let me at least try the job. If I didn't like it, if it wasn't working out, I promised that I'd go back to Northcote and then go to Leeds University.'

Freda was not happy. Barbara had begun to place her own hand on the tiller of her ship of destiny. With a love of glamour reflected in her passion for Hollywood movies she had given Freda's 'educational programme' a contemporary twist which may have seemed frivolous and possibly even reminded her of the pitfalls of her own mother's ambition. At fifteen, Barbara was beginning to operate outside the bubble Freda had made for them.

The interview with the *Post* must have caused quite a stir at Northcote because June Exelby remembers it to this day. 'I remember her going for this interview to the *Yorkshire Evening Post* and Mrs Cox saying, "You make sure you take the job in the typing pool, because once you are in, you are *in*."'

Mrs Cox was right, but it really didn't matter what anyone said about taking or not taking the job, Barbara was showing that at fifteen she could handle herself, she was able to determine the best strategy to get what she wanted, in particular steering clear of confrontation at home. 'I talked my mother into it; I talked them both into it. There weren't rows because I was a little scared of my father; I would never argue with my father because he was very strong-willed.'

Barbara had decided she was going to work on the paper, she was confident that she would soon rise out of the typing pool. More significantly, she had shown that once her mind was made up, nothing and no one could stop her.

CHAPTER EIGHT
Getting On

'And where's all this scribbling going to get yer?'

A Woman of Substance

Barbara's job on the *Yorkshire Evening Post* took her daily into the centre of Leeds, to Albion Street, the then site of the newspaper group, the Yorkshire Conservative Newspaper Company, which published the *Yorkshire Post* and the *Yorkshire Evening Post* and was re-named Yorkshire Post Newspapers in 1969, making it rather less widely recognisable in 1979 as the Yorkshire Consolidated Newspaper Group in Emma Harte's empire. [23]

As a typist, Barbara worked mainly for the advertising and circulation departments and was expected to take dictation. Her first day was a disaster, 'something I would never care to live through again. Not only could I not type the letters because I was so nervous but I couldn't even read my shorthand back. Fortunately, all were standard letters for the advertising department, so the other girls helped me. However, I was still typing away at seven o'clock and everybody had gone home and finally, after the tenth time on the last letter, I sighed with relief. Then, as I was leaving I saw the wastepaper basket full of very expensive notepaper engraved with the Yorkshire Conservative Newspaper Company – never mind printed, it was engraved! And I thought, I'm going to get fired for wasting all their stationery. So, I took a handful, went into the ladies' room, put a match to it and threw it down the toilet. Well, the blaze was so enormous I didn't know how to put it out.

I kept flushing the toilet, and finally I put the blaze out. I then thought, well, I might get fired for wasting their stationery, but that's better than getting fired for being an arsonist. So I took the rest of the paper, smoothed it out and made what was a full wastepaper basket seem much less, before hiding the rest in the bottom drawer of my desk! I went to that drawer every night of the week, transferring paper from it into one of my mother's shopping bags, and brought it home and burned it.

'I hated that job, loathed it. I wanted to leave, I really did, in spite of my ambition. But I couldn't because I had this paper there in the desk. I thought they'd come and get me. What they'd do to me I didn't imagine. I was very young and naive...'

In time, as the whirlwind in the typist pool began to settle, Barbara turned her mind to developing a strategy that would make her a journalist as soon as possible. Part of the week every girl in the typing pool had to spend time in the copy room, sitting in a little booth with a typewriter and headphones, taking down copy phoned in by the *Evening Post's* reporters. 'Suddenly, the telephone would ring,' said Barbara, 'and the telephonist would say it was Keith Waterhouse, or whoever – Keith had brilliant red hair, very unruly – and I would type his dictation. You sat there typing as he dictated. You just put Keith Waterhouse at the top and when he'd finished he'd say goodbye and you'd take off your headphones and go into the newsroom and drop the article on the sub-editors table, which thrilled me because it meant that I got to see the reporters sitting nearby.'

One day, Barbara realised that there was nothing to stop her feeding her own stories through the sub-editors in the same way. 'So I came to write my stories, used the same paper, put my name at the top – Barbara Taylor – and dropped it down on the sub-editors' table. And they ran three or four, and when it came to payday the question went up as to the identity of the writer of these stories and where to send payment. The Accounts Department said, "Barbara Taylor. Is she a stringer that we have in Doncaster or Harrogate or somewhere?" Suddenly, the penny dropped and they realised that I was the new girl in the typing pool. And so it all came out, and the editor was intrigued by this girl whom nobody knew, and he sent for me. This was when I first met Barry Horniblow.

Barry Horniblow was the editor of the *Yorkshire Evening Post*, his name almost ridiculously apt in the then current tabloid revolution to which he lent no small endeavour. 'He had come up from Fleet Street,' Barbara recalled. 'The *Yorkshire Evening Post* in those days was a broadsheet and he turned it into a tabloid like the *London Evening Standard*.' Under his editorship it made all the money that kept the more prestigious morning paper, the *Yorkshire Post*, afloat. But the whizz kid from Fleet Street didn't fit in. 'They didn't like him because he was Savile Row from top to bottom,' Barbara told me. 'Obviously if he was in the newsroom he was in shirtsleeves, but his clothes were impeccable, while the others were tough newspapermen from the North with their sleeves rolled up. Barry was white-haired, well-dressed, always impeccably dressed, except when he was in the newsroom.' And more to the point, he had a reputation for giving youngsters a chance.

'He said to me, "So, you want to be a journalist?" I replied, "Oh, yes sir, but I don't just *want* to be, I am *going* to be." This amused him. This was a man from Fleet Street and he liked that in me. I was about sixteen. Fools rush in where angels fear to tread... I was so nervous I worked my toe into the carpet and lost my shoe, and had to ask whether I could retrieve it from under his desk. He said, "What have you written?" and I told him I had written for local newspapers and all of that. He said, "Oh, some time bring me your cuttings book." Then I said, "Thank you very much, Sir," and off I went.

'Then, at lunch time, I ran all the way to City Square, took a tram home to get my clippings book, dashed into the house and my mother said something like, "Oh, good, you've been sacked!" She didn't want me on this paper, she wanted me at Leeds University. Panting, I got the clippings book, took it back and went to his office. Mr Horniblow, who could see I was out of breath, said, "Barbara what is it?" and I told him what I'd done. He was intrigued, and that was the beginning of my journalism career.'

Horniblow made her assistant to his secretary. Within six months she was a reporter, graduating to women's-page

assistant and then women's-page editor. She was barely a
woman herself, but she wrote the lot anyway: cooking, fashion,
personalities. Two years later, 'Fleet Street beckoned!' as
Barbara put it.

But it wasn't all plain sailing. 'After Mr Horniblow had seen
the stories in my clippings book, he promised to get me shifted
[out of the typing pool], and when he didn't, every time I saw
him in a corridor I'd say, "It's Barbara, when will you move
me?" So, one day I was told that I was going to be a part-
time secretary. I was to help his secretary, Marion Greaves, and
she hated my guts. An older woman, she resented me, she didn't
want me there. I used to help out in the mornings. I had to be
there in the morning and I had to be there when she took her
lunch. The minute she'd gone to lunch Mr Horniblow would
come out and say, "Everything all right?" and I'd say, "Oh yes."'

But in fact Miss Greaves was only giving Barbara letters to
type, while the editor had wanted her to get experience on the
women's page, known as the Kay Boughton page. Why it was so
named has been lost to time. As Barbara explained, 'There was
no such person. It was a name, and the secretary, Miss Greaves,
did it. It was really only a column. After probably about a
month or two, he [Horniblow] said, "You're not getting any
experience, are you, Barbara?" And I said, "No, I'm not." And
he said, "Well things are going to change." I would say I'd
been on the paper eight or nine months when he said one day,
"Instead of coming here to work and help Miss Greaves, I'm
going to have you in the reporters' room. I think you'll get
some better training there." So, suddenly I was in the reporters'
room, and one or two people were a bit suspicious... when he
took this young girl under his wing, can you imagine? It never
occurred to me at the time, but looking back I realise they had
suspicions about him. They must have had. No? Wouldn't you
think?'

'Were you having an affair with him?' I asked her.

'No I wasn't. I know enough to know myself, I was not silly
like that and he was a much older man. It was like a professor
that you would adore. He was enchanted by my attitude...'

Barbara was no longer the little girl with the starched
appearance. I asked Leeds-based Bobby Caplin, a friend of

hers since 1949, to describe her as she had been when they first met. 'She was a beautiful girl, absolutely *beautiful*. If you can imagine Barbara at sixteen years of age, a size eight or ten, slim, long hair –'

Barbara had beauty and, before long, not a little presence. The late Arthur Brittenden, nine years her senior, was working for the *Yorkshire Post*, same building, same group of newspapers, when the fifteen-year-old Barbara first appeared on the scene. Brittenden would rise to become editor of the *Daily Mail* (1966–71), then director of Times Newspapers and later director of Murdoch's News International. He has seen her only once since she left Leeds for London, but managed a crystal-clear recall of the winning spark in her. 'She was very winning, very appealing. I think people who are going to get on tend to show it at some time along the way, and she most certainly did. When she was there in 1948 and '49, I was on the *Yorkshire Post* – it was the prestigious morning paper of the group until it lost some of its character when it absorbed the *Leeds Mercury* [the paper, incidentally, on which Emma Harte gets her brother Frank a job in *A Woman of Substance*]. Barbara was a secretary then. We had these "moments", which I still remember nearly fifty years on, when we came upon each other in the canteen … very romantic. That was how I first remember her. We used to sit at a table having a cup of tea, but there was always something *different* about her. Of course, she was very attractive. Unbelievable. But she had this something different about her and it was very appealing. I suppose, looking back, she must have been – I mean one reads about how ambitious she was and so on, but there was never anything aggressive or unpleasant or whatever about her. It was always terribly likeable. I think we were *all* in love with her probably.

'One other encounter stays with me – actually the last time I saw her. I was on the *News Chronicle* in Fleet Street. She had only recently come to London, and I remember coming down in the lift one day and going through the front hall, and there she was, sitting for some reason in the front hall with another girl. Why on earth would I remember with such clarity walking through the front hall of the *News Chronicle* fifty years ago and seeing Barbara there? But this was the thing about her, that you *did* remember. There was something always special about it – electric!'

Barbara would need all of her feminine wiles to establish her position in the male-dominated *Yorkshire Evening Post* offices, especially after whiz-kid incomer Horniblow backed her.

The newsroom, to which she was posted by Horniblow, was L-shaped. To the right of the door was the long side of the 'L', a long table big enough to seat around six sub-editors: 'waistcoated or cardiganned figures, alternately red-faced or sallow-complexioned, pot-bellied or concave-chested according to whether they drank Guinness for strength or milk for their ulcers; but all of them chain-smoking,' as one of their number described them.[20] Opposite the door sat the news editor, and beyond were the face-to-face desks of the reporters. The passage of copy was from reporter to deputy news or news editor, who having read and passed it would shout 'Boy!', bringing the copy boy over to take it to the subs' table, who would prepare the copy for press.

Barbara was lucky to be given Keith Waterhouse as her mentor, a true pro although only four years her senior. 'Barry loved young people, he was very focused on Keith so he put me with him – his desk butted up to mine, that's how they were arranged.'

It turned out that she and Waterhouse had much in common. His family had fallen into the hands of the Board of Workhouse Guardians when he was a young boy. His father, a costermonger, died penniless after borrowing money to start a business and spending it instead on drink and betting. The bailiffs stripped the family home of furniture, and his mother was reduced to hiding her prized possessions – a pair of fairground vases and a harp zither – from the means-test man in the coal-hole and airing cupboard. Later, the family was moved to a council estate on Halton Moor, actually not far from Temple Newsam.

Another coincidence was that Waterhouse's desire to become a journalist, which he had rehearsed in a paper of his own making as a very young boy, was, like Barbara's, moved by fantasy, an image of himself as the famous journalist and thriller writer, Edgar Wallace, who had begun his working life at the age

---

[20] *City Lights* by Keith Waterhouse (1994).

of eleven selling newspapers at Ludgate Circus in Fleet Street.[21] Waterhouse maintained that he was only three years old when he saw the picture of Wallace that so influenced him. It showed his hero 'wearing the peaked cap of a Reuters war correspondent when covering the Boer War.'

Also like Barbara, Waterhouse wanted eventually to write books. His first considerable literary success would come with *Billy Liar* in 1959, a loosely autobiographical novel about a North Country undertaker's clerk, a working-class dreamer who lives in a world of fantasy in preference to the bleak reality. He had himself known the bleak reality of working in a funeral parlour after his mother insisted she needed him to bring in more than the ten shillings a week he could earn as a newspaper reporter on a local paper. Later, in collaboration with his friend Willis Hall, who also grew up in Leeds, Waterhouse made it into a play starring Albert Finney, and then a film starring Tom Courtenay and Julie Christie. [24] The work reached far beyond the industrial North that spawned it, but no doubt found many sympathetic northern ears for the very reason that Billy himself, and others who suffered the traumas of a northern childhood, needed the fantasy element just to survive.

'So, Keith was always helping me with my copy,' Barbara continued. 'He taught me to write for newspapers... Working on a newspaper at the age of sixteen ... a major, tough, provincial newspaper – a daily – being in that newsroom with a lot of newspapermen on the police beat, at court, inquest court, as a junior reporter. It was a great experience.'

Waterhouse recalled Barbara as 'an ambitious sixteen-year-old ... apt to burst into tears from time to time when bawled out for not yet knowing her job to perfection, and I became her hand-holder-in-chief. Little did she know that it was a case of the blinded-by-tears leading the blinded-by-tears.'

'Keith was very sweet to me,' Barbara remembers. 'We'd go to the Kardomah Café and have beans on toast. I remember he told me not to cry in the newsroom, to cry in the ladies' room instead.'

---

[21] Edgar Wallace went on to write such classic thrillers as *The Four Just Men* (1905), *The Crimson Circle* (1922) and *The Green Archer* (1923).

Being slapped down by Ken Lemmon, deputy news and later news editor, would have been a new experience for Barbara, perhaps a salutary one, and the tears that flowed, which Waterhouse mopped up with such care and attention that it won him Barbara's hand at a Press Ball at Leeds Town Hall 'in a dinner jacket hired from Rawcliffe's, where my mother had bought my school cap', might have damaged a less purposeful girl.

'I was very much in love with newspapers,' says Barbara, 'and being a newspaperwoman, a newspaper*man* I should say, even down to wanting a dirty trench coat, which indeed I got.' Freda, who so wanted her glittering prize to go to university, knew she had lost Barbara to journalism the day she turned up wearing it. 'My mother accused me of having taken it off in the garden and rolling it around in the dirt to make it look used, but I didn't, it just got dirty.

'Stanley Vaughan was the crime reporter, he used to drag me with him. I tagged on behind him – he spoke with an American accent and never took his hat off. I grew up in that newsroom. The nature of the work gives you exposure to life, sometimes life in the raw. Also, one has to have the human element in a news story. You can't just write about the landscape or a room setting in a novel and not have it peopled with real people. I became conscious of the human element in stories when I was a newspaper reporter because that's what it's about, isn't it? A newspaper story is only interesting if it's about people, their tragedies, their dramas, their heartbreak – that's what I'm dealing with [in the novels]. I'm dealing in human emotion and, according to my French publisher, I am able to put it down on paper in such a way that I touch a nerve in the reader.'

There is a clear line between self-belief and delusion, and in her swift ascent Barbara kept herself on the right side of it by sheer hard work, determination and discipline. She often stayed late in the office because she liked to get her desk cleaned up. And later, if she went for a drink with the others at one of the pubs favoured by reporters – the Pack Horse, say, or Whitelock's – she showed her self-discipline by not staying long: 'Frank Shire, deputy news editor at the time, said: "You're smart,

Barbara, you stay for one drink and then you leave." I'd have a drink, buy them a round and then go.'

Other characters among the *Evening Post's* journalists included 'whimsical' Con Gordon, the feature writer, and the leader writer, Percy, 'who kept a cottage piano in his office which he would play for inspiration in his ceaseless fight against the Atlee government,' according to Waterhouse. Idly I mention to Barbara that Waterhouse was a socialist and how odd that he worked for the Yorkshire Conservative Newspaper Company and latterly for the *Daily Mail*, also a right-wing paper. 'Yes,' said Barbara, 'and do you know what he sang walking through the Yorkshire Conservative Newspaper Company? "The Red Flag"! He did all these crazy things. He walked once from Land's End to John o'Groats for a story. And on the other evening paper – the *Evening News* – was Willis Hall[22]. And do you know who else was on the *News*? Peter O'Toole! I didn't know him well. Keith says I did and that I don't recognise him because he had acne in those days and didn't look so good, and that this big movie star, this gorgeous hunk with blond hair and bright blue eyes used to say, "D'you want to come t'pictures, Barbara?" in his Yorkshire accent, but that now he's very posh and he speaks like *this* ... and he's Lawrence of Arabia. Keith used to say all these terrible things to me when *Lawrence of Arabia* came out. He'd say, "Oh, you really blew it when he wanted to take you t'pictures." By then we were both in Fleet Street, [and we] went to a party given by Sam Spiegel for *Lawrence of Arabia* and met Omar Sharif ... but I don't remember Peter well, though I do remember there was a sort of pimply youth that used to hang around. It may have been Peter O'Toole.'

The Leeds newspaper scene does indeed have an extraordinary history of turning out famous people. Former trainee Nick Clarke, late of BBC's *World at One*, recalls a colleague being bawled out for poor timekeeping. 'The editor

---

[22] The *Yorkshire Evening News* was the *Evening Post*'s main competitor and in 1963 merged with the *Yorkshire Post* group. Besides being Waterhouse's collaborator on *Billy Liar*, Willis Hall was perhaps most famous for his play *The Long and the Short and the Tall* (1958).

warned him: "You idle bugger – you turn up on time or one day you will have to make music for your living."' He couldn't have been more prescient: the poor timekeeper was Mark Knopfler, who would found multi-million-pound rock group Dire Straits.

At seventeen or eighteen, Barbara's life beyond home and newspaper tended to revolve around the friends she met regularly on a Saturday morning at Marshall & Snelgrove, as she and Bobby Caplin recalled. On Commercial Street, Marshall & Snelgrove was one of the top Leeds department stores, 'a miniature Harrods'. 'You could go through the circulation department, and there it was across the street,' said Barbara. 'I would go across at 11.30 a.m. when I took my lunch hour. I'd meet Bobby and Ronnie Sumrie and various girlfriends there.'

'There was also a lovely bar called Powolny's, a college bar, in the centre,' continued Bobby, 'and we all met in there. It was a different era. The places to go to were few. There was the odd coffee bar, but there wasn't much social life; well, there was but it was in people's homes rather than going out. Barbara dated a very close friend of mine, came from a wealthy family, very good-looking, born with two golden spoons in his mouth, lovely guy. She was very, very attractive and she's always demanded the best. Ronnie is two years older than me. At seventeen these girls didn't want to go out with an eighteen-year-old, she wanted to go out with at least a twenty- or twenty-one-year-old. I mean we didn't have cars in those days, but Ronnie had a car, and he was a catch. He was known as one of the top catches in Leeds. And he took Barbara out, but then she moved, went to live in London.'

'I didn't think of these boys as Jewish,' Barbara said, but they were among the second-generation of the Jewish clothiers who then ran Leeds industry. Many of the families had fled west out of Russia and Poland to escape persecution and stayed rather than continuing on to America, their original destination. It was a father–to-son inheritance.

In the earlier twentieth century there were Jewish ghettoes and hooligan attacks on Jewish people, and later, when Barbara was a journalist in London her interest was piqued by the

controversial and highly publicised trial in 1961 of Adolph
Eichmann, shortly before she met her future husband, himself
by origin a German Jew. Developing a strong empathy for their
plight and the force of will that brought them through led to an
important element in *A Woman of Substance*. In the company of
Emma Harte we get a description of the Jewish ghetto in Leeds,
and the Kallinski tailoring shop where Emma will come to work,
and altogether it is one of those moments in Barbara's fiction
for which she became famous, because it is researched with
intricate precision. We end up with a complete knowledge of
the divisional labour-system invented by Jewish tailor Herman
Friend, whereby a suit would be made up in parts by different
tailoring outfits, according to the dictates of a factory. Friend
worked with, and made famous, the John Barren factory, 'the
first ready-made clothiers to start in Leeds after Singer invented
the sewing machine'. He wrought a revolution in the industry,
we learn, 'and helped to put Leeds on the map as the biggest
centre of ready-made clothing in the world.'

Discussing this with David, son of Abraham Kallinsky,
patriarch of the tailoring family 'on that hot August night
in 1905', a friendship is born that will endure through the
Emma Harte series: 'Together they would climb, in their own
individualistic ways, struggling out of grim poverty, fighting all
manner of prejudices, reaching for bigger and better things, and
in their rising and their reaching they would carry the city with
them.'

All of this was bred in the bone for the lads who were
Barbara's friends back in the day in Leeds: 'We were hard-
working people,' Caplin recalled. 'I have an elder brother who
was a little bit cleverer than me, who ended up a project director
at the World Bank in Washington, helped to design the first-ever
computer in the UK. My late father started the family business
and it was up to me to go into it. I was never good at school…
I was struggling, I was never academic and I can honestly say
that the happiest day of my life was the day that I left school.
But I was never the boss's son either, I went into the factory at
ground level and had to go to Technical College to get my City
and Guilds. Ronnie was also in the clothing business. Sumrie
Clothes of Leeds was one of the finest clothing companies in the

country, very famous. He never had to work. He was a good-looking guy, sat in the showrooms when people came.'

A 'floor show' was a fashion feature on a Saturday morning at their venue, Marshall and Snelgrove. In *Telling Tales* Alan Bennett describes 'resident mannequins prowling the aisles between the tables modelling outfits on offer on the floor below in the couture department.' This was perfectly in tune with another opportunity that Horniblow lined up for Barbara at the newspaper.

When he made Barbara a reporter, he also hired Madeleine McLoughlin from the *Manchester Evening News*[23] as women's page editor, and soon Barbara would become her assistant. 'Suddenly Kay Boughton's column became Kay Boughton's Women's Pages, and the secretary was only the secretary and no longer writing her page, or her little bit, and there was Madeleine installed as women's page editor instead.'

Immediately, what was most striking to those around her was Barbara's style, the way she carried herself off. But in support of her rise through the ranks of journalism was an unprecedented media interest in women as a consumer force, in their attitudes and opinions, and by women's own interest in the kind of thing she was now writing for the *Evening Post*. It was a mixture of talent, style and publishing environment, which would set her fair into the third millennium and not only in journalism.

Huge changes were afoot in fashion and for women generally. Barbara remembers that even in the early 1950s 'a lot of the fashion was still how to make six dresses out of two pieces of curtain or fabric or towel.' Billie Figg showed me a photograph published in one of the Amalgamated Press women's magazines of herself in a hat made out of a man's old tweed coat. 'It was still war-time "make-do-and-mend". Rationing went on for quite some considerable time after the war, food rationing until 1954. Isn't it funny,' said Billie, 'what was inculcated in us then never leaves you. I cannot waste the ends of soaps, I have to dig them into the next end. When I see youngsters in offices throwing away huge reams of paper that these machines spit

---

[23] A big Lancashire newspaper, on the other side of the Pennines from the *York-shire Evening Post*.

out I'm appalled because I keep every sheet of paper that's got a plain white back to write on. You just can't get over it.' No wonder Barbara had been so frantic at the paper wastage on her first day. Now, however, she had justified her self-confidence and found herself in something of a growth industry.

At this point, Billie was working on the PR side of an advertising agency – Napper, Stinton, Woolley in Great Chapel Street, off Oxford Street in London – with women as her main target. She recalls: 'There was this terrific feeling for the first time that women could get somewhere. People talk about the early 1950s as a depressed time – grey – but it wasn't. Things could only get better. Also, suddenly, women were being listened to. Women were the new market. Their opinion was being sought.'

Billie had professional experience of the old regime, when being a woman held considerably less promise. She cut her journalistic teeth on the Amalgamated Press in the mid-1940s, a group of magazines, 'all of them now defunct – *Woman's Pictorial, Mother and Home* and *Woman's Journal*. The famous publishers Cecil King and Hugh Cudlipp later bought up the company and made it into IPC[24]. It was a marvellous place in Farringdon Street, with this rather ornate doorway and attendants in uniform.'

What is first relevant is why, in 1946, Billie left the company. 'The thing was that Jack and I got married and it was still the time that it wasn't done for the wife to work. As a matter of fact, until a very little way beforehand you weren't *allowed* to be married and work at the Amalgamated Press if you were a woman. There was a woman there then who was still pretending she was unmarried!

'We got married in 1946 and the practice must have been relaxed pretty soon after that. I was there in '44, '45, and right up to our marriage that woman was still masquerading under "Miss". I think it was a protection of men's jobs really. I remembered accepting at the time that once you've got married you've got a bit of support behind you and you

---

[24] IPC stands for International Publishing Corporation. The company would become the largest consumer magazine publisher in Europe.

mustn't occupy a job that could be given to a man. I remember accepting and understanding that,' said Billie. Her husband, Jack, who was brought up on a working-class estate on the edge of London in Dagenham, home of the Ford car industry, echoed this: 'My mother never went to work except later on in the war when a lot of people did. I don't think any woman up and down our road went to work.'

'It was still part of the culture that the wife stayed home,' confirmed Billie. 'After a little while I got very restive and took a part-time job locally. Even so, one asked permission in those days,' she said, cocking an eye at her husband.

Realising too late what a career prospect she'd let slip at Amalgamated Press, Billie became determined to get back into journalism and found it almost impossible. 'I had to do it by steps...' and the job with Napper, Stinton, Woolley was an important one of these. 'I thought, I'll try and get in sideways. I couldn't get straight back into magazines, it was really tough. I'm talking 1950 ... you couldn't easily get into magazines then.'

All of which attests to Barbara's ingenuity in landing a position as fashion editor on *Woman's Own*, though she had what was required, a column on a paper whose banner read 'Largest Circulation in the Country' – and a respected Fleet Street referee in Horniblow, if indeed they called upon him to provide one, for Barry Horniblow left Leeds some time before Barbara. There was also clear precedent for transfer from the Yorkshire newspaper group into Fleet Street. Arthur Brittenden had moved to the now defunct *News Chronicle*, and Waterhouse to the *Daily Mirror*, a move he described with great wit in *Streets Ahead*, the sequel to *City Lights*. Fact was that a successful spell on the *YEP* was as good a setting-off point as any for a journalist, and had even been seen by Horniblow, of course, as anything but a step back in an already booming Fleet Street career.

Billie, on the other hand, was scuppered: 'My record was terribly broken, I hadn't got the cub reporter thing, had missed university because of a bout of TB and didn't even have much freelance. I'd very little and there didn't appear to be any vacancies. But I got into the agency as secretary to Leslie

Stinton, then I drove him mad. Bits of copy for baked beans, on anything the agency was selling, he'd find on his desk each morning.'

She soon realised, however, that she had in fact landed herself in the right place at the right time. 'The office had a woman doing what they used to call "editorial" then, and they decided that they'd like to expand, and they brought in a chap named Ted Jones.' It was through Ted that Billie and Barbara first met. 'Oh, Ted was quite significant in our lives. He came from J. Walter Thompson[25], a journalist who'd got into advertising and PR. He just had a *sense* of a story and we did such exciting things.' Finally worn down by these bits of copy coming from this girl who was supposed to be his secretary, Leslie Stinton decided to despatch Billie to Ted Jones's department. 'We had one hell of a lot of fun. As I said, women had become a market; people wanted their opinions. Suddenly women were being listened to. They'd actually say things like, "Let's have a meeting and get all the women in and hear what they say about it." I was made head of a women's section in the PR department.

'Now, Ted, when he'd been at JWT, had had something to do with fisheries and he'd been up to Hull and Barbara had covered a story for the *Yorkshire Evening Post*. It so happened that Ted had an eye for a pretty girl and he and Barbara had obviously struck it up, so she'd got his name. Barbara was sharp on getting her contacts ready for when she was going to come down to London, and so she'd arranged to call on Ted at his advertising agency when she came down. So, he brought her into the office at some time around 1951, 1952 – before she worked for *Woman's Own*. She would have been eighteen, nineteen.

'Barbara and I had already had dealings, without knowing each other, because she'd been using my stories in her column – the Kay Boughton column. I'm eleven years older than Barbara, so there was quite an age gap, but a friendship blossomed.'

I asked Billie whether she could remember the day Barbara first walked into Napper, Stinton, Woolley. 'I can picture it

---

[25] A famous and highly successful advertising company first incorporated in 1896.

very easily. What I remember is someone very slim and pretty, and with laughing eyes, and my thinking, what a Scandinavian-looking person. My knowledge of Barbara now is putting her in a skirt to calf-length, but leaving me very conscious of very slim legs and ... would it have been stiletto heels?

'Barbara Goalen was the great model at that time, and Barbara dressed to look like that. We wore hats and little white gloves. Couture ruled fashion, the ready-to-wear and the prêt à porter hadn't yet exploded. It was couture, Givenchy and the people that dressed Audrey Hepburn – those were our fashion icons then, and in London people like Victor Stiebel and Hartnell, out of our reach but they were the icons who set the style you copied. You've made me realise that in those days Barbara dressed at a lower price-level than the couturier, but in those terms.'

The Kay Boughton page in early 1952 demonstrates Barbara's by then energetic but easy journalistic style. Readable, well-informed, it captures her preference for elegance, sophistication and the feminine, well in advance of the more youthful, individual influences of the ready-to-wear revolution of the later 1950s.

Those were the days when the public looked to royalty as well as Hollywood to set the tone. Long before she made spicier column inches in her regal Mustique period, with John Binden and other riotous crew playing court, Princess Margaret was about to become one such fashion muse, and Barbara was well on top of it. 'A new note in the Spring trends,' she writes, 'a hint of *the Princess line*, who is so much in the news just now. She was one of the first to adopt the flowing fan line used in coats and suits, and to favour velvet... Some say Princess Margaret will be the new leader of fashion, following in the footsteps of her much-admired aunt, the Duchess of Kent. With an engagement in the air that is more than possible.'

Perceptive stuff. When Anthony Armstrong Jones plighted his troth shortly afterwards, the couple became the Prince Charles and Princess Diana of their day.

By 1952, the year before Barbara left for London, the fashion scene had taken her far from the humdrum realities of home. On 6th February 1952, she was on the case at soon-to-be-crowned Princess Elizabeth's couturier Hardy Amies's London show, introducing us to 'the pyramid silhouette', and recommending 'wider hemlines worn over stiffening petticoats … for fun and games.'

The job also took her to the Paris Collections, and a surprise meeting with Barry Horniblow. 'I remember going to Paris for the first time when I was about seventeen. I went with the WPE [Madeleine McLoughlin] to cover the fashion shows. Paris totally overwhelmed me, I thought it was one of the most beautiful cities – it's still one of my favourite cities – and I came back and sat down at my typewriter and started to write the story of this ballet dancer [she called her fictional heroine Vivienne Ramage] who lived in a garret in Paris and was very poor. It was all very dramatic and I think actually it was probably something like *Camille*. I got to about page ten and thought, "No, I have a feeling I've read this somewhere before."'

Camille had been filmed in 1936, starring Greta Garbo and Hollywood heart-throb Robert Taylor, the actor who reminded Barbara of her father.

'Madeleine McLoughlin wanted to take me to the Paris shows because some boyfriend she had was going to be there, and I could do some of the work. I was quite happy to go, but I realised what she was up to when she said, "You'll have to sit in for me at times", and I said "Why?" And she said, whatever-his-name-is was coming. I think I was quite smart even then because I remember saying to her, "Well, I don't know if my mother will let me go. I could talk her into it, but you've got to promise me that we'll go and see Barry Horniblow when we go to London. So she said, "Yes," but on the way there we didn't. So I blackmailed her – if we didn't see him I'd want my name on what we'd written, and of course I'd written most of it.

'On the way back, she said we'd go. I think Barry was on the *Sunday Sketch* or one of those Sunday tabloids, and I *kept* saying to her (I can be a bit of a nag), "Did you make the appointment?" I remember she finally said, "No, but don't worry, it'll be fine." And I said, "How are we going to get in?" She said, "We'll go through the Circulation Department." Circulation, two girls. I was seventeen so she must have been twenty-seven, maybe a bit older, and an Irish woman – from

Manchester. She's chatting, "Hello, how are you? How are you chaps?" They just let us in as if we owned the place – in and up the stairs. She kept saying, "We've an appointment with Mr Horniblow, which is the way?" And finally we were outside his office door with some woman trying to put us off … and he came out. And I said, "Oh, Mr Horniblow!"

'There he was, white-haired and elegant. And he said, "Barbara!"'

Fade and cut. 'You *must* have been in love with him,' I said.

'No I wasn't, because…'

'A crush?'

'No, it wasn't a crush, it wasn't romantic, it was like…'

'Adulation?'

'Yes, a good word … adulation.'

At the start of 1952, in spite of a keener focus on the women's market generally, prospects for manufacturers in the fashion industry were far from rosy. In January that year the Kay Boughton column reported that women's clothing manufacturers were facing gloomy trade prospects – eighty per cent had had to cut staff in the last three months. Barbara blamed this on 'world conditions … depression in the seven and eight o'clock BBC News bulletins … enough to put any woman off a day's shopping.' The saviour would be her hero, Winston Churchill. He, having been ousted by Labour in 1945, when all fell quiet on the Western Front, had, in 1951, been welcomed back as Prime Minister, and would continue to serve until 1955. '…On Mr Churchill's talks in America, the fashion industry's future lies,' Barbara told her readers. Meanwhile, if one couldn't find the money to dress oneself properly, one should 'Make the most of your voice!…

'An attractive voice is as important as appearance,' she wrote. 'While you will be admired for your clothes, you will be *remembered* for your voice…' It is an interesting thought, apt coming from Barbara, whose voice one does indeed remember. To the broadcaster the late Richard Whiteley, who met Barbara for the first time in the autumn of 1979, when he interviewed her for Yorkshire Television's magazine programme, *Calendar*, her voice spoke of integrity: 'What I found most refreshing was that she hadn't adopted a transatlantic accent, despite having lived in the States for much of her adult life. She had retained a very crisp and rich English speaking voice.'

Barbara is skilful with her voice: she understands that it is a key instrument of style and she will modulate it accordingly and instinctively, so that she is probably not even aware she is doing it. In a crowded room at one of her book launches she wears its formal tones with all the confidence of a sophisticated woman of the world. Then, one-to-one, it can soften to reveal the vulnerable woman beneath. Sometimes – perhaps when she relaxes into her old self or is speaking to a rootsy Northern journalist like Michael Parkinson, the Yorkshire accent re-appears, as three years ago Simon Hatterstone of the *Guardian* ungallantly reported: 'The longer we talk, the flatter BTB's vowels become,' he wrote. 'As the hours pass, I lose sight of the huge-haired New York caricature and find myself talking to Barbara, the bluff, likeable Yorkshirewoman.'

Barbara had worked her voice strategy out years earlier. In the Kay Boughton column, in her youth, she developed a seven-point strategy for an appealing voice: avoid bad thoughts, read aloud for ten minutes every day, control the breathing, make it even, flowing, low, sonorous. Copy a voice you admire, but don't mimic the voice – 'Avoid artificial accents, they are unconvincing and insincere!'

It is a mark of the style of Emma Harte in *A Woman of Substance* that she relinquishes her Yorkshire accent as soon as possible, and the girls at Kallinski's Leeds tailoring shop tease her about it: '"Talking like cut glass," they called it. Emma smiled and didn't take offence, so eventually it stopped, though they never quite became accustomed to her beauty or her air of breeding.'

Today, journalists are wont to assume that Barbara's mode of speech – 'the pleasing tones of the cosmopolitan,' as one put it – are 'the result of having lived her life in many different countries', but Billie Figg recalls that Barbara did not have a pronounced regional accent when they first met in London in 1950–1, though you could 'hear it softly behind'.

Regional accents were not part of the requisite accoutrements of success in the early 1950s, before *Angry Young Man* 'anarchism' took hold, domestic realism came in and working-class values were fêted in so-called kitchen-sink dramas, popular later in the decade.

When Barbara set forth from Leeds in 1953, it was unthinkable that anyone should read the news on radio with other than an arching, upper-crust English accent. But soon Alan Bennett would make a living partly out of the multifarious working-class characters that a Yorkshire accent suggested to him. Bennett does admit, however, that in the Fifties when he went to Oxford University, he, too, made an attempt to hide it. 'Then it came back, and now I don't know where I am.'

In *Telling Tales*, he recalls a particular problem he had in a public recitation of a sentence by Oliver Goldsmith:

Of praise a mere glutton he swallow'd what came
And the puff of a dunce he mistook it for fame

Bennett died when the last line came out first as 'the paff of a dunce' and the second time as 'the poof of a dance'.

Barbara has been known to indulge her Yorkshire accent when returning to her roots, and at other times has been described as – and alternately accused of – putting on a 'power-packed Alexis Colby accent' (this was in 1997) and having 'an almost stagey upper-class English accent'. The fact is that different accents can be called on to send definable signals to different audiences. Empathy is a powerful tool in communication; why not use such a tool if you have the confidence and credibility to do so?

Barbara might say that her experimentation is a sign of the actress in her. None of this is of idle curiosity, for accents have traditionally been connected with identity, and identity is, indeed, the fundamental question of all her novels, her message to her readers being, in her own words, 'to know who you are and what you are'.

Uprooting from a home culture as strong as that of Yorkshire took guts for a twenty-year-old girl in 1953, but had a clear rationale. Roots not only feed a plant, they tie it down. Keith Waterhouse also left, but took his Yorkshire roots with him, wearing them like a badge. He was still alluding to his childhood job in a Leeds undertakers in his final job as a *Daily*

Mail columnist, proud to retain his Yorkshire accent, with its very particular reference points.

On the other hand, Freda made a point of taking Barbara out of the local, post-industrial terraced world of Leeds as a child and into the rural landscape of North Yorkshire, where Barbara mined ideas, lessons of history and values with a wider relevance, ideas which set her up for the incredible international journey on which she would embark. In particular, she mined the abstract idea of beauty – the special spirit of places like Middleham, Studley Royal and Haworth – which impart a sense of the sublime that the industrial revolution had squeezed out of the urbanised working-class in the North with almost Judgement Day finality.

Keith Waterhouse avoided any opportunity to visit the countryside as a boy, his preferred environment being one with 'not a blade of grass in sight'. When called up to National Service at an RAF base at Wombleton he likened the North Yorkshire moors to 'Noel Coward's Norfolk, very flat,' as if he had never set eyes on the real moors, often precipitous. 'The North Yorkshire moors,' he writes, '...even in the driest summers give out such an impression of being marshland that one expects Magwitch staggering across them through the mist.' The fictional setting, where the escaped convict Magwitch appears and terrifies Pip in *Great Expectations*, was in fact based by Dickens on Cooling in Kent. Nothing could be further in imagination from the wild, expansive Yorkshire moors.

Again, Alan Bennett casts a few frogs, a crayfish and the sight of a lizard on a rock as '*it* as far as nature in my childhood is concerned,' concluding that 'with nature, as in other departments, adults *pretended* ... [in order to] conceal the fact that Nature is dull.' Both Bennett and Waterhouse made their way in the wider world still spiritually confined within the cobbled world of bricks and mortar in which they had been brought up, trading on it, sometimes ironically, sometimes to point of caricature.

The Yorkshire countryside to which Barbara's mother turned her was something else. It awakened in her daughter an appreciation of landscape as character – as if it were overwritten with the exploits of its history and the emotions and values redolent of those who had steered it. Being part of this landscape was Barbara's birthright, it reflected something in her and became part of her identity long before she saw the narrative potential and returned to it to articulate her woman of substance.

Imbued with the character of the sublime Yorkshire moors – indestructible, everlasting – her self-belief heightened by Freda's conviction that she was capable of anything, that there were no limits to what she could achieve, she moved out of childhood and shed her working-class skin with the courage and vanity of a Neville, the self-assurance and manners of a Ripon, and the vitality of her maternal grandmother, Edith Walker, to press her game to the end.

The industrial revolution was over. If rising in the world was flying in the face of the working-class rubric, there was no sense of it in Barbara. Prevarication went against her instincts and against all the advice her mother had given to her. Freda had led her daughter back in time to eighteenth-century William Hazlitt's idea that self-belief is the mother of opportunity.

CHAPTER NINE
The Jeannie Years

'There's nothing you can't have if you try hard enough, work hard enough and strive towards a goal. And never, never limit yourself.'

Act of Will

The Fifties were an unforgettable era. The decade saw the exploding of the H-bomb, the coming of TV to the masses, the first exploration of outer space, the beginnings of the affluent society and the start of a period of teenage-powered rebellion against existing attitudes to sex, class, authority and good taste. It was the time of Elvis Presley, Marilyn Monroe, James Dean, Burgess and Maclean, and the papers were full, too, of Khrushchev, Castro and Suez. Feminist writer Simone de Beauvoir used the term 'women's liberation' for the first time in 1953, and, two years earlier, Irish writer Leslie Paul wrote *Angry Young Man*, providing the soubriquet for a radical school of writers that included John Osborne, Kingsley Amis, Alan Sillitoe, Colin Wilson, John Braine and others.

In fact, as we shall see, there were large parts of this Fifties agenda that Barbara never experienced, partly because the 'good taste' and elegance elements that were up for replacement were endemic to her style, which it never occurred to her to change. Nevertheless, the era was an unforgettable experience for her, if quite unlike most people's. It began in austerity and finished up with a Hollywood liaison.

In 1950, twenty Dunhill cigarettes cost three shillings and sevenpence (about 17.5p in modern coinage); a large loaf of bread, two shillings and a penny (10p); a pound of cheese, a shilling (5p); and a bottle of gin, thirty-three shillings and ninepence (about £1.70). On the face of it, that sounds like a cheap shop, but of course salaries were far less then too. A political columnist on the *Sunday Pictorial*, a national newspaper, was earning £1,500 in 1950. Would he be earning forty times as much today? If so, his shopping bill today, at 1950s prices, would be £7 for the packet of Dunhills, £4 for a large loaf of bread, £2 a pound for cheese, and £68 for a bottle of gin. Quite clearly the whole product-cost balance is different today, and there are many more things to spend our money on, but clearly, too, things were not cheap more than half a century ago.

When Freda delivered Barbara to her small flat at 44 Belsize Park Gardens, NW3, between the Finchley Road and Haverstock Hill, she was going to find it hard to make ends meet on a salary that will have been considerably less than £1,500 per annum. Typically, the burden was eased by Freda. Like her persona, Christina, in *Act Of Will*, Barbara's rent was paid by her mother: 'My parents supported me when I was in London,' she admits.

This might be assumed to have had an effect on the frame of mind in which she began her decade in London. Indeed, she makes plain in *Act of Will* that there is a price to pay for her mother's sacrifice on her behalf. Christina is driven by what she now perceives as 'the crucial debt she owed her mother... She must repay it. If I do not it will weigh heavy on my conscience all the days of my life, she thought. And that I could not bear...' Later, she says: 'I have a terrible need, a compelling need, to bring ease and comfort to [my mother's] life. I want to give her the kind of luxuries she's never known...'

This was not, however, the case with Barbara, at least at this stage of her life. 'Of course I was very good to her, financially and in other ways, but I never felt there was a huge debt to repay. I wanted to succeed because I knew it would please her and that it would be wrong somehow if I didn't succeed ... even at Northcote School, for instance, I always knew that I had to, that I couldn't waste time or dawdle or not pay attention to my school work, because I knew that that would be terrible. She expected the very best from me.'

Barbara has also said that she wasn't conscious until some time later of the sacrifices her mother had made for her. Nevertheless, she felt a need 'to prove that I was the best, and that all my parents' love and devotion had come to fruition.' This in no way restricted her or repressed a desire to do otherwise: 'I *wanted* to please her,' Barbara stressed.

It would have been completely out of character for Freda to burden Barbara with thoughts of the debt she owed her, or what it meant to slip quietly into the background when it was time for Barbara to be parted from her. 'My mother never said anything to me at the time, but later I found out that the day I left for London she took a doll I was fond of and put it in her bedroom. She kept it there until she died in 1981. I think she was trying to hang on to a part of me. When she died I found her handbag and my childhood library cards were in it – the handbag in current use! – and I found her diary, all her diaries, and read an entry that said: "Barbara has gone to London today – all the sunshine has gone out of my life." It was all it said on the page. It made me feel incredibly sad.'

Earlier, Barbara and her mother had traipsed around London looking for a suitable place to rent. Had they come by car they would have had little difficulty parking, for, as Billie Figg recalls, many of the Second World War bomb sites were being used as car parks, 'and it was easy to park anywhere. Bombed-out London also became a rich bed for wild flowers.' Billie Figg, born in North London to Londoners who then moved to suburban Woodford Green, became Barbara's lifeline: 'She immediately treated Jack and me as friends,' Billie recalled. 'She would often ring, we would go out together, and she'd come down here first of all.'

Jack remembered helping out at her little flat, putting up a curtain and rail to hang her clothes on. 'It was, as far as I remember, a living room, a bedroom, kitchen and bath,' he said. 'She was certainly living on her own. Looking back, I think we were just slightly stable anchorages in London, a place that was strange to her. She used to telephone us a lot, and so without complimenting ourselves there must have been some sort of comfort in that, whereas maybe quite a few of the other people she got to know, well … perhaps they weren't married?'

Back in 1953, what *Woman's Own* meant to Alan Bennett's mum was columnist Beverley Nichols 'writing about his gardens and chronicling the doings of his several cats', Nichols' life seeming to her one of 'dizzying sophistication'. What it meant to broadcaster Sue Lawley was 'lots and lots of romantic fiction … all those soppy love stories. Did you never want to write one of those?' she asked Barbara on *Desert Island Discs* fifty years later. Listening to the radio programme miles away I could feel Barbara bristling before she answered, 'No, and I never read them actually, to tell you the honest truth.' Lawley stemmed the flow from her lancing cut rather unconvincingly with, 'They were very good.'

Her snipe was in fact off target because it would be quite wrong to suggest that Barbara's lifestyle in London between 1953, when she became Fashion Editor of *Woman's Own*, and 1963, when she married film producer Robert Bradford and left for New York, bore even the remotest resemblance to that recommended by either Beverley Nichols or those romantic story writers. It came far closer to the one described in Barbara's novel, *Voice of the Heart*, which speaks to us of destructive relationships in a glitzy but ruthless world of showbiz, which it took Barbara but a short time to break into.

When she arrived at *Woman's Own*, Barbara discovered that she was in fact one of several fashion editors, and at once did what was required to adapt to their style, the young novice showing just how apprehensive and keen to swim with the stream she was: 'When I got there these women in the Fashion Department all wore hats, they came to work in them! So I went out and I bought a green hat, a pill-box we would call it today, but I always felt rather foolish because I'd worked on a newspaper before in a dirty old trench coat.'

A certain Patricia ('Triss') Lewis was the beauty editor. Brunette, sultry, sophisticated, Triss was extraordinarily attractive and far more experienced than Barbara. Straightaway Triss recognised the special spark in the twenty-year-old and took Barbara under her wing, introducing her to the fast-track world in which she operated from her Kensington flat.

'There were all these good-looking *men*!' remembers Barbara. 'We were a group. There was me and Triss, and because they were all show-business writers they dragged us to the nightclubs and to cocktail parties and that sort of thing.'

The men in the group, somewhat rakish and all of them much older than Barbara, included Roderick Mann, the then show-business columnist of the *Sunday Express*, ex-Fleet Street political columnist Frederic Mullally (*Tribune*, *Sunday Pictorial*), who now ran a Mayfair showbiz PR company – both eleven years Barbara's senior – and their two compatriots, Logan ('Jack') Gourlay (*Express*) and Matt White (*News Chronicle*), also showbiz columnists (both now dead). 'The dashing men about Fleet Street,' as Barbara referred to them. An A&R man from Decca Records, Bunny Lewis, also tagged along.

Partly on account of the preoccupations of the members of this gang, what Barbara landed up in was not the traditional journalistic scene she supposed would envelop her in Fleet Street. It was pure showbiz. 'My friends were mostly in the theatre or movies. I was in a much more writing/movie/showbiz world than I was in any other world when I lived in London.'

Before long, the celebrity culture swallowed up Triss, who was plucked from the Beauty department of *Woman's Own* to become a high-profile personality columnist for the *Daily Express*. 'They called her the Champagne Girl,' recalls Mullally. 'She was given a column of her own by Harold Keeble, who was the great assistant editor of the *Express*, the man who boosted all the great women journalists of his time. He invented page three of the *Daily Express* when it was at its peak. In terms of production, illustration, choice of pictures, choice of columnist, he was more than just Arthur Christianson, the famous Editor's assistant, he was a dominating influence, the fresh wind that blew through the paper. And he *created* Patricia Lewis. Now, she and Barbara were very close. They were the two "glamour girls" of Fleet Street. Fantastic! Beautiful! They went around the West End together.'

Said Barbara: 'It was a particularly glamorous period, the Fifties and the early Sixties, lots of Hollywood stars around, and parties, openings, premières. When I look back, I feel very nostalgic for London as it was then … so different from today.'

Small surprise, then, that eventually Triss would marry classical actor/screen star Christopher Plummer, and Barbara would wed film producer Robert Bradford.

Mullally seems to have been something of a mover and shaker in the scene. He teamed up with (and married) Suzanne Warner, legendary film-maker Howard Hughes's representative in Europe. 'I left the *Sunday Pictorial* under Hugh Cudlipp, where for three or four years I'd had a column called "Candid Commentary", Suzanne left Howard Hughes and we formed this PR operation together in Mayfair. It was at that time that I first became aware of Barbara Taylor. The two girls, Barbara and Triss, were riding high, you see? There was an inevitable gravitation between my position and their interests. You have to remember that I was a more senior figure to these two girls in those days. I'd done my Fleet Street stint. I'd done my column. I'd written two books, political non-fiction. To them I was an attraction to be with, and I had my entrée to all the clubs of London. So there was no problem about calling them, they would call *me*. You know, "What are you doing today?" And I would invite them. I had a great situation in Hay Hill, Mayfair, two floors of a building. Everything happened around those two floors. On one floor I had my PR office, a staff of maybe twelve people, and above that I had my personal apartment. I would give parties there. And round the corner were all the places... I would go out every evening, and it would be cocktails... All the glamour was in that square mile. A little overlapped occasionally into Soho and into Pimlico, but basically it was Mayfair.

'There were not clubs as we talk about clubs today. These were places where you did not show your face before seven o'clock unless you were perfectly groomed and perfectly dressed. You did not show your face if you were a man unless you were superbly groomed and suited. There was a cocktail hour in Mayfair then, as it has never existed since and will probably never exist again. Full of style and grace. This hour was seven till dinner, seven till eight. Mayfair buzzed in about six or eight venues within that square mile, where the crème de la crème suddenly appeared, the actors, the cinema people that wanted to be seen. Most of these restaurants in those days, like the Caprice, had a bar, a tiny bar. You crowded in at about seven o'clock. You didn't even get where you were to sit. You were there in what was a kind of party atmosphere. And gradually the people drifted into the restaurant and the bar would go empty. But for that one moment between seven and eight you were shoulder to shoulder, cheek by jowl with the most glamorous models, the great Barbara Goalens of that time, who were not like the models of today. That was the scene; it was a very glamorous scene. Celebrities were celebrities. Today if you appear on television for five minutes you're a celebrity. In those days they were major, major stars. Actors, models … they got that much publicity, now it's flooded. There were only three, four, five magazines in those days.

'It's the forgotten era. As you came out of the war years into the Fifties, and rationing began to ease up, we were aware of Hollywood and were aware of Hollywood stars, trickle by trickle coming into London, into Les Ambassadeurs, into Ziggi's club … and we treated them as kind of nice pieces we were cultivating and would like to shake hands with, but we were not influenced by them at all. There was a British film industry that was appreciated around the world at this time – the Ealing comedies, and Sidney Box and one or two other greats. It was alive, and I was one of those involved with it. My company had clients like Sinatra, we had from top to bottom, we handled everybody, films by people like the Carrerases, you know, father and son[26], down to the lower end of it, the Hammer Horrors. We made the singer David Whitfield, managed him, got a deal with the A&R man in Decca to get the right songs. But it was tough, it was only just beginning, papers were fewer and smaller, and for a while the major Fleet Street newspapers were totally anti-PR. Express Newspapers had a ban on PR altogether – you were not allowed to mention the name of a club at which someone had appeared last night. Puffs were out, it was very tough. So we had to be more ingenious.

'In the Mayfair bars and clubs it wasn't principally a Hollywood scene, it was an elegant *English* scene, though Hollywood actors came. What happened was that there was

---

[26] James the father and Michael the son. Sir James Enrique Carreras MBE, together with William Hinds, founded the legendary British film company Hammer Film Productions.

an infusion from America. Any Hollywood stars that came to
London were attracted by that particular London scene, that
very elegant London scene. So they would be there, they would
be in and out of these various little places where we met, and
I would meet Errol Flynn for the first time in my life. I would
meet Douglas Fairbanks. They swanned in and out of our
London scene, to which they were attracted by its elegance.

'The great clubs of the day were the Casanova, run by Rico
Dajou, the Don Juan (Rico had the two clubs, they were in
Grosvenor Street), Les Ambassadeurs – upstairs restaurant and
downstairs nightclub (called the Milroy and run by big John
Mills – not the actor), and Ziggi Sessler's at 46 Charles Street,
now Mark's Club. The Caprice of course, a restaurant, but a
top restaurant for the other people, not even really journalists,
the Mayfair crowd. They had a wonderful head waiter. I wrote
about him in one of my novels – *Danse Macabre*. If he hadn't
chosen to be the greatest maître d'hôtel in London he would
have been an archbishop of the Catholic Church. He was that
wonderful a person. Annabel's came later.'

I recognised names out of Barbara's novels immediately. Early
on in *Voice of the Heart*, Francesca Cunningham, Katharine
Tempest and others meet for dinner at Les Ambassadeurs in
Hamilton Place, between Piccadilly and Park Lane. It's also a
favourite lunch-time haunt of stylish film star Victor Mason, who
is a model of what Katharine, Francesca, and, of course, Barbara
consider a man should be: handsome, rough-hewn, suntanned,
'massive across the chest and back', clothes of the finest quality,
chosen with panache, slacks with knife-edge creases, a man who
cares about appearance. Francesca's family, the Cunninghams,
whose aristocratic seat is Langley Castle in Yorkshire, also have
a house in Mayfair's Chesterfield Street, which runs between
Curzon Street and Charles Street, where Ziggi Sessler's 21 Club
was. Maximilian West first walks onto the pages of *The Women in
His Life* from his 'imposing house on the corner of Chesterfield
Hill and Charles Street', and I knew that in the 1980s and '90s,
when Bob Bradford was filming in England, he and Barbara had
an apartment in Charles Street. Annabel's, in Berkeley Square,
which Barbara describes in the same novel as 'the chic-est of
watering holes for the rich and famous, where the international

jet-set rub shoulders with movie stars and magnates and members of the British Royal Family,' actually opened during the summer before she decamped with Bob to New York in 1963. They were still members in 2005. Berkeley Square was also home to bespoke yacht builder of distinction, Camper & Nicholson, where, in *The Women in His Life*, Maxim commissions the 213.9-foot *Beautiful Dreamer* for his wife Anastasia. If you haven't heard of Camper & Nicholson, which traces its history back to the 18th century and claims to be the global leader in all luxury yachting activities, you are not even in the picture. And, as fate would have it, Barbara's English publisher (Harper Collins) was, in the early days, sited within the square mile – at No. 8 Grafton Street.

When she first came to the area at such a tender age in the early 1950s, Barbara could have had no idea that this was to become known worldwide as multi-million-selling author 'Barbara Taylor Bradford's Mayfair' – in every sense, *her* village:

> *Maxim came out of the imposing house on the corner of Chesterfield Hill and Charles Street and stood for a moment poised on the front step... Pushing his hands in his pockets, he forced himself to stride out, heading in the direction of Berkeley Square. He walked at a rapid pace along Charles Street, his step determined, his back straight, his head held erect. He was dark-haired with dark-brown eyes, tall, lean, trimly built...*
>
> *He circled Berkeley Square, dodging the traffic as he made for the far side, wondering why Alan needed to see him, what this was all about... Oh what the hell, he thought, as he reached the corner of Bruton Street. Alan's been so special to me most of my life. I owe him ... we go back so far, he knows so much – and he's my best friend. Crossing the street, his eyes focused on the Jack Barclay showroom on the opposite corner, and when he reached the plate-glass windows he paused to admire the sleek Rolls-Royces and Bentleys gleaming under the brilliant spotlights...He walked on past the Henley car showroom and Lloyds bank, and pushed through the doors of Berkeley Square House, the best commercial address in town and a powerhouse of a building. Here, floor upon floor, were housed the great international corporations and the multi-nationals, companies that had more financial clout than the governments of the*

world. Maxim thought of it as a mighty treasury of trade, for it did hundreds of billions of dollars' worth of business a year. And yet the buff-coloured edifice had no visible face, had long since blended into the landscape of this lovely, leafy square in the very heart of Mayfair, and most Londoners who walked past it daily were hardly aware of its existence. ...Maxim crossed the richly carpeted, white-marble hall, and nodded to the security guard, who touched his cap in recognition.

The Women in His Life

I asked Barbara which her favourite haunts were in the early days. 'I went to the Mirabelle a lot in the 1950s, when it was in its heyday. The maître d' was Louis Emanuelli – Welsh, of Italian descent. Louis was later the man at Annabel's. He was a great pal and would do anything for me. Les Ambassadeurs nightclub, the Milroy, was always full of Hollywood stars, producers, etc. The famous bandleader there was Paul Adams. I particularly liked the Arlington Club on Arlington Street, a tiny club in Mayfair, but an 'in' kind of place with a bartender called Joe who was a character. And yes, we went to Ziggi Sessler's. And there was an actors' club somewhere off the Haymarket called the Buckstone, a minor club, but I used to go there and so did a whole group of actors – Richard Burton, Christopher Plummer, Peter O'Toole and Jason Robards – Richard Harris as well, all dedicated drinkers. I used to love that club... I believe it's still there...

'At this time I became a friend of Jeannie Gilbert, an American woman who was press officer for the Savoy, Claridges and the Berkeley. She was from Kentucky.

'Jeannie had a little house in Minerva Mews in Chelsea and gave lots of parties with guests, sometimes authors – famous writers, like James Baldwin, the black writer. He was around at that time. Unfortunately she had a habit of introducing them sometimes by nickname. One occasion I remember in particular, I was talking to this man whom Jeannie had introduced to me as Snips, or something like that[27], and he was chatting away

[27] Very possibly 'Samuele', the nickname given to the narrator of Wilder's first novel, *The Cabala*, a well-read and classically educated young American of a Puritan mindset.

about writing. I said I wanted to be a novelist and he started talking about books. Finally he said, "You're a journalist, you're very young." – He was a rather portly man, middle-aged. – "You're rather young and pretty." I said, "You know a lot about books, what did you say your name was? Jeannie introduced you as S_____." And he said, "Oh, I'm Thornton Wilder." He wrote *Our Town*[28]! Famous American writer! I was terribly embarrassed when I heard his real name.'

During the Jeannie years, Thornton Wilder might well have been in London promoting his play, *The Matchmaker*, first produced in America in 1954 and adapted nine years later as the famous musical comedy *Hello, Dolly!* Mention of the literary novelist James Baldwin reminds us that Jeannie was dealing with a variety of 'product', their common denominator simply that they were staying in one or other of her hotels. Baldwin was born in Harlem, his fiction exposed taboos in courageous and disarming fashion and concerns both homosexuality and the plight of his disaffected people. His first novel, *Go Tell It on the Mountain*, was published in 1953, and caused a tremendous stir.

But her clientele were not only in the Arts. The man who got her the job in the first place not only at the Savoy but also at Claridges and the Berkeley, was Lieutenant-General Sir Frederick Browning, a close friend of Prince Philip, Duke of Edinburgh, husband to Her Royal Highness Princess Elizabeth, to become Queen Elizabeth II in 1952.

'Boy' Browning, as he was known, an Olympic bobsleigh competitor in 1928, a decorated hero of the First War and husband of the novelist Daphne du Maurier, was, during the Second War, Commander of the 1st Airborne Division and I Airborne Corps, and later Chief of Staff of Admiral Lord Louis Mountbatten's South East Asia Command. After the war he became Comptroller and Treasurer to Princess Elizabeth, and from 1952, Treasurer in the Office of Prince Philip, with whom he was by this time close. It was a period of marital disharmony for both Browning and the Prince, whose domestic situation was explored with a certain amount of tact in the TV series, *The Crown*. The two men enjoyed each other's company socially

---

[28] The 1938 play that won Wilder the Pulitzer Prize for Drama.

in London, the Prince from Buckingham Palace, Browning
from his *pied a terre* just off Sloane Square, when away from
Menabilly in Cornwall, which, besides being home for the
dashing ex-soldier, was of course Manderley, the setting for his
wife's most famous novel, *Rebecca*.

And it was at this point that Browning met Jeannie Gilbert.
Barbara told me: 'When I met Jeannie she was already working
at the Savoy, but at some point, while promoting Diners Club,
she met this man, Lieutenant-General Sir Frederick Browning,
who was very taken with her. He must have been a director
of the Savoy Group because he got Jeannie the job of PR at
the Savoy, Claridges and the Berkeley. She was widely regarded
as the best press officer the Savoy Group ever had ... and she
was very pretty. There was a picture of Browning always in her
house, with him in that uniform. He was living in London and
she saw a lot of him. Now, whether or not they had intercourse
I don't know,' Barbara concluded. 'I wasn't under the
bed. But Jeannie always said to me that that is how she got the
job.'

As I discovered later when researching J M Barrie and the du
Maurier family, this led to Browning confessing all to his wife
and Daphne confessing her infidelities, and in 1957 to nervous
breakdown for Browning and Daphne's dark collection of short
stories, *The Breaking Point* (1959). So, clearly, the currents
radiating from the scene into which Barbara now found herself
were far reaching.

'There were also always famous movie stars floating around,'
Barbara continued, 'people such as Victor Mature, Eddie
O'Brien and other name stars of the day, also high-powered
movie producers at her parties, such as Ilya Lopert (he made *The
Red Shoes* among other films), Gregory Ratoff (also an actor),
Arthur Krim of United Artists, and screenwriters Jack Davies
and Michael Pertwee, who were partners... Other actors around
at the time were Tyrone Power, and Sean Connery, as well as
Lyndon Brooke (son of Clive Brooke) and Terry Longdon –
both English. Lois Maxwell was another friend through Jeannie;
she was the first and most famous Miss Moneypenny in the
James Bond movies. Jeannie had a way of gathering all kinds of
people, from the UK and the US. Eventually she married the

Broadway producer David Merrick, after returning to New York in the early 1960s.'

Mullally also remembers Jeannie as 'the best press officer the Savoy ever had, and she did what most PR people never succeeded in doing, she became friends with every columnist in Fleet Street. At any time you could drop in to her little suite of offices on the ground floor of the Savoy – two rooms – have a drink, ask questions and she would answer them. She cultivated and seduced our columnists. I was one of them. She was a great PR, wonderful; her model was a girl called Jean Nichols, a PR of the Savoy who came before. Jean married the author Derek Tangye, who went to live in Mousehole in Cornwall. They grew daffodils together and he wrote all those books, *A Gull on the Roof* and all that. Jean was another beauty; tragically she died of cancer.'

Jeannie Gilbert became Barbara's best friend and another means by which she came out into this glittering world. 'Because Jeannie did PR for those hotels, she'd always be having cocktail parties. If there were six actors in town and she wanted a pretty girl around, she'd call me up. I could ring her up and say, "Could I do an interview with…?" But I was never a celebrity journalist. I did a couple, Dominguin, the bullfighter, for the *Evening News*, and a few movie stars, and the odd writer, but I was really doing the woman's page. Celebrity journalists weren't quite "in" in those days, I don't think anybody was ever called a celebrity journalist.' Nevertheless, quite clearly, the Fifties opened the door for them.

What so astonished Billie Figg, and will have appealed to Jeannie when Barbara stepped into a room full of her clients, was the way this twenty-year-old girl from the North 'felt very at home with all these famous people, as if it was only a matter of time when she'd be one of them.'

Said Billie's husband, Jack: 'I noticed that she'd come into a room and suddenly you'd find that everybody was looking her way. It was the laughter in the eyes, they had enormous magnetism, they were *full* of laughter.'

'Her style is such,' continued Billie, 'that the feeling I always had was that Barbara, from her school days, had wanted to be famous and wanted to be successful and without thinking

about it just had *an inborn acceptance that she could,* and that
whatever she turned her hand to she would be good at. She had
enormously high expectations of herself and a lot of assurance. It
didn't cross her mind that anything she did would be second rate
and she knew that she would work hard to ensure that it wasn't.
I don't think she ever thought, I'm not very good at anything.
I think it was built in. She says that her mother built that in to
her, doesn't she? It was very obvious to me what a fuel it is to
have that kind of confidence. It never struck her that she would
in any way be boring to any of these people or that they would
feel that, established though they were and up-and-coming
though she still was. It didn't cross her mind that they wouldn't
be entirely dazzled by her, and indeed they were, because Barbara
had, without knowing it, a very good repartee, and she had the
kind of huge sense of humour and comeback that makes very
good conversation for men as well as for women. Certainly there
was an immediate rapport in any conversation with men, and not
just because she was sexually attractive.'

Soon Barbara's diary was studded with appointments at the
smart places of the day, as some of those whom she met at
Minerva Mews became part of her life. For example, she got to
know Jack and Dorothy Davies particularly well, and from the
mid-Fifties would live in a flat next door to them. Jack was the
father of child star John Howard Davies, who played in *Oliver
Twist* when he was nine, and was in *Tom Brown's Schooldays* at
eleven, later directing *Fawlty Towers, Mr Bean, Reginald Perrin*
and *The Vicar of Dibley,* among other comic masterpieces. Jack
Davies had worked as a staff writer on the Will Hay films of the
1930s, before making his name on the semi-satirical *Doctor in
the House* movies, hugely successful in Britain, the first of which
was released as Barbara arrived in London, in 1953. It starred
Dirk Bogarde as medical student Simon Sparrow, who runs foul
of consultant Sir Lancelot Sprat, played by the robust figure of
James Robertson Justice.

Mention of Justice jogged Mullally's memory of occasions
when the actor joined him and Jack Gourlay at the Colony Club
in Berkeley Square for an extended session, reminding us what a
significant, often devastating, role alcohol played in the fast lane
in the 1950s.

'In those days it was bottle parties after 11 p.m. You had to have your own bottle, due to licensing laws. Whichever club you went to, you bought a bottle of whisky the night before and they marked it up as to how much you'd drunk and put it in a cupboard with your name on it. In the Fifties that was it! You would go back to your club at eleven o'clock and they'd send for your bottle and put it on your table. You couldn't order another bottle that night because it was past the hour. That was the crazy licensing laws in those days.

'So, there I am with Jack in the Colony Club, we're with the owner – we only ever drank with the owners. And Jack and I were both after birds all the time. The owner would summon a girl from the show... Then, about 3 a.m., Jack would stagger off and I'd be left with Justice, and I'm living in South Audley Street, having split with my wife. I've got rooms. All I can do is offer him a couch. Biggest mistake of my life. I offer him a couch before he got the mail train to wherever the next day. Mistake, because when this giant of a man started to snore, the whole place shook...'

This must have been before James Robertson Justice, who found fame on stage, television and in films, from comedy (*Doctor in the House*, 1954) to adventure (*The Guns of Navarone*, 1961), teamed up in a long-running affair with a young art scholar of both Goldsmiths and Brighton art college, Molly Parkin. Soon to become a successful painter in her own right, before rising to dominate the worlds of fashion and style in the Sixties as fashion editor of *Nova* and *Harper's Bazaar*, and then for four years *The Sunday Times*, Molly was twenty-five years younger than Justice and when she came to write her first novel, *Love All* (1974) we got a snapshot of this era of decadent, sexually promiscuous 1950s celebrity, to be overshadowed in the popular consciousness by the Swinging Sixties. Molly is one of a select few who receive a civil list pension from The Queen, although she confesses she does not know why she was chosen to receive the annual grant.

Of those Barbara met at Jeannie's was the movie star Victor Mature. I knew this because Billie Figg had mentioned an occasion when Barbara and Billie returned to her flat to find Victor Mature there, 'and we all went out to dinner'.

Then, on a separate occasion, I happened to ask Barbara
what the derivation was of the phrase '*the whole enchilada*',
which readers of *Voice of the Heart* will know Victor Mason
uses repeatedly when he wants to say that something is 'the
complete works'[29]. Barbara replied: 'That was a saying used
constantly by Victor Mature. He always said, "the whole
enchilada". I really didn't know what it meant until I came to
live in America.' A coincidence not only of initials, VM, and
first name of Victor, made me wonder how far I was expected
to stretch similitude between movie star Victor Mature and
movie star Victor Mason in the novel. Victor Mason falls
in love with Katharine Tempest's best friend Francesca,
whereupon Katharine hurts Francesca terribly by suggesting
falsely that he is the father of her baby. Francesca, being
Yorkshire born, a writer and something of an ingénue in the
fast, showbiz scene in which she found herself, had always
struck me as drawing on the vulnerable side of Barbara, fresh
from the North and less experienced than her new showbiz
friends. Katharine was altogether the more complete operator,
generous and loyal on the surface, but, as Barbara described
her to me, 'a woman of great calculation, ambition, a degree of
ruthlessness, and self-justification to a certain degree... Always
doing things for her friends, but somehow they all seem to
serve her own ends.' Katharine dominates the book even
when she's not on-scene, just as, quite clearly, the experienced
Jeannie Gilbert dominated Barbara's life at this time.

I knew that there had been a falling out between Barbara and
Jeannie in later years. Did Francesca and Katharine represent
the young Barbara and Jeannie respectively? Had there been
something between them and Victor Mature? Had I stumbled
on a real triangle of passion?

Barbara confirmed only that Victor Mature had come to her
via Jeannie – 'He actually was a boyfriend of Jeannie's, that's
how I knew him.' But she denied that she had an affair with
him or that, like Victor Mason in the novel, Mature had been
the cause of bad blood between the two women: 'I had quite
a number of male friends who were not my boyfriends, if you

---

[29] An enchilada being a tortilla stuffed with a variety of things.

know what I mean. Most people would think that if you knew a man that you were sleeping with him, but that wasn't the case.'

In that extended interview with Allison Pearson in 1999, Barbara was quoted as saying, 'I interviewed all sorts of men – movie stars – and they tended to chase me.' Pearson told us: 'The PR at the Savoy introduced her to Omar Sharif and Sean Connery. There is a photograph of Barbara and Sharif taken at this time and you suddenly realise that all those ridiculous clichés about beautiful people on which her novels rely were, for the gorgeous young girl about town, the height of realism. I congratulate Barbara on the heroic restraint clearly required to not sleep with Omar Sharif and I get a wry, knowing look. "I wasn't prim, Allison." "Weren't you?" "Not at all, but I was cautious. I wasn't a big sleeper-arounder. I was scared of getting pregnant. Mind you, I'm not saying I didn't sleep with anyone before Bob, but I worried what people would think, mostly my parents."'

This is so telling a comment, too apparently unlikely a claim (given the distance that at the time it was given separated Barbara from her parents) not to be true. Admitted was an affair with the photographer Terry O'Neill, who would later, after his marriage to Faye Dunaway, become involved in Hollywood and movie producing. 'But mostly I seemed to go out with actors. In fact, Mummy often teased me, said I always fell for the pretty face. My father would ask, "And what's this man's intentions?" like some Victorian, and I'd laugh and answer, "I don't know, Daddy, but my intentions are to have a career.'

The parental involvement reminds us how young and inexperienced Barbara was, and, however independent she seemed, how tied to her roots she remained at this early stage. Freda's strategy for her daughter's rise in the world had left little to chance in matters appertaining to her mother Edith's fall.

Sex is often bound up with ambition. It is itself a Hollywood cliché – 'All the little girls were scalp hunters,' said Frederic Mullally, who would not be described as 'woke' today. Barbara's youth, beauty and laughing eyes might have been in danger of steering her into the path of trouble of a sexual nature had she not had the personality to deal with unwanted approaches.

The first oral contraceptive – the Pill – was not available until 1961, but that doesn't seem to have reined in the expectations of Mullally and the other male members of the gang, for whom, if they are to be believed, sex was always available, if often in rather seedy fashion: 'It was Mount Royal or White House (Regent's Park),' Mullally said to me. 'Those were the two places where you didn't have to bring your luggage with you.'

Sex is a relatively unimportant aspect of Barbara's novels. She was once asked about this in interview, and replied: 'Well, I do labour over the sex scenes, yes, a lot. I do a lot of rewriting. I try really to work from the point of view of the emotions of the people involved in the scene, rather than describing parts of the anatomy or using dirty words or being that explicit. It was shocking at the time of Harold Robbins when Harold started writing very, very explicit and rather dirty sexual scenes. It's really *feelings* that I'm writing about.'

Billie Figg recalled Barbara seeking security in the group culture. 'There was no shortage of boyfriends,' she told me, 'but they weren't a terribly important element. She was something of a loner herself, in a way, in that she was "*getting on*", she was fashioning herself, and she was a great *crowd* person. She would go round in a crowd, she loved collating people and creating groups.'

The late Lois Maxwell, who played Miss Moneypenny in the Bond films, from the first, *Dr No* in 1962, to *A View to Kill* in 1985, went to many of the parties at Minerva Mews and remembered Barbara's gang mentality in particular: 'Barbara was always beautiful and vivacious and full of mischief, and I am sure she has forgotten, but one day I was walking along the Kings Road with the man I thought I was falling in love with, and all of a sudden there was a dreadful whistle and who was on the other side of the road but Barbara and the two Jeannies and various other pals of ours, and they all looked at me, and she started to sing in high dulcet tones, "Love and marriage…" – And "Love and marriage" followed poor Peter and me all the way down the Kings Road! I was blushing and he was a little bit put out about it. But I don't think this incident ruined anything because he did ask me to marry him, and I did…'

There was safety in numbers, and Barbara preferred relationships that kept her ambition the commanding focus, rather than diversionary instant satisfaction, although that didn't mean that sex was off the agenda. Memorable relationships were those that were chummy and kept her career centre-stage, as had always been the case at home. Later, she would date film director John Berry, who was, like so many other of Barbara's male friends, significantly older than her.

Born in 1917 of a Polish Jewish father and a Romanian mother, John Berry had been a member of Orson Welles's legendary Mercury Theatre from 1937, and in charge of it until 1943 when he followed Welles to Hollywood, directing a number of films including *He Ran All the Way*, a thriller but also something of a statement on American life, starring John Garfield. 'It was a film noir,' Barbara recalls, 'and the last movie Garfield ever made. He died just after it was completed, at the age of thirty-nine.'

At the House Un-American Activities hearings into Communist Party influence within the film industry, Berry had been blacklisted and couldn't work in the States. In 1951 he had directed the documentary that supported those accused of communist ties, *The Hollywood Ten*, and had gone to live and work in Paris before arriving in London, where Barbara met him. 'He came to live in London in order to write a script with his great pal Ted Allan, the Canadian playwright/screenwriter, author of *Lies My Father Told Me*, among other plays and films. These two were hilarious together, and played lots of pranks on me, but we were great chums.' She went out with Berry, 'but ultimately we became just great pals. He and Ted loved having me around, probably because I fell for all their jokes and pranks, and cooked dinner for them … although they insisted they were the better cooks! The two of them had sort of taken me under their wing.'

Again it is the group culture, safe, fun, and *useful*: 'What a lot I learned from those two men! They were both in their forties … and I was by then, what, about twenty-seven? It was like going to a theatrical movie school. I remember many of the discussions about *Oh, What A Lovely War*, which Joan Littlewood produced.'

The famous stage musical about the First World War later became a film, but is known far and wide as having been composed by Joan Littlewood with her fellow artists in her Theatre Workshop at Stratford in East London. Ted Allan is generally only credited with coming up with the title, but apparently he was more completely involved with its genesis. 'Ted had written the original treatment,' Barbara told me, 'and there seemed to be quite a lot of dissension between him and Joan about the credits.'

In pursuit of her ambition to become a novelist, Barbara took every opportunity she could to talk to writers and to seek their advice. Jack Berry and Ted Allan encouraged her. 'I was writing a novel called *Florabelle* at the time … they pushed me to finish it. Although neither of them liked the title, they did select one from a list – *The Things We Did Last Summer*. She told everyone she met that she intended to become a novelist, and no doubt many of them gazed into her laughing eyes and, like Thornton Wilder, gave her all the encouragement she needed.

She was far from being alone in this ambition. In the gang, Roderick Mann published novels from the early 1960s; one, *The Account*, was actually published by Barbara's own UK publisher and involves a PR lady for a hotel who is not unlike Jeannie. Meanwhile, Mullally was in print even earlier with his fiction and has a dozen novels to his credit.

Barbara also became good friends with the writer Cornelius Ryan. Mullally remembers him as 'a movie photographer for one of the studios, a very sociable guy.' From 1941 to 1945, Ryan worked as a reporter for Reuters and the *Daily Telegraph*, covering World War Two battles in Europe and the final months of the Pacific campaign. His first book, *The Longest Day*, was published in 1959 and sold four million copies in twenty-seven editions, before being made into a film by Darryl Zanuck in 1962. His second book, *The Last Battle*, was published in 1966, and he finished a third, *A Bridge Too Far*, in 1974 while terminally ill with cancer. The phrase, 'a bridge too far' was taken from 'Boy' Browning, who, during the planning of Operation Market Garden in September 1944 memorably said: 'I think we might be going a bridge too far.' He was right. Field Marshal Montogmery's brainchild succeeded in liberating two

Dutch cities and many towns but failed to secure a bridgehead over the Rhine.

With O'Neill and Ryan both being photographers, we should not be surprised to see the profession figuring in an important capacity in Barbara's novels. I asked her if Clee in *Remember* (1991) had been based on O'Neill, but no: 'Not really, although Clee was awfully good-looking too... I made him out of whole cloth with a little bit of Robert Capa thrown in. And like Capa, he was a war photographer. In fact, so were the two male leads in *Where You Belong*. I enjoy writing about newspapermen and women, and photographers, because I know them well.'

The great thing about Cornelius Ryan's books is his painstaking research and attention to detail. He built up a 7,000-book library, and kept 'four or five hundred of the absolute best at my fingertips – a synthesis of the perfect World War Two library,' as he told Barbara in an interview in 1968 for an article that appeared in a syndicated column she then wrote called 'Designing Woman'. She and 'Connie', as friends knew him, became very close.

Barbara's own research is a strength – be it the divisional labour-system of the Leeds clothing industry in *A Woman of Substance*, or a highly detailed salad and omelette-making scene in *Where You Belong* ('readers love to have food'), or the procedure of an English coroner's court in *Hold the Dream*, or her meticulously drawn real-life environments: her Manhattan interiors, Yorkshire millworkers' cottages, French châteaux, or the dark waterways of Venice which inspired *A Secret Affair*.

She said to Billie Figg after publication of *Voice of the Heart* in 1984 that she suffered terrible embarrassment after she'd given the manuscript in to her American publisher, Doubleday. Her editor had criticised it for being too minutely descriptive. But her English editor, the late Patricia Parkin, who was with Barbara from the start, said: 'Don't you dare change that! That's what people want.' Time has proved it. 'I think that being a journalist has helped me greatly in many areas – not just the observation of people, but also in research,' says Barbara today, but she is happy, too, to acknowledge a debt long ago to Cornelius Ryan in this.

'We became good friends, before I knew Bob,' she told me. 'He taught me a lot about research. There was something of the teacher in him. He was always lecturing me – if you really want to write books you've really got to be serious about it and you've got to write so many pages a day and so on...' There may be something of him in Nick Latimer in *Voice of the Heart*, who gives Francesca five Ds of which every writer should be aware:

> *Dedication, discipline, determination and drive. You've got to be obsessed with a book... And there's another D. D for desire. You've got to want to write more than you want to do anything else. ...[And] there's a sixth D, and this one is vital. D for distraction, the enemy of every writer. You've got to build an imaginary wall around yourself so that nothing, no-one intrudes. Understand me, kid?*

'We liked each other a lot and he was a bit of a mentor,' Barbara remembers. 'He was very Irish. He actually introduced me to the agent Paul Gitlin who represented me when I sold *A Woman of Substance*. We stayed friends off and on, and he and Bob became good friends, and then Connie got very sick with cancer, as you know...

'Dick Condon also became a good friend of mine. He wrote *The Manchurian Candidate*, and I met him through Jeannie Gilbert when Dick was Head of Public Relations for United Artists. He wanted to be a novelist, and he and Cornelius Ryan encouraged me, said that I really had to stick at it. They both were singing the same song.'

Condon's *The Manchurian Candidate*, a political assassination thriller set in North Korea and America, prophetic and of great social and political significance, came out in 1959 and was a storm of a hit as book and film. Earlier Condon had written a play (*Men of Distinction*, 1953) and a novel (*The Oldest Confession*, 1958) and went on to write many more of both. Back in the Fifties, at least until *The Manchurian Candidate* met with such success, he was one of the wider group of Jeannie's people.

'That was the Wardour Street PR guy,' recalled Mullally, 'drinks for journalists and so on. That's how he would have met Barbara and myself and everybody else. Now, Richard went on, to everyone's surprise, to become a very good novelist. And I followed him and we met in Mexico. I went to live in Mexico in the late 1950s, rented a villa. Richard had just done two big things with two novels. And on my way up through Mexico City I had a little party... Wonderful character, big, expansive character, dominating the communications, and we're sitting in a little circle in my sitting room and he's telling one of his stories, or we were telling a story against him, and there comes a point when in the middle of his story he falls over from his chair and there's a very slim little barrier between him and eight floors to Mexico City. I promise you I leapt across the table and caught him, stopped him from going through. Now everybody starts roaring with laughter, but Condon, who did not find it funny, got up on his feet, went into the bathroom and stayed there for about a quarter of an hour. I knew what was happening. He had lost it.'

Every occasion in the Fifties seems to have been attended by drink and cigarettes. There were none of the health scares, they were the essential accoutrements of style, and alcohol in particular became reason for deep unhappiness and the kind of tragedy that Condon narrowly avoided. Barbara didn't start to smoke until she was twenty-nine, and with her *Yorkshire Evening Post* strategy well in mind, alcohol never lured her into serious problems. But it did for both Jeannie and Triss in the end. Their respective marriages, to David Merrick and Christopher Plummer, both ended not only in divorce but in tragedy on account of it.

In Jeannie's case there was a legal tussle over her child. Merrick got custody after Barbara was subpoenaed to appear in Court on his behalf. As a result, she and Jeannie didn't speak for years until, as Barbara recalls, a mutual friend 'asked me if I would see her because she was actually dying and I said OK. We had, the three of us – this other woman and me and Jeannie – a very nice dinner and then she said, "Can I come back and talk to you?" and the minute we were alone she said, "Why did you testify against me in a court of law?" I said, "I didn't testify against you, I testified *for your child*."'

There is a section at the beginning of *Voice of the Heart* inspired by this moment when two sometime very close friends – Francesca and Katharine – who haven't spoken for years come back together, Katharine returning to seek forgiveness from all the friends she has hurt. 'Jeannie wasn't the model for Katharine,' says Barbara, 'nor did she do anything to hurt anybody like Katharine did, who actually ruined Francesca's life by lying. But that section was the whole thing with Jeannie Merrick, as she had become, and it was the idea of a friend trying to become … it was two friends *becoming* friends again.'

In Triss's case, her very marriage to Christopher Plummer was cast in tragic circumstances, as Mullally recalled: 'One night they were driving back to London and opposite Buckingham Palace there was a terrible crash. She went through the window and her whole face was taken apart. She had to go to the top plastic surgeon who did the job in those days for the Airforce in one of the great hospitals for reconstructive surgery. They literally put her face back together again. I saw her after months of surgery and she had wires coming out of her head and scars all over her face. She nearly died. They were not married at that point. He then said, would you marry me. So, in between surgeries, they married. It was a bad way to get married and their marriage was never a success. I knew them both at that time... She followed him wherever Christopher was making movies: Madrid – they stayed in the next apartment to me there – New York. Then they divorced. He had bought a house in Park Street, Mayfair. She gave a New Year's Eve party at Park Street where she invited... Barbara wasn't involved at this stage, must have been in America...Triss invited two or three big Hollywood stars, there was haggis and whisky... It was a disaster. I was invited with my then girlfriend. The butler was drunk. The Hollywood stars did not like the haggis, didn't know what it was all about. And dear Triss kept boozing and trying to forget what was happening. That was a typical post-Christopher event. But that house, a big townhouse in Park Street, was left to her as part of the divorce proceedings, which she flogged and has probably sustained her.' Triss retreated to Brighton and died in October 2003.

Barbara is the one survivor of the gang today. Frederic Mullally died at 96 in 2014 and Roderick Mann at 87. It is interesting to look at what it was in Barbara's make-up which may have ensured her survival of this opportunistic period in her life. First, she didn't lose sight of home. Her mother would come and stay at regular intervals, and Barbara made a habit of going back to Leeds whenever she could. It was important to her to keep the two worlds in some way co-existing. The glitzy world in which she was moving she knew to be all about appearance, and she was not ready to agree wholeheartedly with Oscar Wilde that 'Truth is entirely and absolutely a matter of style', even if the next few decades would be a push-pull matter of indecision on that score.

Whenever Freda came to stay, Barbara made a point of taking her out with her. 'What was very nice, I always found in Barbara,' said Billie, 'was that every so often she'd have her mother come up and stay in London with her and she took her to all the places she frequented. You hear what I'm saying? All those places, whether her mother appeared to fit or not she was going to take her and she came.'

When Barbara returned to Armley it was always a tremendous occasion, but one that also emphasised the difference between their two worlds, as Barbara's Ripon-based childhood friend Margery Clarke remembers: 'Barbara always brought her parents presents, like hampers from Fortnum and Mason... Her father, being a Yorkshireman, found out how much they cost and shook his head and said, "Now then, our Barbara, they've seen you coming!"'

A Fortnum and Mason hamper comes to Francesca's rescue in the making of a meal in *Voice of the Heart*. There is caviar, pâté de foie gras Strasbourg, aged Stilton cheese with port, and three tins of turtle soup – goodies not exactly compatible with Freda and Winston's simple diet, one presumes. Billie remembers having Freda and Barbara for dinner one evening and serving a vegetarian meal, quite daringly radical in suburban London in the 1950s: 'I suppose it was a bit ingenuous of us. Freda ploughed through this meal and was saying: "Yes, it is very interesting this," but at the end she really couldn't contain

herself. She said she was not one hundred per cent for it –
"Daddy likes meat!"'

These were little markers, a few of many that showed
that however much Barbara might want to keep her past,
present and future as one, it was going to be a challenge. It
is one to which she admits even today, although she couldn't
survive if she didn't return to the land of her birth at regular
intervals. 'It's just that when I go there I am a totally different
person than I am in Manhattan, than I have become. I have
to go back into the Barbara people knew, and it is difficult
sometimes.'

On another occasion, she brought Freda home a squirrel
coat, something she had always told Barbara she wanted, a kind
of symbol of what her life had been sacrificed for. When Barbara
gave it to her, Freda said, 'Where will I ever wear *that*?' The
story seems to resonate with the differences between Armley
and Mayfair, and Barbara made a point of telling me: 'You must
remember, I became a completely different person when I went
to London. I lived there for ten years... I'm very far removed
from Leeds now.'

To all appearances, Barbara was becoming what her mother
always dreamt she would, and what grandma Esther Taylor
feared would do her no good. Yet, the mutation, while titanic in
terms of where she'd come from, was peculiarly out of step with
the way the world of celebrity and fashion was now turning.

Women's fashion was poised for a big change; clothes
design would, for the first time in history, be directed towards
the youth market and set a whole range of diverse off-the-peg
trends. *Haute couture* and the upper-class world of privilege
that supported it – once central to the Studley Royal-style
pretensions of 'the beautiful Edith Walker' – would no longer
feature in most young women's life even as fantasy.

In fact, it is interesting to see just how oblivious to modernity
was the whole stylish Mayfair scene into which Barbara had
fallen with as much relish as if she had been coming home –
which, in a sense, she was: home to the fantasy world of Edith
Walker, the family myth which, consciously or not, she was
fast making reality. Meanwhile, just across Regent Street from
Mayfair, in Soho, things were happening that would change

the world, but to which the Mayfair set remained disdainfully oblivious.

'All the glamour was in that Mayfair square mile,' said Mullally. 'A little overlapped occasionally into Soho and into Pimlico, but basically it was Mayfair. Soho was crumby. Nothing was happening in Soho. It was just crumby.'

'What about the French Pub and all that?' I asked. 'What about Ronnie Scott's? What about the Colony Room?'

'Soho wasn't dressed up for *cocktail-Mayfair*,' he replied. 'You'd go slumming in Soho.'

Soho had long been London's Bohemia. During the war, artists, the military on leave, intellectuals, black-marketeers, prostitutes, pimps and local working people made merry together in its pubs every evening, the painter Nina Hamnett occupying a central role and acquiring almost mythical status. 'After the fall of France, the York Minster, already a popular watering-hole with the Bohemians,' wrote Judith Summers in her book entitled *Soho*, 'became the unofficial London headquarters of the exiled Free French.' It became known as The French Pub, its host Victorienne Berlemont, whose name, since the First War, meant something to squaddies all over the world.

Then there was Dylan Thomas's famous watering-hole at the Café Royal on Soho's western border, and drinking clubs beating the tight licensing laws – the Horseshoe in Wardour Street, the Byron in Greek Street and the Mandrake in Meard Street. 'Since the turn of the twentieth century London's so-called Bohemians had been associated with Soho and [on the other side of Oxford Street] Bloomsbury and Fitzrovia.'

But now, in Barbara's day, during the 1950s, Soho was once more a magnet for the eccentric, the creative, the unconventional and the rebellious. 'To the young especially, Soho is irresistible, for it offers a sort of freedom,' wrote Daniel Farson in *Soho in the Fifties*. 'When I arrived there in 1951 [to take up a job with *Picture Post*], London was suffering from post-war depression and it was a revelation to discover people who behaved outrageously without a twinge of guilt and drank so recklessly that when they met the next morning they had to ask if they needed to apologise for the day before.' Soho was a place for characters and conversation, for ideas and revolution.

It no more mattered whether you had wealth here than it had at La Coupole in Montparnasse in Paris from the late 1920s, where poets, painters, intellectuals and revolutionaries gathered in similar fashion.

In Soho, painters such as Francis Bacon, Robert Colquhoun and Lucien Freud, writers like Colin MacInnes (*Absolute Beginners*, 1957), Frank Norman (*Fings Ain't Wot They Used T'be*, 1959), and jazz musician and writer George Melly. Gaston Berlemont now had the York Minster, and the famed drinking club the Colony Room in Dean Street had opened in 1948, the eccentric, warm but ruthlessly selective Muriel Belcher its soon-to-become-legendary owner. For here, as in the key meeting-places on the other side of the tracks in Mayfair, you had to be a member.

And now a new and soon to be defining mark of 'Fifties Soho' was the emerging coffee-bar scene, where, as Summers writes, 'for the price of a cup of frothy coffee, Teddy-boys, Rockers and skiffle fans could sit for hours behind a steamed-up window listening to the latest Elvis or Chuck Berry hit on the jukebox, accompanied by the loud hiss of an espresso machine.' Soho coffee bars were the music Mecca for the young, and youth was, for the public at large, what the Fifties was all about.

Barbara was never trendy, although her close friend, Billie Figg wrote the first article about Britain's original home-grown rocker, Tommy Steele. It appeared in *Picturegoer* in 1956 and was headlined, '*The* Coffee-Bar Sensation'. Steele, the piece tells us, was discovered by John Kennedy in the *Two I's* bar in Soho. When Kennedy, who ran a picture agency and happened to be in there drinking coffee, heard him sing, he immediately arranged for a Decca A&R man to come and listen to him. Kennedy became Steele's manager, and Steele took the charts by storm. After that, Soho, and the *Two I's* in particular, was the place to be discovered. Tommy Steele, Terry Dene, Adam Faith and Cliff Richard could be seen performing here in their earliest days. As Bruce Welch of the Shadows recalled: 'If it was good enough for Tommy Steele it was good enough for us ... we almost lived there... If we were lucky we'd play downstairs four nights a week, from seven till eleven – mostly Buddy Holly and Everly Brothers numbers. It was a small place, very hot and very sweaty, with a tiny eighteen-inch-high stage at one end, a microphone and a few old speakers up on the wall … always packed.'

When Kennedy flipped through a sheaf of photos of Tommy Steele during Figg's interview, he stopped at one showing his charge playing a gig at London's swanky Stork Room, and said: 'But Tommy's not interested in Mayfair Society. He wants a girl just like his mum.'

The comment showed agent Kennedy's nose for a good photo caption, but it also pointed up precisely the breakaway nature of the scene Tommy Steele was setting. Glamour was no longer the dream. Hitherto, Mayfair Society had been the thing. It, royalty, Hollywood and couture fashion were all the news on the society and women's pages. But now a music scene was about to erupt onto the pages of newspapers and magazines, which would change all that. Hollywood kept producing stars like Ava Gardner, Elizabeth Taylor, Rock Hudson, Grace Kelly and Stewart Granger in the old glamorous tradition, but the male iconography of the period belonged to Marlon Brando dressed in leather and sitting astride a motorbike in *The Wild One* (1953), or, in mid-decade, to the smouldering, challenging youthful features of James Dean in *East of Eden* and *Rebel Without a Cause*.

Barbara left London on the cusp of a change which dealt a killer blow to Mayfair glamour as the dream of the young. Brian Epstein first heard the Beatles at the Cavern Club in Liverpool in October 1961, the year that Barbara and her husband, Bob, met. In 1963, the year that she married and left England for America, they topped the charts for the first time with 'Please Please Me'. Beatlemania was upon us. The world would never be the same again.

Yet, for Barbara, despite being a decade younger than Billie, change was never even on the cards. She may have felt the difference between the Leeds Barbara and the Mayfair Barbara, but in fact she was caught up in the family myth of 'the beautiful Edith Walker' and never left it. She continued to wear conservative, classic, smart clothes, and 'just as she was conservative with clothes, there's a parallel with her taste in music,' observed Billie. 'At that period the other music that was square dancing, which had come over from America, bop and bee bop and all those sort of things ... they were nothing to do with Barbara.'

Far away and yet so close geographically was the glamorous Mayfair tradition to which Barbara belonged, and for which Freda's educational programme had prepared her. On the face of it, what was established in Leeds was built on in London, not discarded, and contrary to Barbara's insistence that she was a completely different person when she went to London, there was no great change. 'But the person *did* change,' insisted Billie. 'The appearance and the person were not the same...'

'On the outside,' Barbara says, 'people see a part of me and that's the part I allow to be seen. I think I'm a very shy person in many ways. I think the profession I've chosen should tell people that. It's private, it's an interaction between the author herself and characters. My typewriter is my psychiatrist ... the Barbara Taylor Bradford complexities I save for my work.'

Identity defines a distinction between the real person and what she appears to be. Getting to know who we really are is Barbara's constant theme. Freda's concentrated purpose during her childhood was to give Barbara a glimpse of who she truly was. Who it was her birthright to be. Then there was Barbara, the only child of an unemployed labourer and a nanny. No wonder she needed a typewriter as her psychiatrist to sort it all out.

In the novels she gives us characters who are forgers, like Camilla Galland in *The Women in His Life*, who believes we can only ever have an unnatural identity, that we create a life out of more or less conscious choices, adaptations, imitations and plain theft of styles, names, social and sexual roles, that we write our own scripts and live by them. And she gives us others alongside them who are deeply centred on their natural, 'real' selves, like Anastasia in the same novel, or like Francesca in *Voice of the Heart*, and still others who, dispossessed of their own identity by dint of fate to create themselves new natures, like Maxim West, only to find there is something missing, there is a vacuum where his real self should be.

Barbara was, however, still a long way from this level of perception. In the 1950s and early 1960s she saw herself as writing a script of her own to live by, drawing on the values she had imbibed in her youth, which Freda believed were her inheritance, which gave her a resilience that others around her – Jeannie, Triss – lacked, and which inured her from the danger of becoming sick with celebrity narcissism. She used the self-assurance Freda awakened in her, she found security in her mother's conviction of her perfection, her superiority over her contemporaries in Armley, her extraordinary qualities, but always knew it was something she needed to prove, if it were to be true of her real self.

'One of the charming things about her,' remembered Jack Figg of Barbara in the 1950s, 'is that she never took all of that glamour very seriously. She did appear to, she was involved, but there was always a twinkle in her eye, as if to say, isn't this fun, all these people, who are not really part of us, but we are joining them.'

Occasionally the diverse scenes (Armley, suburban London, glamorous Mayfair) in which she moved did intersect and Barbara would have no difficulty in making it work, whereas Jack Figg was quick to admit, he did not. On the few occasions he did find himself 'standing about with a wine glass in hand and chatting at one of Jeannie's bigger receptions,' he made 'quite a lot of booboos. I remember once I was speaking to a chap about Norman Wisdom [the slapstick comedian] and I said that I thought he was very, very clever, very funny, but his material was absolutely appalling and I felt that he needed better writers, one thing and another. And then Billie took me aside and said, "You are talking to Jack Davies, he IS Norman Wisdom's scriptwriter."'

An ability to rumble the celebrity culture was the best protection any girl in it could hope for. A sense of humour, an ability to laugh at oneself, and to find genuine friends beyond her circle, would give the necessary objectivity – and in this the Figgs were so important. They regarded themselves as definitely off the celeb circuit: 'Sure I was a journalist,' Billie said, 'but I was a journalist who was coming home every night to a suburb. She'd obviously got these several circles of chums, which is healthy. I remember, Barbara often used to come down in a pale-blue Ford Zephyr that she had rather early on, a lovely pale-blue Zephyr, very stylish, and she'd come down to our other house, which was even more suburban than this. She stayed for a few days and I was away working, and Jack had just taken a new job – a travelling job…'

Jack seized the opportunity to develop what was, after all, his story. 'Yes, Barbara was staying, and Billie, I think, had gone to Paris to the Collections. So this chap, who was showing me the ropes at my new job, said, "Can we go somewhere quiet and go over some paperwork?" So I said, "Let's go home." He said, "Will your wife be there?" I said, "No, she's in Paris at the moment." So that was all right. So, we were sitting in this bay window we had at home, going over this paperwork, and Barbara roars up the drive in this pale-blue Zephyr with a mink stole that she used to trail around, and she had her own key and she came in, and I said, "Oh, Barbara, this is Maurice Brown," and Maurice Brown's eyes were popping out of his head. Barbara, who was a great prankster, her eyes twinkled and she said, "I'm going upstairs, darling, I'll be up there if you want me." Maurice was waiting for an explanation as to who this other woman was. Nothing was ever said. I just left it. But I'd arranged to meet Maurice Brown the next morning somewhere, at some station, and Barbara said that she would take me and drop me off, which she did. There he was waiting as we roared up in this pale-blue Zephyr, and she got out and put her arms round me and drew my head down and kissed me full on the mouth, and put her leg back as people do, and said, "Bye darling, see you later!" Well, I just sat in the car with Maurice and said, "Good morning, Maurice," and off we drove.

'That was typically Barbara really. It was the way she twigged immediately that there was a very funny situation to be made out of this.'

Although Jack is wont to describe himself and his wife as 'loose-end people … someone for Barbara to lean back on', it is quite clear that they were family. They were close enough for Barbara and Billie to go on holiday together to Paris, and indeed to indulge, on a few unlikely occasions, in the Figgs' sport of camping.

'We were campers,' said Billie, 'and we went away every weekend at that time, with a tent and our car. If Barbara was at a loose end, as happened on some of these weekends, she came with us and we brought a little tent for her, a separate tent. I can tell you, she didn't stay under canvas. When we got there the first time, she looked at this thing we erected … Well, it was all right during the day, but then when we decided to prepare for retirement (it was quite early when we made the beds) there was this sudden scream and she shot out saying there were beetles in there. We said, "Oh yes, that's part of it, you often get beetles, you just brush them out." But no: "Oh, I'm not staying there!" So we had to go and find her a pub to stay in. On another occasion she came to a little piece of land my father had down on the River Crouch in Essex and we all camped on there. She was very tickled because my father had said, "It will be very nice to see you on our little estate!" When we got there, there was this tiny bit of land that we pitched our tent on. They were fun times. We roamed over half of Essex with Barbara.'

Typically, Barbara turned the Paris holiday with Billie into something of a journalistic coup. There never was a distinction between the worlds of work and play. As far as Barbara was and still is concerned, they are a seamless whole. 'We agreed that we'd like a holiday, a week in Paris,' Billie recalled. 'We just thought that would be nice to do. We took a hotel, which was a pretty run-down sort of Left Bank hotel. It had a bed in the wall, you had to press a button and the bed comes down. Somehow it worked out that Barbara was going to be on the side near the window. There was a fire escape outside which went right past the window, and I remember Barbara saying, "Oh, Billie … what if somebody comes down that fire escape? What if some man breaks in?" She paused and looked across at me and said: "I'm first!" And then she said, "I don't mean I want him first!" I shall never forget that. Did we laugh! Anyway, it was a pretty run-down kind of place, but Barbara had fixed with a man she knew, called Escarti – he worked for a film company – to get an interview with Ingrid Bergman. This was an incredible coup because she'd only just come in out of the cold, as it were, after the seven years' banishment that Hollywood had treated her to. She'd run away with Rossellini seven years previously and America had shunned her. [She had left her husband Peter for director Roberto Rossellini and ignored the moralistic machinations of the Motion Picture Association of America to bring her to heel. Incredibly, Senator Edwin Johnson declared she should never again set foot on American soil.] No American film company would deal with her. But now, only that year [1956], they had starred her in *Anastasia*, and the British Press – us, if we got it – would be the first to interview her. It was a scoop! We did get it! Amazingly, it was agreed to! We fixed up that *Woman* magazine would take the article.

'Bergman was at the Théâtre de Paris playing in *Tea and Sympathy*, and we turned up about ten minutes before she did. She came in looking very ordinary with her hair in pin curls and a scarf over them, frightfully mumsy really. The story we wanted – the sort of thing that everyone wanted at that time – was Bergman's philosophy of life. Barbara and I each had some questions ready. We sat in a place full of sofas, so many we had one each, I remember, and we just fired questions at her as we went. She answered them all.'

The article begins with a comment about Bergman's characteristic lack of affectation, that she was a complete natural, not into the appearance culture – 'it is impossible to imagine that what she says is part of a pose', and knowing that 'is important when you are talking to an actress,' wrote our two reporters. Then Bergman tells them about the early childhood loss of her mother – she died when Ingrid was two – and of her father, who died when she was twelve. Truth, appearance, loss, loneliness, the very themes that would, years later, dominate Barbara's novels, and already dominated her life now. The positive theme of the interview is about courage … the courage to do something with your life and not be 'put off by other people's advice or opinion … the courage it takes to stand on your own feet and do what you think is right … It is a duty,' says Bergman, 'each of us owes to the rest of the community as well as to ourselves… You have only to look about you to see a world full of people with chips on their shoulders. They wanted to do something with their lives, but were put off by other people's advice or opinion. And so they feel cheated. They are impossible to live with because they have built up resentment within themselves. If I had not gone ahead and studied for the stage in Stockholm, my disappointment would have poisoned my whole life.'

Barbara and Billie hung on her every word: thinking 'of the people who felt they could have been artists or writers, but were afraid of the insecurity,' as Ingrid Bergman's philosophy of life became clearer. For Barbara in particular, this was completely on song. She must have left the theatre walking on air, more determined than ever to move her own plans along.

By the time she interviewed Bergman, Barbara had been out of *Woman's Own* for two years. In 1955, at twenty-two, she had been hired as columnist and celebrity profiler by Reg Willis when he became editor of the *London Evening News*. At that time it was London's largest circulation newspaper. 'I was working with a woman called Gwen Robyns, who you must have heard of because she wrote many books about Grace Kelly. She was married to a Dane or a Swede and she was this plumpish, jolly, nice woman. She was our boss and it was a room full of women. We did all sorts of features, and I used to be sent out to do stuff for the diary page, too.'

As usual with Barbara, the move forward was serendipity; she got the job in the course of what today might be termed networking, but was for Barbara simply an evening out. 'I met Reg Willis when he was features editor. It was probably a movie thing. Roddy Mann was probably there and Jack Gourlay and Matt White, and my little group of people that we all went around in. I noticed there were mostly men there with me, and I remember I had a blue hat, a knitted beret; it was a sort of bluish purple, but it had sequins that were like long tails; it was a glittery beret and very pretty. And that's how I met Reg. He came over and he said, "I love that hat, who are you?" And I said, "I'm Barbara Taylor." We chatted and he asked me who I worked with, and I said, "I'm with *Woman's Own*, but I really want to get back on a newspaper, I'm beginning to hate this." And that is how Barry Horniblow's name came up. I told him about *YEP* and my great editor Barry Horniblow, and we spoke about how Barry had gone out to South Africa, and eventually he said, "I'll see you around and if you ever – you know my number, it's the *London Evening News*, give me a call some time." Then, of course, I kept running into him and finally one day I did call him and said I really would like to come and have an interview for a job on his newspaper. So I went down to see him. I remember Reg interviewing me about my experiences in Leeds and what have you, and then he took me in to see the editor and when we left the editor's office, Reg said, "How long notice do you have to give, how many weeks?" So I said I'd have to find out, and he said, "Well, better give your notice anyway." Now nobody had offered me the job, the editor didn't say he was giving me a job. Reg just said, "Don't worry about it, Barbara." Then I found out I had to give two weeks' notice to *Woman's Own*, and when I told Reg, I don't remember how I said this, but I was nervously saying to him, "Are you sure I've got this job because the editor didn't tell me that I had the job." I wanted to hear it from the boss man, not the features editor. He said, "Barbara, I promise you, it's really all right." So, I gave my notice in with trepidation, and then I got a letter from the *News* and it was signed, "Reg Willis, Editor". He knew that the other chap was on the way out. So that's how I moved to the *London Evening News.*

'Then one night, after I'd been there maybe a couple of years – I often stayed late because I liked to get my desk totally cleaned up and do all the things that get neglected if you've been out doing stories, and Reg often used to look in – on this day he came in and said, "I see you're still here, Barbara, come on, I'll buy you a drink." And I do remember him standing in the doorway with a funny look on his face. He had some papers in his hand and I don't know what the words were – it's too long ago – but I must have said something like, "Is something wrong?" I knew … I always could read people. And he said, "I've just got something on the wire service, Barbara." He looked at me and said, "There's only one way to say it – Barry Horniblow just died." Well, of course, tears … I got sort of choked up. I didn't start sobbing or anything. I'd got tears in my eyes and I started to cry and he said, "Come on, I'll take you out for a drink." And I don't recall going for that drink, but maybe we did – El Vinos, somewhere like that. Horniblow … of course I worshipped him … Although then he was white-haired, he must have been a man in his fifties when I was fifteen, or maybe in his forties, I don't know.'

How far the death of Horniblow widened Barbara's perspective on what was going on in her life I cannot say, but he had started her off professionally, had been the first impetus, and his passing may well have encouraged her to look hard at where she had taken herself since. She had built up a great deal of journalistic experience, and contacts, too – perhaps now was the time to make a play for something more her own, or to buckle down and realise her ambition to write novels. Had she done so, it would have been no surprise to her friend, Billie: 'I always knew she was fiddling about with plots [for novels of her own] and trying them. She was very up on all the new books coming out. She had a knack, the books she chose – I remember Bud Schulberg's *What Made Sammy Run* in the early Fifties, things like that. They were the big bestsellers.'

However, instead of pursuing her ambition to write novels, as Keith Waterhouse, Roderick Mann, Frederic Mullally and Richard Condon were doing, and as Ingrid Bergman would certainly have advised her to do, Barbara looked for independence in what she already knew. She went the journalistic route with a new newspaper, which turned out not to be a good idea.

The paper was a weekly, geared to appeal to Americans living in London (there were some 80,000 at the time), and to American troops stationed in the UK. No doubt the thrill of the start-up appealed. As Barbara recalls: 'The staff was small and we all had to pitch in,' she as woman's page editor. An American, Bill Caldwell, was the first Editor. He had the distinction of appointing a youthful Bob Guccione, an artist and cartoonist before he launched *Penthouse* magazine.

Embellishing a story she had recently given to Anthony Haden-Guest (*New York Magazine* and the *Observer*), Barbara recalled the day Guccione first stepped into the office: 'I saw this man in reception when I went to lunch,' she told me. 'He was still there when I returned.' When she asked the receptionist who the visitor was and what he wanted, she replied 'Robert Sabatini Guccione. He's waiting to see the editor, but he doesn't have an appointment.'

Barbara, yielding to courtesy – 'It's so impolite to leave someone waiting for two hours' – conceded that she had 'better have a word with him'. The receptionist grinned, 'Oh yes, he just said he'd like to talk to the beautiful strawberry blonde,' and delivered the Sicilian to her door.

They became friends. After Bob Guccione had made *Penthouse* a success, Barbara would attend dinner parties at his New York mansion, the walls hung with his collection of Van Gogh, Matisse, Renoir, Chagall, Degas, Modigliani, Picasso …

Meanwhile on their first meeting he showed her his 'rather clever cartoons, with a feeling of Jules Feiffer about them', and she set up an appointment for him to meet Bill Caldwell. 'Bob told me he could also write, and that he had an idea for a political column called "Foggy Bottom",' she recalls. Caldwell hired him on the spot the next day. 'Everyone on the paper liked Bob Guccione,' Barbara remembers, 'and his column became very popular with the Americans.' His work routine was rather singular, however: 'He wouldn't come in until one or two, but he would stay there very late. He often worked all night.'

It was while Guccione was so doing that *Penthouse* began to take shape in his mind. Caldwell had by this time been replaced as Editor by Derek Jameson. 'After he had been there a few months, Guccione tried to press sexy material on him,' Barbara said. 'Derek, a real dyed-in-the-wool newspaperman, declined. He told Guccione: "Look, we can't put tits and arse on our front page. We'll all end up in the nick!"' Given that Jameson would later become editor of the tabloid *News of the World*, and Editor-in-Chief of the *Daily Star*, his protestations must surely have been influenced by the prevailing, rather different market perception of *The London American*, though one can't help wondering if a move, however tentative, in Guccione's direction might have enhanced the newspaper's appeal to Americans, who were already being well prepared for it by Hugh Hefner.

'Later, Bob brought in a dummy of a magazine he wanted to start. It was beautiful. He was very professional in everything he did. I said, "Bob, it looks great, but isn't it a total copy of *Playboy*?" He said, "If there's one, there's always room for two." And he was right.'

Penthouse went on to sell five million copies a month at its peak.

The London American fared less well. It ran for sixty-six issues between March 1960 and June 1961. '*The London American* lacked advertising revenue,' Barbara states today, 'and this in the end was the cause of the paper's failure. It couldn't justify its existence. The owners had other business commitments. So they finally lost interest. The paper closed down. I felt sorry for some of the people who were without work, and we were all sad to see it disappear. We'd all enjoyed being together, there had been a lot of camaraderie.'

Barbara returned to freelance work, moving in behind a desk in Billie Figg's 'funny little office on the fifth floor in Covent Garden, overlooking the *My Fair Lady* show in Drury Lane,' as Billie herself described it: 'At that time I had a PR company with Shirley Harrison, the author. Barbara used to come and use a desk, not as part of Shirley's and my business but as a friend.' This was, without doubt, a low point for Barbara, the demise of *The London American* a terrific blow. 'By the end of the Fifties I think she was feeling disappointed that she'd not brought off anything very big,' recalls Billie. 'I remember, and Barbara agrees with me, she had an uneasy period. What she was up to was not meeting her aspirations.'

'I did feel out of sorts,' Barbara admits. 'I was rather irritated with myself, disappointed that I hadn't written a novel. That was my dream.'

Initially, she had begun to freelance for a Belgian magazine, specialising in celebrity-type interviews, while at the same time working on *Florabelle*. Soon, however, another reason not to pursue her declared ambition to be a writer of fiction would present itself and she would grab it. She was offered a job with a magazine called *Today*, a title from the IPC stable for whom Billie had once worked. 'I was a big admirer of the editor of *Today*, an energetic and talented American called Larry Solon, so I took the job immediately… I enjoyed it there, and perhaps that's why *Florabelle* never got finished. I was back in journalism full-time again.'

Then, not long afterwards, fate played Barbara a winning hand. Jeannie Gilbert, who by this time had made New York her home, was staying with her fiancé, the Broadway producer David Merrick, at the Beverly Hills Hotel in Los Angeles, where she ran into an old friend, a movie producer who was waiting to meet a colleague for lunch at the pool where, famously, the Hollywood glitterati met. As he was about to go to London, Jeannie told him he must call on her best friend, Barbara Taylor. But she didn't have her telephone number, so she scribbled on a piece of paper the number of Barbara's then neighbour, the screenwriter Jack Davies.

Barbara had recently moved to a swish address in Bryanston Square, Marylebone, the very place where Edith's Studley Royal contemporary – her mother's rival in Frederick's affections, the Most Honourable Constance Gladys Marchioness of Ripon – died less than half a century earlier. She was occupying No. 13 at the time. 'Jack Davies and Dorothy, his wife, had a duplex apartment there,' she told me, 'what you would call a maisonette in London. You went in on the street level and then they also had the downstairs that opened on to a garden. I had the garden apartment next door to them, and next door to me was Sean Connery with a garden apartment... Dorothy was an interior designer, and we sort of did it up together. It was warm, cosy, with a living room, kitchen, bathroom and bedroom, just right for a single girl.'

Robert Bradford, the film producer who'd been dining with Jeannie Gilbert at the Beverley Hills Hotel, takes up the story: 'When I got to London I was inundated with work on a movie called *The Golden Touch*, a costume picture about the Louisiana Purchase [the transaction in 1803 which saw the sale of the French-speaking Mississippi state by Napoleon I to the US for $15 million].'

Forget the coincidence that the love of Barbara's life had adopted Bradford as his surname after the war[30], there couldn't have been a more apt title for the project that brought them together than *The Golden Touch*, though it was a couple of weeks before Bob came across that bit of paper with Jack Davies' number on it: 'I phoned it and they invited me over. It was a Saturday night. They had promised to get Barbara in for a drink, but when I arrived there was no sign of her.'

---

[30] An industrial Yorkshire city a few miles west of Barbara's birthplace, Leeds.

Many miles away in Gloucestershire, Barbara was attending a friend's birthday party, unaware of what had been cooked up. Jack and Dorothy had failed to make contact. But they and Bob got on well and that night they asked him to join them for dinner in Soho. 'I did, and then when the bill came Jack discovered he'd forgotten his chequebook. So I lent him some money. Dorothy then insisted I come to lunch the next day, so they could repay the loan, and she promised to have Barbara for lunch as well.'

Barbara drove back from the country early that Sunday morning. No sooner had she parked outside her flat when she heard the phone ringing. 'It was Jack asking me to come to Sunday lunch. I explained I had a deadline to meet [but] he brushed it aside, said a friend of Jeannie's was in town, that he was a handsome man with lots of charm. I just laughed, explained I couldn't miss the deadline… Then Dorothy called and explained what had happened the night before. They would be embarrassed if I didn't show up… So I said, "Oh all right, but I can't stay long. *I have a deadline*!"'

When she made her way next door she was told to expect three people, one of whom would be this Bob Bradford. When the three arrived, there was an attractive red-head in a green suit, a smaller man, somewhat nondescript, and another man. It was quite obvious to her that the taller of the two men just had to be with the red-head, and that Bob – the one for her – was this smaller nondescript fella. As it turned out, she was wrong and not to be disappointed. The woman was Pat Lasky, the smaller man screenwriter Jesse Lasky Jnr, who was working on the script of *The Golden Touch*, and 'Bob just came across the room with Dorothy and was introduced. He sat down next to me, started to talk about Jeannie, and how he had run into her in the Beverly Hills Hotel. We got on immediately: he was so warm and friendly, and he had the loveliest brown eyes; they were kind. I can remember thinking what a nice man he was, and also how attractive he was as well. I'd been led to understand that we were having lunch at the maisonette, but Jack announced that we were going to a restaurant. And so, half an hour later, we went to a nearby Indian restaurant. I'll never forget Bob leaning into me, whispering in my ear that he wasn't too fond of Indian food. Neither was I.'

What had been Bob's immediate reaction to Barbara?

'She was twenty-seven, twenty-eight. What did I see in her? I can't really say. She was very pretty, an attractive young woman. She was bright, and I put a lot of value on intellect, intelligence. She was *outcoming*, and I guess that really caught my attention. After lunch I asked her what she was doing. And she said, "Nothing."'

'That's true,' said Barbara. 'I'll never forget Dorothy's face. It was a picture, as silently she mouthed, "*What about the deadline*?" Of course, the deadline was forgotten. I went with Bob to the movies, and we've been going to the movies ever since.'

CHAPTER TEN
Change of Identity

'Most nights he lay awake, prowling the dark labyrinths of his soul, seeking meanings for his life and all that had happened to him.'

Maxim West in *The Women in His Life*.

In *Voice of the Heart*, people are not what they appear to be. Immaculate, wealthy superstar Victor Mason started life as 'Victor Massonetti, construction worker, the simple Italian-American kid from Cincinnati, Ohio,' and tempestuous leading lady Katharine Tempest has also changed her name. She was born Katie Mary O'Rourke in Chicago. They have both become something else by their own efforts; they have risen in the world and have changed their names to signal their new identities.

For Katharine in particular this becomes quite an issue in the novel, her lover Kim reading her concealment of her true identity as a sign of emotional shallowness. Then we learn that her decision to change her name signals something dangerously repressive, a desire to blot out her past. As a child she was alienated by her father, sent to boarding school in England because of her influence over her brother Ryan, an influence which is benign but at odds with their father's plan to turn Ryan into a politician. Katharine isn't even allowed home for the school holidays. Then she is abused by her father's business partner. She changes her name in an effort to make a fresh start.

Through Katharine we get to understand the effect that dire childhood experience can have on a girl, but that it isn't possible to wipe the slate clean by changing your name, whatever cosmetically salutary effect it may have on self-image. There is more to identity than appearance: a name change will not suffice to put things right; this is the theme too in Barbara's novel, *The Women in His Life*, which reflects her husband Robert Bradford's early experience.

He, the only child of a German Jewish family living in Berlin had fled the Nazis and changed his name. Barbara's old friend and fellow Jew, Bobby Caplin, made the point that name change was common among Bob Bradford's generation. 'Having come through the holocaust maybe you don't want to be reminded... I mean it's not just a name, there's a whole lot of other baggage that comes with that. It's all very well saying, well I wouldn't do it, but we haven't been through those circumstances, where you do not want to be acknowledged as a Jew, which I can thoroughly understand.'

Robert Bradford was born in 1925[31]. His father, Sigmund, was a banker. The boy was eight years of age when the Nazis seized power and his mother, Doris, arranged for him to be smuggled out of Germany and placed with a relative in Paris. In May 1940 the German Wehrmacht invaded France and the following month occupied the capital city. Meanwhile, teenager Robert had set off with a cousin to walk the 480 miles south to Marseilles, joining the Resistance and in due course learning to speak English from American soldiers. From there, at the end of the war, he had travelled to America in search of his mother who had made it to New York, but she died shortly before they could be reunited.

'His father had already died. He never saw his mother again,' Barbara told me. 'He prefers not to talk about it. I cried quite a lot when I wrote *The Women in His Life*. I suppose I thought of Bob as he was as a child. I think he found the book very haunting, very moving.'

---

[31] There is, as I write, a degree of uncertainty about Robert Bradford's birth date and no readily accessible certificate, which is hardly surprising given the extraordinary events of his early life. Barbara originally told me that he was born in 1930. Then, after he died in 2019, her UK literary agent, Jonathan Lloyd said, 'Bob was older than people realised. Barbara told me two nights ago that he was 92.' The *Times* obituary placed his birth in 1925 and his age on July 2, 2019 as 94.

By the time Barbara met Bob in 1961 the last thing she read in Bob's brown eyes was any of this. He was already highly successful in the movie industry, and a sophisticated, cosmopolitan figure. Plainly, he knew who and what he was. He was the epitome of the suave Hollywood producer, with all the outward accoutrements that she had always deemed essential in a man. He had style, he dressed well and he gave the impression of being able, like a fine batsman, to deal with the swiftest of balls at his own pace, a master of timing with no small amount of wit, playing with an accent which encompassed every stage of his extraordinary hybridisation process and relieving any possibility of confusion with a sardonic twinkle in his eye.

Friends of Barbara could see immediately that they shared something in their personal style, something of the glamorous tradition, but then one also commented, 'I think my feeling, when I very first met him, was that he was someone I couldn't access, if you know what I mean.'

This was the key comment, if not immediately the most obvious one. There was an existential detachment, inscrutability even. One can see this as an alienating factor or as a sign of a fine intellect and/or the necessary accoutrement of modern man. There is no way you can be successful in the high-powered world of movie finance, where tens of millions of dollars are at stake, without a certain indifference to anyone who is a distraction to the game you are playing at any particular moment. 'And he *was* a major player,' agreed Bobby Caplin. 'He is certainly very shrewd, and I think in the part of the film business he was involved with, you have to be.'

Jack Figg observed Bob's 'detachment' when Barbara suggested Bob take Jack and wife Billie to dinner, when she had to be elsewhere. 'I was flattered [that Bob had invited us],' said Jack. 'We went to a place – I think it was in Charles Street – more or less opposite the flat they had there. It wasn't a restaurant, it was just a big black door.'

'Mark's Club?' I suggested.

'That's it. The door was opened by a chap with white gloves and we were shown in. We sat at a table and I was making small talk, "Nice place this, etc." Billie and I suddenly felt very uncomfortable as nothing [came from Bob] … and I was saying,

"Do you want us to order, Bob?" "No, no, no," he said. And we sat there and the atmosphere was charged with some sort of tenseness and after a while I just said, "What's happening?" He said, "Well we're in the wrong place, we're down in the B Room. We've got to go into the other room." And there was a little flight of stairs leading up into it. He said, "That's the A Room." So we said, "What does it matter we're in the wrong room, aren't we all right here?" "No," he said, "And I can't be seen here. If I'm seen here everybody will start talking about Bob Bradford, did you see him there, etc."'

Mark's Club was business, where appearances mattered. There is a prerequisite in business to be accepted somehow into the inner sanctum, and to that end personal style may be as important as the product you are selling. Also, there is no way you can carry off the big deals, or handle the prima-donna personalities, unless you can exhibit that you are free from random attachments, distractions or intrusions that compromise your style in any way. It had been a bad choice to take two of Barbara's dear friends to a place where neither he nor they would have felt comfortable in each other's company.

If you'd known Bob, you would wonder how the above scene could even have taken place, so accommodating was he – genuinely good company and kind. I half expected him to ask me to leave the story out, but he didn't, because first and foremost Bob was at ease with himself. If, at one and the same time you are an island to yourself but also able to disarm your business client with a sense of humour, you are surely in, and Bob had this very nice, quiet, sardonic sense of humour, which Barbara loves and made a point of stressing to me: 'No day goes by when he doesn't make me laugh.' That is something for a wife to say of her husband after more than fifty years of marriage.

In 1961, others were soon shown this side of him, as Jack Figg recalled: 'I discovered, as we would see him more and more personally, that he's very easy to get on with and rather warm – and I thought, how odd!'

The period of Barbara's first meeting with Bob was especially poignant, for it occurred at precisely the moment that the world was examining the dispossession of German Jewry at the hands of Adolf Eichmann. 'I was stupendously aware of what had happened to the Jews of Europe under the Nazis,' Barbara said. 'I suppose because it was the persecution of innocent people. Though I was always into history... I couldn't bear the thought of it.' There could have been no more powerful a delineation of the loss that Bob had suffered (to be so tenderly described in Barbara's novel *The Women in His Life*) than the real-life re-enactment of the horrors of the Holocaust daily in the English newspapers as Barbara first met her future husband.

SS-Obersturmbannfuhrer Karl Adolf Eichmann, head of the Department for Jewish Affairs in the Gestapo from 1941 to 1945, chief of operations in the deportation of millions of Jews to extermination camps, was brought to a controversial and highly publicised trial in 1961. It lasted from 2nd April to 14th August. Eichmann was pronounced guilty, sentenced to death and, on 31st May 1962, hanged in Ramleh Prison.

> *Stepping over to the table, she grabbed the paper, stood staring at the headlines and the photographs, her eyes widening with shock, her face freezing into rigid lines of horror.*
>
> *Names of places leapt off the page at her. Ohrdruf ... Belsen ... Buchenwald. The most fearful words stabbed at her eyes. Death camps ... atrocities ... inhumanity ... extermination ... Jews ... millions murdered ... genocide.*
>
> *She lowered her eyes to the pictures. They stunned and horrified her, so graphic were they in the foul, inhuman story they told of the most unspeakable brutality and cruelty, a terrible testament to the pitiless torture and mass murder of innocent people.*
>
> Teddy (Theodora Stein) in *The Women in His Life*

Barbara was drawn deeply into the reportage. It had a marked effect on many, but especially those involved with Germans. Bob Bradford told Barbara little about his own history, but the Holocaust recurs frequently in her novels. 'I do have strong feelings about it because I'm a child of Europe,' she explains. 'I grew up in England during the war, and my husband Bob was born in Berlin and taken out of Germany to Paris when he was a boy, because he was Jewish. Unlike many German Jews who didn't ever believe they would be hurt or touched, this family did. His mother got out, but all the aunts and uncles disappeared.'

Just how deeply Barbara mined the emotional strata of Bob's early life in her book was shown years later: 'I was somewhere in Ohio to give a little talk, most likely Dayton. Seats had been set out in a bookshop, you know the kind of thing, you could have a coffee, a soft drink. And this woman came and sat down and put her copy of *A Woman of Substance* on the table. She said: "I'd like you to sign it, but I haven't read it."

"Don't worry," I said (as I do). "Millions have."

'She then pulled the book from her bag and said that she had been going to Switzerland by plane when *The Women in His Life* had just come out. She tried to read it on the plane, but figured from the opening that it was another business story like *A Woman of Substance*. She'd got to Zurich and her husband had become involved in a lot of business meetings so she had picked the book up again. "I picked it up in desperation!" she said (which was good to know!). "When I got into the part in Germany when Maxim is a small boy I became enthralled … the part when his mother and Teddy got on the train and said goodbye [to his family] … when she worried about the Germans on the train" – it was full of uniforms – "and Maxim was saying all sorts of Jewish things about what he had been eating. When I read this," she said, "I had cold chills, and when they got to Paris I felt tremendous relief … I started to cry and I cried and cried for hours and I didn't stop. You see, I was taken out of Germany like that and I had my mother's jewellery stitched into my clothes too. And you, your book, was a catalyst for me. I had not been able to cry since I was taken out of Germany in the 1930s. You're not Jewish, are you?"

"No," I said.

"How can you understand?"

'"Because I am a human being," I said.'

The women in the title are those behind her hero, Maximilian West – his mother, his grandmother, the woman that subsequently brings him up (Teddy), his first wife, his daughter, various women who have helped to form the man or are important to the man. As he grows up, he wonders whether his dear parents are still alive. After the war, Teddy goes to Berlin literally to unearth Maxim's identity in the bombed-out rubble of the city, searching among the *Trummerfrauen*, the rubble women, who play their laborious part in the rebuilding of the city, counting out the bricks they retrieve at the storage depot every Saturday afternoon, to be paid accordingly. It is among the rubble that Teddy finds the Russian princess, Irina Troubetzkoy, a friend of Maxim's parents. She takes Teddy into her squalid cellar room below ground and informs her that Maxim's parents have gone to their death, his father in Buchenwald, his mother in Ravensbruck. When, finally, his worst nightmare of their murder is realised, 'Maxim suddenly understood that the sadness inside him would never go away. It would always be there. For the rest of his life.' His loss becomes the driving force in his life. He makes a pact with himself that he will become a dollar millionaire by the time he is thirty, and does so with time to spare.

Exiled from country and family at so impressionable an age, brought up by another family in Paris, his relations themselves victims of the death camps and his mother lost to him even after she had passed over to freedom, Bob, too, was deeply alone, bereft of loving parents, but also of the value-system that's part of the baggage of a national or religious culture. Like many other German Jews, he felt dispossessed as much of his German as of his Jewish heritage by the Nazi onslaught. Likewise, in *The Women in His Life*, Maxim's father, Sigmund, and mother, Ursula, are from 'great and ancient families', real Germans, as well as being Jews. Bob would need courage to attain the inner sense of unity on which a personality can normally count when rising out of the culture of his birth to make his way in the world.

Somehow he found it, and worked his way into the movie business. He was a protégé of Jesse Lasky Sr, founder of Paramount, and was employed at one stage by the Hal Roach Studios in California, famous for stars such as Charley Chase, Will Rogers, Harold Lloyd and Laurel and Hardy, and for seeding the careers of the likes of Jean Harlow, Janet Gaynor, Fay Wray, and Boris Karloff, before their post-war TV production of classics like *The Lone Ranger*, Groucho Marx,

Abbott and Costello, *The Life of Riley*, and *The George Raft Show*.

The late 1950s found him in Spain as Executive Producer for Samuel Bronston Productions. Among his film credits from this era are *John Paul Jones*, *King of Kings*, *El Cid*, *Fifty-five Days at Peking* and *The Fall of the Roman Empire*. From this time, producer Samuel Bronston, a sometime official Vatican photographer, developed Spain into a European capital of movie-making out of massive studios near Madrid. But when, in 1964, the big-screen epic *The Fall of the Roman Empire* failed to meet audience targets demanded by its enormous budget, Bronston went bust, was sued in court and forced out of production, still owing $4 million as late as 1975.

The Sixties saw Bob as Executive Vice President and CEO to Franco London Films S.A. in Paris, making among other films *Impossible Object* with Alan Bates and *To Die Of Love* with Annie Giradot. By then Barbara and Bob were married, and there was a period in the late 1960s to early 1970s when they lived together in the French capital at the Plaza Athenée, an elegant hotel off the Champs Elysée that appears in *Voice of the Heart* and *The Women in His Life*, and where she and Bob stayed regularly until recently. It is where Max, his mother and Teddy stay when first they flee Berlin to Paris. *The Women in His Life* is redolent of those days, Bob's childhood in exile, places that he came to share with Barbara in the early years of their marriage.

Barbara enjoys and nurtures her association with France in her books, in 2002, of course, in *Three Weeks in Paris*. A decade earlier she attributed her success there to being one of the few foreign writers who paints an accurate picture of the country 'and actually gets the Eiffel Tower in the right place'. In *The Women in His Life*, Paris is a magnet to Maxim West, because he is the fictional persona of Bob Bradford as a child, and Monte Carlo is where later he moors his magnificent yacht, *Beautiful Dreamer*.

In *To Be the Best*, Paula and Emily go to Monte Carlo to meet their cousin Sarah, who has been living up the coast, near Cannes, for five years. Barbara used to holiday in Cannes before she met Bob. In *Her Own Rules*, Meredith Stratton's quest for her mother takes in parts of France within Barbara's best-remembered experience: Havens Incorporated – the American-English-French group of upmarket inns, hotels and châteaux, which Meredith inherits – has its Paris office in rue de Rivoli, which is where eligible architect Luc de Moutboucher lures her to his château Clos-Talcy between Talcy and Menars in the Loire.

A Sudden Change of Heart is set partly in Paris. In *Angel*, the heroine, Rosalind Madigan, returns us to the Loire Valley, to a band of country running 'from Orléans to Tours ... through a verdant landscape known as the Valley of Kings,' and gives us Montfleurie, 'the most magical of all the Loire châteaux'. Rosie looks into the dust of history for the spirit of the place, 'where once violent battles had raged when Fulk Nerra, war lord, predator and ruler of the area, had stalked this valley.'

And so on... Was it here, too, that Barbara began to paint? 'I remember we called in one night to have dinner,' Jack Figg told me, 'and she greeted us with absolute excitement – "I've learned I can paint!" She had just returned from a holiday in the South of France, where she'd met a Portuguese man called José, and she painted him at home. Suddenly she realised she could paint! She had these pictures expensively framed and they looked absolutely terrific.' Such is the power of France for this writer.

Bob Bradford's childhood experience may have been less happy there, at least to begin with, but together they have enjoyed many happy times in Paris since. In any case, in 1961 his life was set on an upward trajectory. If being cut off at the roots from his family had amounted to an existential challenge as a child, he had by this time met it with success in his film projects. If you had asked him, he might have said that his idea of 'roots' wasn't Berlin, but the things that led up to the work he was doing now, things which, like unlikely tributaries from afar flow together to make the river – his life – what it was. It is a significant conceptual difference to the traditional roots metaphor, which carries with it the burdensome possibility that precepts of your birth culture tie you down.

In 1961 Bob's past had ceased to exist for him, he had only a future – a feeling perfectly in tune with his new girlfriend's own ambitious nature and particularly welcome following the failure of *The London American*, which had temporarily sapped her drive.

If there was a feeling of disappointment that she hadn't measured up to her own demanding aspirations in the late Fifties, by the early Sixties, with Bob, 'there was an infusion of new excitement,' as Billie recalls, 'and then she went off to live in New York, which had got far more "go". Although London had got a lot of "go" in the Sixties it wasn't Barbara's scene. But New York was, and they loved her.'

Bob was the tonic she needed. Life for such men is all about flow, change, movement *to* somewhere. The modernist concept challenges the old idea of rootedness and static identity and, indeed, the whole notion of loss, which is why deep down the post-war scene appealed to him. In place of roots and family and community, there was freedom – man constantly on the hoof, constantly *in change*, man whose environment of airports and hotel rooms delivered the extraordinary *emotional detachment* that Barbara's friends had noted about Bob, while in his future-orientated projects he sought to deliver the sense of unity within that we all require – his autonomy, his values, his new-natural *identity*.

Maximilian West, the hero of *The Women in His Life* and the character whom Barbara has said, 'I truly love as if he exists,' and who, unusually for her, she brought back in another novel, *A Sudden Change of Heart*, is just such a man. His personal style is immutable, forged out of the materials of loss that his genetic and historical background has engineered, but he, like Emma Harte before him, makes it an uncompromising *philosophy of life*, which women in particular find irresistible.

New York is an environment which fairly crackles with the belief that anything is possible. Bob Bradford took Barbara physically out of England, where making money and having ideas above your station were still frowned upon (particularly in the case of young women), into an environment where these things are a patriotic duty. A journalist once put it to Barbara that her personal claim never to have felt inadequate is rare in England. She replied: 'Don't you think that's why I live where I live today?'

At that stage in their lives, when Barbara had been left feeling dissatisfied and unfulfilled after the demise of *The*

London American, and irritated with herself, disappointed that she hadn't yet written a novel, she would have found Bob's altogether pragmatic approach attractive. One can sense in her response to it the ambitious daughter Christina's need for a pragmatic set of values at a similar stage in her life in *Act of Will*. Christina's mother, Audra, has a perception of a *moral hierarchy* against which she deems her daughter, who has given up her art and become a commercial dress designer, a failure. But in *The Women in His Life*, in Maxim's modernist 'project-culture', there is no such moral hierarchy. Instead, project-goals achieved are used to elaborate a value system to replace the deep-truth culture in which Audra lives in *Act of Will*. There are no absolute values, no ultimate rights or wrongs, there is only *project* and the value of *action*, which is defined in value terms by where the action will lead. The Ten Commandments are justified on the altar not of Judaism or even on that of Yorkshire working-class culture, but on the altar of pragmatism – you abide by them for no other reason than if you don't, no one will deal with you again.

In Maxim's world, morality has a *cash value*, which doesn't mean that you do whatever makes the most money in the short term, any more than his project-orientation suggests that he is mad for making money (which he is not – he is at ease with money but not overly impressed by it). Cash value in the moral context means, simply, pragmatism – what a decision will flow on to. The point in being morally pure is that no one will trust you if you are not.

Once the heart is taken out of morality and replaced with the head, art and commerce are on a level pegging. There's a particularly pertinent moment in *Voice of the Heart* when Victor Mason gives Francesca (the character who appears most like Barbara) an antique copy of *Wuthering Heights*. Because Emily Brontë's work was always central to Barbara's aspirations as a novelist, the idea reminds us that in this high-powered milieu, art is a collector's item – a thing's cash value is not considered to be at odds with its artistic value, nor less intrinsic to it.

It is no longer 'better' to write a great novel or paint a beautiful picture than it is to put together an elegant deal. In the world of film (art at its most commercial), Maxim's flair as a

financier is likened to that of an inspired artist. His father-in-law
Alexander Derevenkjo observes, 'I can no more explain to you
the creative impulse, what it is inside a painter that makes him
capable of producing a breathtaking work of art ... than I can
explain to you what it is inside Maxim that enables him to put
together an incredibly successful company or a stunning deal.'

It may seem amazing that such a man as Maximilian West
should consider marriage at all, let alone to sensitive Anastasia
Derevenkjo, whose life is centred on the deep-truth-culture
that his modernist approach is set on replacing. But then, as we
later discover, Maxim is not so secure in his new project-identity
as his outward display suggests, and it is the play between his
philosophy (modernist) and Anastasia's more meaningful deep-
truth philosophy, with which the book ultimately deals.

As for Bob, he seems to have been a similarly unlikely
candidate for marriage in 1961. At thirty-six he had already
been married before, and, for all the reasons I have given, was
well suited to an autonomous, self-sufficient, single lifestyle.
I remember Barbara telling me that her friend, the writer
Cornelius Ryan, had said to him: 'If you don't get on and
marry Barbara, *I will*!' It had been a joke, but the point is made
that Robert Bradford had not been looking for marriage when
he was swept off his feet by Barbara Taylor. That, however, is
precisely what they did. Bob and Barbara were married in
London on Christmas Eve, 1963. [25]

CHAPTER ELEVEN
Coming Home

'The city of his birth and childhood. It had forever pulled him back.'

Maxim West in *The Women in His Life*

Having a man behind her is what Edith Walker had lacked in her intended rise in the world, and 'a man behind her' is what Emma Harte in *A Woman of Substance* is given by her creator to get her project going.

The man Emma Harte selects to expedite her business is Joe Lowther. His considerable portfolio of property, which 'included eight shops in Town Street, a row of cottages in Armley, several terrace houses in nearby Wortley and … two large plots of land near St Paul's Street in Leeds itself,' was built up by his mother and her mother before her. When 'his ancient great-aunt' dies he inherits an additional £150,000, a large house in Old Farnley and 'four commercial properties in the centre of Leeds.'

Pursued by Lowther, Emma agrees to marry him, even though she doesn't love him. She is honest enough with herself to see that in marrying Lowther she is 'cheating him' of love, but that doesn't stop her. It is a bad match. Even the physical side of the marriage is unsatisfactory. The marriage is simply part of Emma's wider business strategy, although she tells herself that she needs him to 'protect her and Edwina' (her illegitimate daughter, you will recall, by Edwin Fairley). We have to conclude that she is using Lowther and that her action is completely unethical, but Emma then exercises her extraordinary business skills to turn the Lowther properties into an enterprise beyond his wildest dreams. Hers is an intricate and powerful strategy, which she executes with ruthless precision. We can only marvel at her performance.

There are some aggressive, apparently feminist traits in Emma Harte, particularly in her treatment of Joe Lowther, and one is tempted to hail her as something of a heroine of the feminist movement, which was gathering pace during Barbara's own rise, peaking as she wrote the novel. In 1953, the year that Barbara uprooted from home for London, Simone de Beauvoir first coined the phrase 'women's liberation' in her book, *The Second Sex*. In 1963, the year she uprooted from London for New York, Betty Friedan set the feminist fuse alight in *The Feminine Mystique*. Seven years later came *The Female Eunuch*, Germaine Greer's bitter landmark examination of women's oppression. Then, leading up to publication of *A Woman of Substance* in 1979, came associated bestselling novelists like Judith Rossner (*Looking For Mister Goodbar*, 1975), and upfront commercial ones like Erica Jong (*Fear of Flying*, 1973) and Judith Krantz (*Scruples*, 1978), their all-woman themes leaving Jacqueline Susann standing, and characterising 1970s New York women as forceful, funny and free – figures epitomised by Diane Keaton in movies such as *Annie Hall* and *Looking For Mister Goodbar*.

None of this was quite *Woman of Substance* territory, however. When Barbara picked up her pen in 1976 to write it, she did not pick up the feminist gauntlet as well. Emma, like many of her other heroines, is ambitious, disciplined and self-possessed. She can be ruthless, and is when crossed; she wants to win, and she is not averse to using her feminine wiles, but she always needs a man behind her. In the novel, she says: 'Being underestimated by men is one of the biggest crosses I have had to bear ... [but] it was also an advantage and one I learned to make great use of... When men believe they are dealing with a foolish or stupid woman they lower their guard, become negligent and sometimes even downright reckless. Unwittingly they often hand you the advantage on a plate.' She uses men, but she does not get her kicks out of crushing them or castrating her male lovers. I was reminded of what a commentator once wrote about Margaret Thatcher: 'Her femininity added a frisson of sexuality to one's engagement with her and disturbed the public-school code of conduct and decorum formerly operating within the all-male preserve of the party's higher echelons.' Henry Rossiter, Emma Harte's financial manager in *A Woman of Substance*, is a paid-up member of just such a code of conduct and his loyalty to it is clearly disturbed by the allure of a woman whose 'mind was logical and direct. She did not think in that convoluted female way ...'

A Woman of Substance showed Barbara's female readers how to go out and take up the opportunities that the feminist revolutionaries had opened up for them, but Barbara was not arguing the politics of feminism or any other movement. She already had her vehicle – the style to which she was born. She believes we all have this, if only we can find it, as Freda found it in her. The novels do not tell women what to believe, only to know themselves, thereby to put themselves in control of their own destinies. Movements are out. Feminism neither appeals nor appals. Barbara advocates not feminism but a brand of existentialism in which the feminine principle is preserved: 'I think that you have to *do it yourself*. I did it myself and Emma Harte did it herself ... and it can be done without being abrasive.'

When Barbara married Bob in 1963 she was nowhere near ready to pen the character that would make her fortune. It would be thirteen years before she was. So, what did happen in the intervening years to bring Barbara to Emma Harte?

Marrying Bob meant weighing anchor altogether – on her family, on England. A picture on the author's website captioned 'The Bradfords in Morocco on the set of *Impossible Object*' suggests that she slipped effortlessly into Bob's rootless world, travelling with him on location. The film, made in the early years of their marriage by the company Bob ran, Franco-London Films, was based on a novel by Nicholas Mosley about a writer who finds it difficult to distinguish fact from fiction. When a journalist asked Barbara whether she had had difficulty in adjusting to life in the Manhattan glamour world, she was able to reply, quite truthfully, 'No, I'd been in it in London.'

But there were real differences in her life, which cannot have been met without some measure of emotional insecurity.

Contact with Yorkshire and London friends like the Figgs was necessarily now limited. 'We lived in New York, in Manhattan, and in California in Beverly Hills. Bob had the apartment in Beverly Hills before we were married, so we went backwards and forwards, and then he gave it up because he ran a film company in France, so I commuted from New York to Paris and stayed three months in Paris then went back to New York for a month.'

Also, the irony was that, through marriage to Bob, she no longer needed the ambitious drive that defined her personal style and set her apart. She needn't have bothered with a career at all. She was able for the first time in her life to buy antiques of her own, and began to design and decorate their homes, capitalising on all those childhood trips with Freda to the country houses of Yorkshire. Bob saw to it that she wanted for nothing. Right from the beginning of their marriage he took a practical interest in the clothes that Barbara wore. In Paris, she was introduced to Ginette Spanier, the *directrice* of Pierre Balmain, who became a friend. 'I was very much into *haute couture*, but only a couple of pieces a year. Later, many of my clothes were by Pauline Trigère, the great American designer who was French born. Pauline and I were great friends until the day she died. She made the kind of clothes I love. Very sleek, very tailored, no frills and flounces... I also get clothes from Place Vendôme in London. Most of the things I choose there are by Italian designers. The owner, Seymour Druion, buys his collections in Rome and Milan, and picks out things for me which he knows I'll like and which Bob will like as well – dark colours for winter, no patterns; pastels, especially blue and pink, for summer.'

So, back in 1963 she had already made it. Becoming a multi-millionaire in her own right nearly two decades later apparently required little adjustment: 'I have always had quite a good standard of living and it hasn't made all that much difference,' she was able to say when asked what she was doing with her royalties from *A Woman of Substance*. 'I bought some English antiques and paid too much for them in New York, but the rest is simply invested carefully. I already had two fur coats and I didn't want any more. How many fur coats can you wear at one time?'

But, of course, the difference was that back in 1963 Bob was sourcing the finances of 'the whole enchilada'. He was strong, with definite ideas about the way he liked things to be. How far did he exercise control? How did the balance of power work then?

In 1994, the *Orlando Sentinel* quizzed Barbara as to how she and Bob had got on during their thirty years of marriage. She replied, 'We're both very bossy, so we lock horns a lot. So he calls me Napoleon, and I call him Bismarck. At Christmas in Palm Beach I saw an embroidered cushion that carried the words: "Napoleon lives here, I married him." I bought it and crossed out "him" and put "her". And I gave it to Bob. Well, I've resigned my generalship now, I've come down to a lieutenant colonel.'

This story was retold in numerous interviews, and it happened so long ago that no one is quite sure whether Barbara bought the cushion and crossed out 'him' or Bob bought it and crossed out 'her'. But on one occasion she did speak plainly: 'I always think Bob is controlling and I know that I like to control.' But it was usually she who gave in: 'I'd say: "Oh, to hell with this, it's not worth arguing about."'

It was in these pre-*Substance* years, too, that Barbara wrote a trio of manuals for the American publisher Simon & Schuster which seem to suggest an uncharacteristic compliance in Barbara's style: *How to be the Perfect Wife: Etiquette to Please Him, Entertaining to Please Him* and *Fashions That Please Him.* When a journalist discovered these in the 1980s, the cry went up: Can this really be the same woman who created Emma Harte?

'Yes, I laugh about that these days,' Barbara told Sue Lawley. 'They sold like crazy and, having written *A Woman of Substance* about this warrior woman who goes out to conquer the world, people have teased me about it, especially the press who have managed to dig up these books and say, but Barbara this is terribly *opposite*, and I say, well I meant it when I wrote them … now my attitudes have changed.'

She meant it when she wrote them, so what does this tell us about Barbara as young wife? Was it a period in which she luxuriated in pleasures of which most women dream, or one in which she was fighting to retain her self-respect and autonomy? Was it one in which she learned to play Lettice Keswick in *Everything to Gain*, 'a woman a lot like me ... a homemaker, a cook, a gardener, a painter, a woman interested in furniture and furnishings and all those things which made a home beautiful'? Or was it Emma Harte to the rescue in the mid-1970s when marriage threatened to cast Barbara forever in the role of second fiddle? One novel in particular plays over the whole range of possibilities for just such a woman in her situation.

The two really interesting wives of Maxim West in *The Women in His Life* are Anastasia Derevenkjo and actress Camilla Galland. After Anastasia's chance meeting with Maxim in Paris they fall deeply in love. Maxim gives her everything she could possibly want materially, but in time it is not enough. 'Maxim could not give all of himself to her.' We are not talking impotence here on a sexual level, rather on an emotional level. A dam holds back Maxim's emotions, and the block is to do with his childhood loss, to do with his being cut off from his roots by the war. For all his commercial genius, his successful projects, there is, deep down, a vacuum where his real self should be.

He cannot give Anastasia what she truly wants, for what she wants is *him*, but he is out of touch with himself. One night on their luxury yacht, after a spectacular party at which she wore his gift of a diamond necklace, she feels 'something cracking and splintering inside her... "That's all I am to you these days, isn't it? The giver of your parties, the decorator of your homes, the wearer of your diamonds," she exclaims coldly.'

This is a crucial point in the novel. Two sides of a coin are made to face one another. On the one side is Anastasia, whose nature encompasses a deep sense of truth and beauty and love; on the other is Maxim's project-obsessed psyche, which provides their riches but denies her access to his true self.

Maxim reels at her onslaught. Anastasia accuses him of infidelity, even though she knows he is a faithful husband, and she leaves him in the early morning. She attacks him because her womanly intuition tells her that what's missing is the crucial element of life: love. Maxim's script is not rooted in his true nature, he is still running away from who he is, which is why he is afraid to let anyone in, even the woman he could truly love.

In his second wife, Maxim finds someone who is able to meet him on his own terms. He and Camilla Galland live a kind of parallel existence, each engrossed in their own projects and deriving a shared exultation in their mutual success. 'If you marry me,' says Maxim to Camilla, 'I wouldn't want you to give up your career... I need plenty of space. In fact I must have it in order to do my work properly. I don't want you clinging to me, making me the core of your existence. I have to travel a great deal, and I hope you understand this. Of course you can come with me on the extended trips. I'd love it, love to have you with me. But not on the short, quick trips. They're too hectic, and I'm always locked up in meetings. I don't want distractions. Or to be deflected from what I have to do – because I am worrying about my wife. I've always had great direction, concentration. I can't change.'

Theirs is to be a project-marriage. There are to be 'ground rules', and we are conscious that the rules are set by Maxim not by Camilla, his very name a synonym for a rule of conduct. Nevertheless, Camilla is happy at the prospect: 'I have to work, Maxim, just as you have to ... they'd take me away in a straitjacket if I didn't.' She feels like 'the luckiest woman in the world,' and then fate steps in to end it – Camilla breaks her neck by falling down a steeply pitched basement staircase.

Maxim replaces her with Adriana Macklin, who, like him, is consumed with business projects. He becomes unhappy, in fact he becomes impotent, though not with beautiful blonde Blair Martin, who wears pale-green silk pyjamas by Trigère, and lives in Sutton Place, Barbara's own apartment, overlooking 'the East River and a portion of the 59th Street Bridge'.

We shouldn't get too sidelined by matching up the biographical elements, which have been scattered across the canvas so that no real-life colours attach to any one character in particular. What we are dealing with here is a theme which does have relevance to real players, indeed to us all, and has to do with life in the modern world in which, too often, truth is no more than the opposite of a lie.

Camilla and Adriana share Maxim's thoroughly modernist outlook. For all three, *project* – making things happen – is all. There is no great depth to their relationships, or if there is, as might have been possible in the case of Maxim and Camilla, both parties agree that it is not the priority. Emotional complications have been eradicated by ground rules, or, in the case of Adriana, by the fact that she is a similar operator to Maxim. But, as Anastasia knows, emotions cannot be so easily dealt with. Anastasia haunts Maxim, and Adriana attacks him for always 'flinging that ex-wife of yours in my face'.

The rest of the novel leads up to Maxim's moment of truth. He is softened up for it by an accident, which delivers the crucial volte-face that 'there are more things in life than big deals.' He returns to his roots, finds his birthplace in the post-war rubble of Berlin, 'the city of his birth and childhood, [which] he had always believed held a secret for him.' Finally, he learns the secret, and 'the sadness inside him slipped away.'

Appropriately, when he discovers his true identity (a complete surprise, in which Barbara cleverly discovers the absolute value of love at the core of the concept of identity) he becomes whole again in Anastasia's arms, just as the Berlin wall comes crashing down and his homeland is made whole again too.

Barbara and Bob had themselves crossed into the Eastern sector of the city in 1986. The trip had sparked the idea for the novel. 'I had always had this compulsion to go to the East zone,' she said at the time. 'So we went through Checkpoint Charlie and when we were there I had this flash in my mind's eye of a woman in a white satin evening gown in the style of the Thirties, blonde and very ethereal. Somehow I knew that her name was Ursula [the name of the woman in the novel who we believe to be Maxim's mother], and I asked Bob if he had ever mentioned anyone of that name. But he just kept telling me it was my writer's imagination!'

The dam against emotion had been holed, the message was once again about identity – to remember where you came from, because 'it defines who you are'. By the time Barbara wrote *The Women in His Life* it had been revealed as the lesson of her own life, for it was Barbara's imaginative return to her very deepest roots in the landscape of Yorkshire in the mid-1970s that enabled her to write the novel that would define her. Her return brought her back to the values of the landscape of Yorkshire to which her mother had introduced her as a child, 'a sense of honour, duty and purpose', the need for 'integrity in the face of incredible pressure and opposition' and 'not only an honesty with those people who occupied her life, but with herself.' It is for this reason that her woman of substance is not quite the model of modernism which, at face value, she seems.

So, what led Barbara back?

For her part, soon after marriage to Bob, Barbara decided that she must have a project of her own: 'Bob was busy being a movie producer – so if I didn't work, where would all my boundless energy go? I couldn't just sit at home and do nothing, I've never been one of those ladies who lunch and I loathe shopping.'

But she didn't immediately buckle down to writing a novel, the one that would define her. Instead, she pursued a freelance journalistic career, writing about the homes of the famous in a syndicated interior-design column called 'Designing Woman' – first for *Newsday*, then, moving with editor Tom Dorsey, for the *New York Daily News*, and finally the *Los Angeles Times*. Her column went across America to 185 newspapers and she wrote it for twelve years. She also wrote a number of interior design books. I have seen them in her drawing room, now beautifully bound in leather, including the bestselling *Complete Encyclopaedia of Homemaking Ideas*.

Appearance, design, beauty – an arena in which the aesthetic and the commercial are indistinguishable – all absolutely in tune with the world in which she was now moving, and all the time she was learning, building up her knowledge base in an area that would, as it happened, prove useful for the novels, for she realised how compellingly she could write about the most exquisite artefacts of European origin – her favourite Biedermeier and Art Deco furniture and Impressionist paintings. America was looking to Europe in this arena, in which indigenously it could not of course compete. Barbara was unmistakably English, and brought up to the task. As she said: 'Mummy gave me this eye for antiques. She taught me to look.'

The design column and books became her project, which ran parallel to Bob's in the film world, and so began a pattern of life that in time would bring Bob and Barbara project-bound together in the marketing and filming of her novels, something

Maxim and his wives never quite achieve in the novel. This became the pattern of their lives. Bobby Caplin summed up the position well: 'I don't think either of them would have been as successful without the other.' Bob tends to get what he wants, he is a tough negotiator, but what he wants is now what Barbara wants. [26]

They made a formidable team, now that their project was a shared one. Bob engineered some unbelievably good deals for Barbara in America, involving many millions of dollars. Her personal wealth was quoted in 2004 in the Rich List as £95 million, which put her at 419th position in the world.

But this was only one side of the coin, the other was the fulfilment of those contracts. Her first English publisher, the late Mark Barty-King, became seriously concerned in the early days that she was working so hard, never seemed to go out because she did little *but* work: 'She was riding high on a worldwide reputation and there was always such big pressure to produce something,' he told me.

The picture that came to mind was of the miller's daughter confined by the king to her room and spinning gold thread out of straw, the beautiful girl working away, working away, spinning a golden yarn according to magical directions from Rumpelstiltskin. But Bob would have none of it.

'*A Woman of Substance* was her first book. She sweated the book for two years, twenty-four hours a day. I used to go to Hollywood to work and she worked twenty-four hours a day on that book. It's unbelievable and thank God she's not doing that any more. She doesn't have to...'

Barty-King remembers that the second book, *Voice of the Heart* was another draining experience. Running to 928 pages in length, it was not published until 1983, and yet Barbara had a contract and started writing it more than six months before *Woman of Substance* was published.

In an interview with the broadcaster Richard Whiteley, she once set out the regime that her life had become by this time: 'It's the salt mines. I do ten or twelve hours a day, seven days a week. I get in here [her study] at six o'clock in the morning. I'm wearing a pair of cotton trousers and a tee shirt, winter and summer, in winter I put a cardigan on, no make-up, no jewellery, just my glasses, very underdressed. And I edit what I finished yesterday, and at about seven thirty to eight o'clock I take Gemmy [the dog] out. So I've already done about two hours' work. I start at six a.m. in here, and then I work till noon, and then she [the dog] has her lunch and I have a salad and I take her round the block, bring her back, and go back to work till 6 p.m.'

I asked Bob how Barbara would relax. 'She doesn't like cocktail parties because you stand around and talk nonsense, totally idiotic stuff, and she'd rather sit at home and read a good book. She loves to read and to think and to work, and she likes to go out to dinner and she likes to be with close friends and relax. Particularly when she's working on a book, she doesn't want to sit around with people who talk nonsense. They have nothing to say but blow hot air and for her it's a total waste because her head is in the book, thinking, thinking out the plot.

'Although what we do keeps us apart we are not shut out of each other's lives. When Barbara is shut up in a room writing for days, I am her window on the world, telling her what I've seen, who I've met. She tells me about her next chapter and uses me as a sounding board. I am very proud of her and what she has done. I'm a very secure individual, unworried by her fame and fortune. I had mine before her. She was my back-up and now I'm hers. My greatest relaxation is long weekends. I leave our New York apartment, take a plane and fly to Miami or Puerto Rico. I swim, I read and be away from people. You can't be a happy couple if you are always in each other's way. Barbara doesn't like the sun; I do. When she is "off the book" she travels with me.'

From the start of their marriage, Bob was himself project-bound in a difficult and highly commercial industry, and it was ever a two-career household with no idea of working nine-to-five. In the early 1970s, still some years before she started work on the novels, Barbara made a move to escape from the relentless urban vortex into the country, and one is minded how much she must have been missing her regular trips home to Yorkshire that she had always made from London.

In 1971 she persuaded Bob to look for a country retreat in northwest Connecticut. She told *Architectural Digest*: 'Our search began when my husband, Bob, and I were guests of conductor-composer Skitch Henderson and his wife Ruth, at their house in New Milford. We were instantly entranced by the region, seeing elements of England and Europe in its scenic, sweeping beauty composed of rolling, tree-covered hills and shining lakes.'

Everything to Gain (1994) began a series of books with narrative set in Connecticut, continuing with *Dangerous to Know* (1995), *Her Own Rules* (1996), and *A Sudden Change of Heart* (1999). She accords the place great significance in the novels. In *Hold the Dream* it is the place selected for the long-awaited coming together of the Hartes and the O'Neills. Emma Harte's granddaughter Paula first realises she loves Shane O'Neill, grandson of Blackie O'Neill (Emma's dear friend from the start of *A Woman of Substance*), when she is visiting Shane's converted barn in the country town of New Milford, near where Bob and Barbara's new home would be. In *Everything to Gain* it is where Mallory Keswick retreats to consider her future before she yields to the pull of the Yorkshire moors, where her late husband grew up and where she gets her idea about what to do.

'I fell in love with [the house] the moment I saw it,' says Barbara of the one they finally bought, 'a wonderful old Connecticut colonial, classically elegant in its design, surrounded by ancient maples and smooth green lawns flowing down to a large pond. Dominating that pond, and adding to the decidedly pastoral feeling of the property, were two regal white swans floating on its surface against profuse pink water lilies.

'The first thing we did was hire Litchfield architect Paul Hinkel, whose work we had seen and admired. Paul is an authority on colonial architecture, and since he was nearby he could supervise the construction daily. He was quick to understand our requirements, agreed with us about the restoration and remodelling, and made other good suggestions. After much consultation and endless refining, Paul presented plans that turned a thirteen-room house into one with eighteen rooms, plus a wine cellar and storage space. He also redesigned the guest cottage.'

They could not have settled for less. However, this weekend retreat did not come as a release valve during the early years of their marriage. Though the search began in 1971, it would be twenty-one years before Barbara and Bob made the purchase. 'He bought it for me in May 1992, for my birthday,' said Barbara. It followed a spectacular deal Bob made with her American publishers, at the time the biggest author contract in history.

So, the much-needed weekend escape took a long time coming. And even after they did buy it, 'We didn't go there much,' said Barbara. 'It wasn't Bob,' as Bobby Caplin pointed out, 'that home in Connecticut – magnificent, quite unbelievable, but it certainly wasn't Bob. That was one hundred per cent Barbara. Bob is a city man. This was maybe one of Barbara's dreams, with the lake and the swan. They were in the middle of nowhere!'

The Connecticut episode delineated once more Bob's pragmatism on the one hand, and Barbara's unfulfilled emotional needs on the other. 'Ten thousand square feet, enormous house,' Bob said when I asked him about it. 'It was wonderful! Paradise! But it was too big for us and we were never there, it was just draining us of money. The pool men, the tree doctor, the gardeners, every day there was something else. And it was two hours' travelling, over two hours to get there.'

'I think Barbara loved it,' I began. 'I remember…'

'She loved the country, she is a country girl, she is English, but I mean she is also a very practical lady and she works best at her home in New York.'

That may be so, but the novels give an impression that Connecticut meant something important to Barbara in a creative, imaginative sense. When she writes about the countryside around the Litchfield hills, the brilliant skies of the region are described in a manner not dissimilar to that in which she refers to Yorkshire. When I took this up with her she agreed: 'Connecticut has that very special kind of light, a clarity of light that I talk about in *A Woman of Substance*, *Hold the Dream* and *Voice of the Heart* – the part set in Yorkshire – because it's like Northern light and it seems to emanate from some hidden source like the light in some of Turner's paintings. It's also rather an undulating countryside – I like moors and hills, though it's not, of course, the moors.'

That light of Yorkshire is a symbol of creativity – Barbara says as much when she finally returns to it in imagination to write *A Woman of Substance*. It is 'quite extraordinary. It's almost as if it comes from another source. A writer must turn inward in order to write – everything comes out of me and this is what I remember, that extraordinary clarity … that love of the light.'

Their work was indeed their life and vice versa, and Barbara would never have wanted it any other way. But there was this emotional side that did need an avenue if Barbara was ever to achieve her expression. Was part of her being denied? It was an unlikely bedding ground for a traditional family, of course, and there would be no children.

I detect a sadness that she and Bob didn't have children, but also no shadow of regret at the lifestyle they chose, which they are both so good at. 'I don't have any regrets at all,' said Barbara twenty years ago, and she says the same today. 'I don't think you miss a person that you haven't known. Bob and I got married in 1963 and I was then thirty years old. We didn't want to have children immediately. We said, "Well, maybe in a few years." Then somehow it was suddenly too late. It's the luck of the draw. I'd have loved children but I didn't have them. I've got a wonderful marriage, I've got Bob, who is a great supporter of mine in every way, as I hope I am of him, and we've got to be content.'

There is a touching moment in the old nursery at Pennistone Royal, towards the end of *Hold the Dream*, where Paula, Emma Harte's granddaughter, sings her twin children, Tessa and Lorne Fairley, to sleep with 'The Sandman' song, for which Barbara proudly claims authorship. 'I wrote that! That's my creation!' she says excitedly. 'I also wrote a children's book and edited a couple for a publishing house. They had bought the most beautifully illustrated book I've ever seen for children. It was in Czech – each page had an illustration and a poem in Czech, and they asked me to write a little poem for each of these wonderful illustrations, and I thought, well, why not? I drove Bob crazy! I'd ring him up at the office and say, "Just listen to this for a minute." And he thought something wonderful was coming –'

The sandman has the swiftest wings and shoes that are made of gold;
And he comes to you when the first star sings and the night is not very old …

'– Bob would say, "Do you mind, I'm in a meeting!" It was a lovely children's book, I enjoyed doing it; it was a challenge. It wasn't that we set out not to have children, you know. And I didn't say, "Oh I'm going to have a big career." I had a miscarriage and I never got pregnant again.'

I talk to Bob about Barbara's relationship with her own mother, the love she gave her, and he says, 'That's why Barbara is so keenly interested in working with children today and with literacy problems. She works with Literacy Partners in New York, a charity that raises money and opens centres to teach people to read. She is on the Madison Council of the Library of Congress in Washington, and has worked with the president's mother Barbara Bush and First Lady Laura Bush on literacy and the National Book Festival. Over eighty million Americans can barely read, or can't read at all…' Today, she is an ambassador for the National Literary Trust.

She has also been on the committee of PAL, a children's charity (the letters standing for Police Athletic League) which has, at different times, attracted Barbara Bush and Hillary Clinton to fundraising luncheons. 'PAL is a charity devoted to underprivileged children in the New York area,' Barbara told me. 'It was started in the 1920s to get poor kids off the street, but it is run more by business people today. Recently we opened one centre in the Bronx, a tough area of New York, and I sat in on a session and listened as fifteen-year-old girls talked about wanting to get their boyfriends out of the Latin Kings, a gang. "The only way you can get out," one girl said, "is to commit suicide or they will kill you because they don't want you to leave – they won't let you leave."'

It's a world Barbara drew on in *Everything to Gain*, where Mallory Keswick's husband and children are fatally shot in a tough area of New York. Their killer had been smoking crack cocaine.

Again, in her charitable work in the UK, children have been in focus. She has been on the board and a trustee of PACT – Parents and Abducted Children Together. Again it is her fundraising capability that is to the fore. The charity was started by Lady Meyer, wife of the former British Ambassador to Washington. Catherine Meyer is a good friend of Barbara, and it was she who asked her to become involved. 'Catherine's children were abducted by her first husband,' Barbara told me, 'and I can't imagine how she lived through it. It must have been harrowing.'

In this context, suggestions often proffered by journalists that Barbara's dogs are substitutes for her unborn children seem in poor taste, although it is perfectly true that she made her beloved bichon frises part of the family, and she explores the entire history of the breed in *Voice of the Heart*. Barbara thought it mean of reporters to question her affection for her dogs, given that most pet owners shower affection on their animals. It is, after all, the point, isn't it? Beaji and Chammi, now deceased, had a very good lifestyle and they shared all Barbara's secrets, for they would sit under her desk while she worked her characters and stories out loud.

When her first, the late Gemmy Bradford, fell ill in 1987, Barbara flew home on Concorde straightaway. 'I went immediately to the vet, where the housekeeper had taken her. She was operated on, and miraculously lived. She died when she was twelve. She wrote a lot of books with me. Gemmy was short for Gemini, even though she was a Scorpio. My parents were both Gemini and so is Bob, and my agent. So I'm surrounded by Geminis.' Astrologers may be interested that Barbara herself is Taurus, and Taurus and Gemini are the two most likely signs for members of the Rich List, followed by Aries.

Beaji and Chammi undoubtedly enabled Barbara to express a side of her that otherwise got scant exercise, although it is of course the writing that provides the real fulfilment. Why then did it take so long after marriage to Bob, which had, after all, removed the need to earn money by other means, to start the novel that would make her name?

It was not for want of trying. She worked on four novels during the period up to 1975–6 – four false starts. 'I didn't like them, I'd get halfway and be bored with it, and I thought, if I'm bored then obviously the reader is going to be bored, and I'd put it away and start another one. I did this four times, four different novels before I got the idea for *A Woman of Substance.* I had been trying to write romantic suspense like Helen MacInnis.'

Helen MacInnis wrote espionage thrillers with romantic sub-plots, which benefited from her extensive research skills into political events of the regions in which the novels are set. After her husband was assigned to intelligence work in the British army during the Second War, there was even suspicion that she had inside information. Once again, Barbara would not have been blind to the fact that research was a key element in the bestselling mix. By the time of MacInnis's death in 1985, more than twenty-three million copies of her novels had been sold in America alone, and they had been translated into twenty-two languages.

However, the reason why Barbara Taylor Bradford came to write the eighth most popular novel in the history of the world had nothing to do with an editorial analysis of what was currently selling well, and everything to do with leaving that side of her thinking alone.

With the distance of time, her own development away from the person she had once been, and the geographical distance from home that marriage to Bob entailed, and with a growing sense of frustration, as I have outlined, Barbara began thinking about her past and her family more.

'I only really began to understand my mother's life when I was in my forties,' she told me. Barbara turned forty in 1973, three years before she put pen to paper on her first published novel. She had begun to talk to her father about his relationship with Freda. 'I know that she rejected him constantly. No, she didn't talk about it, but I knew about it somehow when I was in my teens and the only person I discussed it with was my father. When she used to come and stay with me in London, when she first arrived she'd be saying, "Your father is terrible" and he is this and that, and she'd be sort of running him down – and after about a week, when she was supposed to stay for ten days, she said, "Oh, I really have to go home, your daddy can't manage without me and

I miss him," and I looked at her in amazement. I never actually said to her, "Why did you stop sleeping with him?" but once, when I was in my twenties, I did say, "Why are you like that with Daddy? Sometimes you seem so cold with him."'

This was the occasion Freda told Barbara that she had wanted only her, that if she had had other children she would not have been able to give her everything, and that she was glad that Barbara had not been a boy because then she would have gone off more with her father. It must have begun to come clear to Barbara, now that she was thinking about these things with the benefit of some distance and objectivity, that there was more to all of this than met the eye.

So, in her forties, Barbara was going back into her roots more, and recognising that Freda was a person in her own right, not simply a mother with whom she was joined at the hip, and she was set on the road to realising that Freda's extraordinary mothering was a response to some deep loss of her own. Although she did not talk to Freda about this, maybe pieces of the mosaic – the 'bits and bats that I picked up over the years' – began to fall into place. Her subconscious will have set to work, and because her childhood, her parents and the landscape of her beloved Yorkshire were so far distant, these things would soon begin to occupy her imagination as well as her thoughts.

'There is something about Yorkshire which is deeply ingrained in me and I am moved by the beauty. It stirs me inside,' she says. 'I had this joy in it as a child, but I didn't know I had it. Being away from it, on this side of the Atlantic, and looking across the Atlantic in my mind's eye, I see it with great perception … There's also a lot of nostalgia in it, that yearning, the memories of my childhood are bound up in it, so to me it's very emotional … A writer draws on memories.'

In Manhattan she was looking out through the window of a completely different culture and her emotional side was beginning to understand that she had left something important behind.

Then, at some time in the mid-1970s, she read an interview with Graham Greene in *Time* magazine, which suggested a bridge between her writing and what that something might be: 'Greene said, "Character is plot."'

That one sentence marked a turning point in her approach to writing fiction. 'It made me understand what writing fiction is all about. I realised why I'd gone wrong in those four books that I'd started and never finished. It was because I'd come up with a plot and then tried to fit people in. Character is destiny. Develop character, *then* the story comes.'

As in life, so in fiction. We are what we are, character is what you are; it is what determines our lives. 'We live our characters, don't we? One lives one's basic character. If you're a weak person then you're going to have a quite different life from someone who is strong. Then, also, adversity can develop your character or shatter you. So many of the strong characters grow from adversity. I'm fascinated by the indomitability [of life]. Life is hard, it's always been hard, it doesn't get any easier and it's not important that life is hard, what is important is how we overcome that adversity, or the adversities we have in our lives. I think I'm writing often about courage, conflict, inner and between people.'

So, marriage to Bob, which took Barbara away from her roots, ironically served also to refocus her on them. Yorkshire was the bit of deep-truth reality that produced their first offspring, Emma Harte, her unique character forged in the landscape of her youth.

Marriage to Bob also served to internationalise the arena in which the woman of substance would operate, which is why Barbara is able to write about people and place beyond her homeland, and appeal to readers beyond the country that formed her. By the time she came to write her first novel, Barbara was able to call up the spirit of place that imbued character not only among the crags of Ramsden Ghyll, where she ran as a teenager 'on her beloved moors high above Fairley village', but also among Manhattan's skyscrapers, 'a living painting of enormous power and wealth and the heartbeat of American industry'. Cut off in her Manhattan eyrie, free from the cultural baggage of either Yorkshire or America, she was in touch with the spirit of both. So it was that when she came to write *A Woman of Substance* it featured a woman in tune with Manhattan, but with her roots in the gritstone hills of the Yorkshire moors.

Barbara's imaginative homecoming – her writing of novels which mine the two cultures in this way – was an emotional experience of rediscovery, and determined that the books would themselves have strong emotional and psychological dimensions. It meant that she would put her characters in touch with their true selves, as she had done herself, releasing them from the value-vacuum of their modernist world by returning them to their roots, often to Yorkshire, her own home culture, but in Maxim West's case first to Berlin, where he discovers that his parents are not even the German Jews he had supposed to have been lost to him by the war. Then, finally, Barbara returns him to the love of the one woman, Teddy, who has been a true mother to him but is not even a blood-relation, thereby returning to us the notion of absolute love at the root of identity, the value which will henceforth organise rich and powerful Maxim's life along other than pragmatic lines, and to which he will refer for his values. This was the point of the homecoming.

One morning in her early forties, Barbara called up her subconscious and provoked her imaginative homecoming with a series of questions: 'Well, you haven't liked these four books you started and you put them away. So, what do you want to write and where do you want to set it? And what kind of book would it be? And what is it about, basically? And who are the characters?

'I didn't ask the questions out loud, obviously, [although] I do that of myself today. Walk around muttering to myself. But my answers were: set it in England because I'm English and I know the English. No! Set it in Yorkshire, because you really know the Yorkshire people. I want to write about a woman who makes it in a man's world … when women weren't doing that, at the turn of the century maybe. I realised as I answered these questions and wrote them down on a yellow pad that what I was describing … was a saga. I was really talking to myself about writing a traditional, old-fashioned saga.'

'That's what I did write. And when I realised I was going to write about a woman who makes it in a man's world when women weren't doing that, and that she'd be a businesswoman,

I thought I wanted to write about a woman who becomes *a woman of substance*. And I looked at that and I knew at once that I had my title, and I also knew that this would be the novel I would finish. I thought it was a damn good title, especially since it can have two meanings, substance: money, and the development of her character. You know, certain people didn't like this title! And I said: "Well, I'm not changing it. I love this title. And I didn't ask your opinion."' Barbara laughs. 'I mean, Bob loved it, but people are funny, you know? They think they know better than you if they're in the business. I said: "I will never change this title."

'A week later I had written a twelve-page outline and I was on my way. For the next three months I sat at my desk in our Manhattan apartment creating Emma Harte in my imagination … and I dug back into my memory for the countless details about Upper Armley and other parts of Yorkshire where the story is set. After I had written 190 pages I went back into the past in the novel. I was suddenly at the turn of the century, when Emma was a little girl. I swiftly realised that I had to make a trip to Yorkshire to discover more. I telephoned my father and asked him to look for old books on Armley and Leeds in the local library, which he did. It was rather fortuitous for me that my mother had been clipping out a series on old Leeds, which the *Yorkshire Evening Post* was running at the time. I talked at length to my parents, relatives and older friends and spent hours in Leeds Public Library studying old copies of Leeds newspapers, histories of Leeds and Yorkshire, interviews with local people who had worked in the mills, and visited old mills in Armley and Stanningley, drove into the Dales, and tramped around Ripon, Middleham and Studley Royal.'

Bobby Caplin remembers this period well. 'I remember Barbara came back to Leeds doing research into the old mills for *A Woman of Substance*. She had gone away a provincial lady and come back a very, very smart and intelligent person. It was great to see. But basically she was still Barbara. This friend of mine had a birthday party during the time she was here. This was Ronnie Sumrie, her old boyfriend, and Barbara contacted Ronnie as an old friend (he was well married at the time) to come and explain to her about manufacturers and to introduce her to the top mill-owners.'

There's a story attached to Barbara's meeting with her old boyfriend after so long. 'I ran into Ronnie on a Saturday, on a Pullman train from Kings Cross. I was coming up to Leeds to see my parents, and to do more research for *Woman of Substance*. It must have been about 1976. Ronnie and I found ourselves sitting in the same carriage; it was the restaurant car. I was further down but facing him, though I didn't immediately recognise him, and then this most enormous girl sits down with him. And it's a totally empty carriage. And I see this flick of horror enter these eyes and he looked across at me, those blue eyes full of horror. I thought, My God it's Ronnie Sumrie! And I stood up and sort of edged towards him and said, "Aren't you Ronnie Sumrie?" And he leapt to his feet and said, "It's Barbara, isn't it?" And as the train was pulling out I answered, "Yes," and so we sort of embraced in this rolling carriage, and I asked, "Do you want to come and join me?" "Oh yes, I do!" he exclaimed. And he was sort of polite enough and gentlemanly enough to say to this woman, "Oh would you excuse me. I've met an old school-friend." We have often laughed about that.'

It was a homecoming that determined her future as a novelist and would in years to come be reciprocated by the city of her birth. In 1990, two years after the scholarly Brotherton Library in Leeds had been granted their request to become the Keeper of the Barbara Taylor Bradford archive (her manuscripts sit next to ones by Charlotte Brontë), she was honoured by Leeds University with the degree of Doctor of Letters, presented by the Duchess of Kent. (Five years later, the city of Bradford would bestow on her an honorary DPhil.) The great coincidence was that Alan Bennett was similarly honoured at Leeds on the very same day – 12th May 1990. They hadn't set eyes on one another in more than half a century, and had no notion that they had attended the same school until broadcaster Richard Whiteley pointed it out backstage, 'and,' stressed Barbara, 'we are both the same sign – Taurus!'

Bennett at once slipped comfortably into character, his ear for dialogue, on which he had made his reputation, as deft as ever. 'Alan was so funny,' said Barbara. 'When we were getting robed, he suddenly looked down, looked at his feet, and he said disconsolately in this broad Yorkshire accent: "I wish I had known it was going to be this posh. I've got dirty suede shoes, Barbara." I followed his gaze and he did have on a rather mucky pair of stained suede shoes, and there we were being put in these velvet robes! Tremendous talent, and his father a butcher in Tong Road!'

The idea of *A Woman of Substance* had brought Barbara home. Suddenly, yesterday was now, the past was about to become a part of her present time. It was the psychological unity she needed to move forward. Acknowledging her anchor in Yorkshire had given Barbara back her centre.

CHAPTER TWELVE
Creating a Brand

'No matter what the publishers do, they'll never stop this book. It'll go through the roof.'

'When I came up with the idea for *A Woman of Substance* I wrote a twelve-page outline and showed it to Bob,' said Barbara. 'After he read it, he said it was a great idea, but that I was undertaking something quite enormous ... the story of a woman's life from childhood to old age. I agreed, and he nodded and said, "You'll do it." He always had confidence in me.

'Although I had an American agent, Paul Gitlin, who had been introduced to me by Cornelius Ryan and had sold my design books, I decided to show the outline to my English agent, George Greenfield.' Greenfield was a leading literary agent in the rather traditional agency of John Farquharson, and had represented Barbara since she was a journalist in London. He liked the outline, but the first bite he got was ironically from an American – editor-in-chief Betty Prashker of Doubleday, when she was in London scouting for new authors. They'd had lunch, she'd told him she was looking for traditional sagas, and he had given her Barbara's phone number in New York. A week later Barbara received a phone call from Carolyn Blakemore, senior editor of the firm, who invited her to have drinks with her and Prashker.

'When we met, they were very cordial,' Barbara remembers. 'They told me they wanted to see the outline as soon as possible; I agreed to messenger it down to Doubleday the following morning. Within two hours of receiving it, Carolyn was on the phone telling me, "It's the best outline I've ever read, bar none! When are you starting work on it? When can we see pages?" I remember saying, "It's now early June, I'll give you at least one hundred pages the first working day after Labor Day Weekend."'

In early September Barbara kept to her promise, actually delivering 192 pages, 'which was the whole of Part One and the beginning of Part Two. Three days later she called me and said she loved it... They wanted it. I told her to get Paul Gitlin to make the deal. That was in about 1975–6. I delivered the book two and a half years later.'

Inevitably, with a book about a character who had so many parallels with that of its creator, Barbara was an important element in the sale of it to publishers. In London, Greenfield had shown the original outline to Mark Barty-King, the then editorial director of Granada Publishing, part of Lord Bernstein's media empire, which included the Granada TV company. Then, by chance, Barty-King bumped into Barbara on a street corner in New York City. He already had the treatment and was intrigued, so, when he was in town on other business and caught sight of Greenfield walking along with a beautiful blonde companion, he was pleased to discover that she was none other than its author. 'I was so pleased to meet her,' recalls Mark, a handsome six-foot-four operator whose nickname in publishing circles at the time was Captain Marvel. 'She was an attractive woman of course, but what was palpable when she spoke about the manuscript of *A Woman of Substance* was her determination. Call it Yorkshire grit or whatever. I had no picture in my mind of her until that day, but I went back to England determined to buy that book, which we did for what was then the highest advance ever paid for the right to publish a book in the UK – £55,000.

'What swayed me was her cold certainty that it would be a success – it was determination rather than enthusiasm. There's a subtle difference. You trusted her judgement. She did not for one moment doubt that it would be a success. The only question was whether one wanted to be a part of it, and there was no question as far as I was concerned.'

When I described the scene to Bob, he replied, 'That's the way she's always been. You cannot take her off the track; once she's on the track she's like a locomotive... I mean, she goes. She puffs away and it's very hard to move her or to stop her.'

In due course (1982–3), Bernstein sold the publishing side of Granada to the old English firm of William Collins Ltd and it became known as Grafton Publishing, with Mark still heading up the editorial side, the late Patricia Parkin as chief editor (fiction) and Ian Chapman, from the Collins side, its managing director. Before long (1989), they, with the rest of Collins, would be bought by Rupert Murdoch for £320 million, and the firm re-renamed Harper Collins.

'We met Ian Chapman,' Bob recalls. 'Ian became a great fan. We were introduced by Mark, obviously, and Ian was a great champion of Barbara's because he was running the company. So, everything seemed to be rolling along, everybody was with us. She has never had any real problems with the UK publishers, I must say. They are the same today as they were then, though the people have changed.'

When Bob saw the enthusiasm both in New York and London, he became involved in the book's marketing, but there was some delay before publication. 'I finished *A Woman of Substance* and delivered it to Doubleday, New York on May fifth, 1978,' remembers Barbara. 'I know it was May fifth because it was just before my birthday. It was very long, it was 1,520 pages, the weight of a small child. Then they took a year to publish it, which was perfectly normal in those days. We had to cut three hundred pages without it showing,' she laughs. 'Try it! You've got to do a page here and a page there and five pages there and you usually do description and I actually did lose three minor characters whom we felt we could get rid of. That took them a few months. Then the Doubleday editor Carolyn Blakemore said to me: "We still haven't lost enough pages. There is one chapter where Emma's not in it." So, she took out a chapter in its entirety.'

The dropped chapter was about the First War. 'And I said, "My favourite chapter!" It wasn't really my favourite chapter, but I wanted her to feel bad because I really didn't want to cut any more pages. Anyway, she said: "It lifts out and you don't know it's gone." I read it and it was true: Emma waves goodbye to Joe Lowther and Blackie on the railway station, they go off to war and the next chapter is six months later, she's there with her children, she's going to work, she's doing everything she normally does. Then of course one of the reviewers said: "Bradford goes into great detail about" – whatever – "and yet hardly touches on the First World War!" But there is a funny story attached to this. When Bob was making the film of *Hold the Dream*, which was the second book in the *Woman of Substance* trilogy, some magazine in London asked me if I would write them a short story about the Emma Harte family and I said: "I can't. I'm in the middle of a novel… " They came back and said: "Are you sure you haven't got anything? It doesn't have to be about the Hartes. Anything at all will do. What about a short story?" And I told them I didn't write short stories any more. Only when I was a child. And they said: "Oh! We'll have one of those." " *No*," was my answer.

'But then Bob was at the studio in London and he called me and said: "Try and find them something. You must have something somewhere because they're driving me crazy and it's very important that we get this big spread about the mini-series." So as I'm talking to him, I said: "Oh, Bob. There's the lost chapter." I sent it. They ran it. And then the British publisher said: "Why have we never seen this chapter! We want this chapter. We're putting it in the book." And they had reason to bring out a new edition, which said: "For the first time, the missing chapter", with a big medallion on the jacket. Then they did the same in America, they put that chapter in the book. It is a good chapter, actually, and it was one that I liked because it was the war.

'So, they took a year with *Woman of Substance*, it was delivered May '78 and within a few weeks I had also sold them the idea of *Voice of the Heart*, so I actually embarked on that book without knowing that *A Woman of Substance* was going to be successful. The first novel came out in May '79 in the US, and by that time I'd worked since the previous September on *Voice of the Heart*.'

'In England [*Woman of Substance*] was published in 1980. This delay had something to do with Mark holding it back because he wanted to get a deal with the book club.'

Mark remembered serious problems in getting the jacket right. The jacket of a book is of course crucial marketing territory, and the marketing on a first-time author is key. If the publisher goes light on that aspect you don't stand a chance. Bob didn't think twice about pitching in on Barbara's behalf. 'She really put everything she had into that book and when it was finished I'd already taken over a great part of her promotion, supervising the marketing of it, working with the American publisher. I was always concerned, right from the beginning, that I didn't want her to be buried. When you are a new author coming in they don't want to spend the money unless the book takes off right away. If you're not careful, they can put you on the list and let the book ride by itself – good luck! So, I was very attentive to that, and she was on the road for the book. She did ten cities promoting the book, and I made sure that when I wasn't there, there was always somebody with her. I mean, it was the first time round, you know?'

I asked how Doubleday took to that. As a mass-market-paperback publisher myself at that time I knew that with no track record in Barbara's career it would have been deemed interference on Bob's part. Most husbands of new authors would have been shown the door.

'The publishers,' he began. 'They get a little nervous. They don't always like me.'

'I haven't heard that,' I said encouragingly.

'I don't know,' he said, flicking his eyes up at me, wondering just where I was coming from. 'I think that they are a little nervous of me.'

'How did you handle it?' I asked.

'I am always very polite and have no case against them. The point is that I do push. I was up in Doubleday and I met with the marketing people, advertising people, and if I saw this wasn't moving I came in there every day, made my phone calls till I got what I wanted. Barbara and I, we had a good relationship with Doubleday, a friendly and good relationship once she got going. In the meantime I had to ask to see advertising and marketing. You know, the guy working on *A Woman of Substance* and the next one, *Voice of the Heart...* I saw them failing in terms of marketing. I didn't see the energy there, so I was up to see the Vice President of the marketing and advertising. I'm afraid I used to drive the guy nuts. "What's happening? Show me what you're doing." I couldn't understand what they were doing. He was telling me, "Well, we're going to do publicity [as opposed to advertising]. That was nothing. So I finally had to go down the hall to see Nelson and get him on board and get him to give them more money.

'So I was with Nelson Doubleday. This was in 1979, when Nelson Doubleday owned the company, and I was sitting with Nelson in his office. Not too many people do that. I always remember he took off his jacket, I was off with my jacket and he said, "Let's talk." I said, "Listen, I treat a book like a motion picture, so let's start from that point of view. I know you don't have thirty million dollars to spend on a book, but let's start from that point of view: you are selling a motion picture, that's the way you tackle it. He was telling me that he'd allocated about fifty thousand dollars to promote the book and, you know, I said he had to do more. He didn't like it, but I think down the line he quite admired me for my persistence.

'We also – that's me and Barbara – took a big risk because I spent money. I believe my statement is correct when I say that I was the first person in the publishing business in the United States to take full-page ads in the *New York Times*. There was nobody before me who did that. I started it and I'm sure there were heads turning in the publishing industry thinking this publisher is spending a lot of money, because at the time we didn't tell anyone. I didn't want the publishers to be embarrassed, so we wouldn't tell and the publisher always got the credit, they got their name on the ad, but I paid for it. I did it on most of the books. Sometimes the publisher paid. Every book Barbara has ever written has had a full page in the *New York Times*.

'*Recognition* factor. It explodes on the scene, people see the name, they see the book, I don't know whether they buy the book or not, but the key point was the media in New York, the media in Washington. They saw. They saw that huge advertisement and you didn't have to call them and explain to them what you were talking about, they knew it, they had all seen it. I also bought spreads in the *Publishers Weekly* [the trade magazine of US publishing], so everybody in the business would know.

'My key market, target market, where work was needed, was always the United States, never England. I hired PR firms in England, but I never got into the advertising. I only did it in the United States because you've got three hundred million people to collar there.'

As Bob was only too aware, everything follows on from the American market. First publication in hardcover was by Doubleday in 1979. There was so much noise that paperback publishers were alerted to the possibility of offering to publish in that format, and foreign publishers took the trade magazine *Publishers Weekly* and saw the spreads Bob had placed. He was doing the bedrock business, from which everything, even interest from the movie industry, would flow. And as one by one people picked up on this interest and made offers for rights in their territories and markets, the whole thing began to snowball. He knew what would happen and never doubted for one moment that the product could carry the interest forward.

'I didn't know it was going to be a bestseller; in the US nobody knew,' he said to me. 'In fact, the hardback only sold 55,000 copies, but 55,000 copies in 1979 was a damn good shot for a hardback book when you are unknown.'

Separately, I asked Barbara what she remembered about the book's first publication. 'In hardcover there was a rush for the book in some of the big cities like New York and Florida, and in Texas and California where I went to promote it in person. Surprisingly, for not a lot of money being spent by the publisher, it did get to the middle of the bestseller list, about number five or six, and did very well for a first novel with very little money spent either on advertising or promotion. They did do an ad, which was very clever. The person who did it actually ran all the Doubleday stores because in those days Doubleday had bookstores of their own, and he was so convinced it was going to be a huge bestseller that he did this ad saying that if you don't like this book we guarantee your money back. They had no returns on it. I remember going to one bookstore in Atlanta and the buyer said to me, "No matter what Doubleday do, they'll never stop this book, it'll go through the roof." It did well, and then it was bought for paperback by Avon.'

Avon was Bob and Barbara's prize for all the hard work. With the paperback publisher's interest came another Bob into Barbara's life, a man I knew well at the time and was making serious waves in the business. 'Bob Wyatt discovered the book;' Barbara said. 'He was the one who bought it for Avon from Doubleday for quite a lot of money in those days,' she remembers. 'They paid about $400,000 for paperback rights. It's not a lot today, but in those days it was. He discovered the book; the book somehow came to his desk, they bought it and he did a very clever commercial for television where they had an actress dressed up as Emma, as a little maid, with a white apron and a frilly cap. I remember the commercial very well because first of all it was a very gloomy moorland setting and then it became a village street with cobblestones and the sound of horses, and a carriage and horse going down. Then suddenly it cut to this – well, actually to the inside of a grand room and a young girl carrying a tray piled up with a silver pot and all that. Then it flashed some other actors' faces and there was a voiceover which said: "A great family saga in the grand tradition. The story of the servant girl who became a world power..." or whatever it was. So, it was Bob Wyatt and whoever he worked with who made the book – he remained my friend for years. When the book came out it quickly went up to Number One on the paperback list and it stayed on the list for more than a year. Everybody talked about it staying there so long, it just never went off the list. It sold three and a half million copies in that first year in paperback. That edition came out in the summer of 1980 and it came out in England in hardcover at that time, too.'

The ball was rolling. In 1985, with publication of *Hold the Dream*, Barbara's third novel, her English publishers were boasting that '*A Woman of Substance* has been in the top twenty listings since its publication'. [27]

Bob Wyatt remembers the Avon TV advertisement as 'a first for fiction at least,' but he was wary of taking too much of the credit for spotting the book's potential. 'Page Cuddy was also important to *Woman of Substance*. She was maybe the first reader on it,' he said. 'And that whole women's fiction thing was Nancy Coffey's at Avon. She invented it.'

Avon, through the 1970s and early '80s, had been enacting a publishing revolution, putting out romantic historical novels with explicit sex scenes known in the book trade as 'bodice-rippers'. Authors such as Kathleen Woodiwiss, whose first novel, *The Flame and the Flower*, they published in 1972, and Rosemary Rogers (*Sweet Savage Love*, 1974) were sweeping the market with sales in the millions.

These authors had a huge impact on the marketing of women's fiction in paperback form in both America and England, where they were marketed by a company called Futura, founded in 1973 and taken into Robert Maxwell's BPCC nine years later. Hitherto, the big-selling fiction titles on a paperback publisher's list had been bought in rights deals from hardcover publishers. Paperback publication had relied on publicity generated by the hardcover a year earlier. But now paperbackers were publishing their own original lead titles and had learned how to market and promote them in far more bullish fashion than any hardbacker.

Particular attention was paid to the cover artwork. Bob Wyatt remembers how Coffey gave the Woodiwiss bandwagon its initial momentum with a 'certain look, a very specific, hand-drawn typeface which became the standard for the industry. No one had done things like this until then. After the soft Woodiwiss books came Rosemary Rogers, and another entire look and feel was established for that writer.'

A Woman of Substance was no more akin to *The Flame and the Flower* or *Sweet Savage Love* than was Maeve Binchy's *Light a Penny Candle*, the first novel by another soon to be huge bestselling name, first published in England in 1982. But both Maeve Binchy and Barbara benefited from the powerful marketing techniques that had been developed in paperback publishing with the bodice-rippers. Maeve was marketed by the paperback publisher of Woodiwiss and Rogers in England,

and Avon would not have had the sophisticated conceptual reach via cover artwork and TV advertising for *A Woman of Substance* had they not built up to it with these precedents.

Far from a bodice-ripper, *A Woman of Substance* 'was looked on [in the publishing industry] as a saga,' Barbara remembers. 'It was the first time anybody had written a *matriarchal* dynastic saga.' It was deemed a new twist on a respected genre that had been enjoying a resurgence of interest. The family saga had been popular since the 1920s. John Galsworthy's *The Forsyte Saga* was first published in 1922, the second part of the family chronicles, *A Modern Comedy*, followed in 1929, and, in 1931, a further collection appeared called *On Forsyte Change*. Galsworthy established the Edwardian family saga as a genre of its own and had many imitators. In the 1960s an English television production, *The Forsyte Saga*, became such popular Sunday night viewing that vicars changed the time of Evensong to accommodate it. It also swept across North America.

The Edwardian era was very much in vogue for another reason, too. *The Country Diary of an Edwardian Lady*, a naturalist's diary for the year 1906, found first publication in 1977. It remained at No. 1 on *The Sunday Times* bestseller list for an unprecedented sixty-four weeks, and, again, was similarly popular in America. Then, in 1978, *Dallas*, the family saga of the oil-rich Ewing family, started life as a five-part TV miniseries and ran for thirteen seasons. Small surprise, therefore, that the two biggest audience hooks in Avon's TV advertisement for *A Woman of Substance* were 'saga' and 'Edwardian'. The Yorkshire tag was not forgotten either, a draw in America, where in 1972 Tom McCormack of St. Martin's Press, famously an anglophile and later a publisher of Barbara, had begun a massively successful American publishing programme for James Herriot.

But while the roots of Barbara's woman of substance are in the upstairs-downstairs Edwardian era, Emma Harte is a woman of our times. The opportunities of which she avails herself are those made available to many as working-class exploitation was eased by socialism and socialism in turn gave way to meritocracy with an emphasis on the individual –

self-respect, self-belief, autonomy and self-sufficiency – the coming values at the very moment that the book was published and Margaret Thatcher, who had risen from the lower middle classes to become Britain's first female Prime Minister, arrived at No. 10 Downing Street.

Barbara's novels, which encourage women to believe they can conquer the world, whatever their class or background and despite the fact that they are operating in a man's domain, tapped into the aspirational energy of this era and served to expedite social change. Indeed, it might be said that Barbara Taylor Bradford would have invented Margaret Thatcher if she had not already existed. When they met, there was a memorable double take of where ambition had led them. 'I was invited to a reception at No. 10,' Barbara recalls. 'I saw a picture of Churchill in the hall outside the reception room and slipped out to look at it. Mrs Thatcher followed me out and asked if I was all right. I just said: "I never thought a girl from Yorkshire like me would be standing here at the invitation of the Prime Minister looking at a portrait of Churchill inside 10 Downing Street," and Mrs Thatcher whispered: "I know what you mean."'

Emma Harte, woman of substance, was in the vanguard of this great change and we see clearly in her character what will be required to survive and prosper in the modern world. It is what helped make Emma so popular and inspiring. In interview in the early 1980s, Barbara said: 'I hadn't realised how much people find Emma's story inspirational. I've had almost 2,000 letters. Many of them said, "Emma Harte has been an inspiration to us – we lead this kind of life, very tragic, very difficult, and if Emma can get through it, we can." The strange thing is that they spoke of her as if she is a living person.'

In later novels, such as *Voice of the Heart* and *The Women in His Life*, there is a keener focus on the psychological downside which attached to having it all, uprooting and rising in the modern world. Weighing anchor altogether may leave you bereft of a sense that there is anything beyond the projects you're working on so obsessively in your effort to get somewhere. The projects become you. Once again, Barbara could write about it because she understood the problem: 'These characters couldn't have been created without my own development,' she has said.

She resolves her characters' trauma by a return to their roots, but the return is no retreat – Barbara doesn't see herself as Yorkshire, any more than she sees herself as American. Her life has taken her out of belonging to any one culture. Hers is the emotional circle she believes we all need to make, to live and be loved, to break free and grow to a position of autonomy and independence from which we can assess independently, use and not be used by the values on which we were bred and which formed us.

So, in the first major project in her life, everything was falling into place. What had seemed good from Doubleday, now seemed fantastic from Avon, but it was still only the start. Between 1984 and 1999, Bob set up no fewer than ten TV miniseries based on Barbara's books, producing nine of them himself (*Hold the Dream* (1986), *Voice of the Heart* (1989), *Act of Will* (1989), *To Be the Best* (1992), *Remember* (1993), *Everything to Gain* (1996), *Love in Another Town* (1997), *Her Own Rules* (1998) and *A Secret Affair* (1999). The impact of such television exposure – six hours in the case of *A Woman of Substance* (1984)[32], starring Jenny Seagrove and Deborah Kerr – was astronomical in terms of book sales. But Bob was not simply building sales of books any more. He was creating a brand. [28]

Very wisely he kept out of the first film, retaining only approvals of locations, stars and script on Barbara's behalf: 'I didn't want to be the one to produce *Woman of Substance* as it was her first book. Since it contained so much of her Yorkshire childhood and youth, she was very emotionally attached to it, so I backed off making the mini-series, believing we would have terrible arguments as she was so emotionally involved. I flew over six or seven times while the series was being made in England and watched at arm's length. There wasn't a great deal

---

[32] Distributed in 2012 as *The Woman of Substance Trilogy* with *Hold the Dream* and *To Be the Best.*

of financial experience on the part of the producer, and there was another company, a British company, involved. So when I stepped in they had somebody to talk to about business. We were able to pull it together. I gathered some money and we pulled it together and got out.

'And, yes, the film promoted the book. There was a line-up of about 165 independent stations in the United States who locked together as a network for two nights. Very unusual. The independent station in New York was WPX; in Chicago it was The Tribune. 165 stations, it was enormous. They were all independent programming, but they locked into CBS, ABC, whatever, to show *A Woman of Substance*! Very unusual. We were going against the networks!'

Both he and Barbara became more closely involved in *Hold the Dream*. It again starred Jenny Seagrove (this time as Paula Amory, Emma's granddaughter), Stephen Collins as Shane O'Neill and Deborah Kerr as the ageing Emma Harte. 'Barbara had just finished the book, *Act of Will*, when I flew her into London and talked her into writing the script for *HTD*,' Bob said. 'Four writers had not been able to give me the screenplay I wanted. I was in trouble. Barbara had her mind still full of *Act of Will* and practically had to start writing *HTD* again. It was unbelievable. I've known a lot of writers, seen some of the great ones in Hollywood. She'd never set foot in a studio in her life, at least not to work in. She'd never written a script. I put her in a studio – Shepperton – locked up in a room with a script typist. Her routine was 6.30 a.m. to 9 p.m., seven days a week for six weeks. We were already in production. I had over one hundred people waiting to get a script, a proper script. The typist who I had for her, who was typing the script, waiting for dictation, she said, "I think, Barbara, we've got to start doing something here. You can't just sit there and think! We have to start somewhere, so what's the location, where are we, where do we start?" Barbara says, "We are in Yorkshire. Outside scene, country." The secretary says, "Who's talking to whom?" That's the way the script was written. It turned out to be a brilliant mini-series. And Barbara was amazing.

'She did it twice – she did it with *Hold the Dream* and *Voice of the Heart*.' The latter starred Lindsay Wagner, James Brolin, Victoria Tennant and Honor Blackman. The film of *Act of Will* (Liz Hurley, Victoria Tennant, Peter Coyote), Barbara recalls as more madness: 'Bob had a line producer at that point called Aida Young, and together they got a script of *Act of Will* developed, but for some reason he suddenly found himself with two mini-series going – he was doing *To Be the Best* (with Lindsay Wagner, Anthony Hopkins, Stephanie Beacham, Christopher Cazenove and Fiona Fullerton) at that time, and had to go to Hong Kong to shoot it. Naturally, Yorkshire Television didn't want to do *Act Of Will* – God knows why, I've never been lucky with Yorkshire Television – so he let it go to Tyne Tees Television.

'He is extraordinary. He not only makes the movies of my books but he manages my career... Bob's the one who deals with the publishers on a day-to-day basis. My only sadness is that he's never been able to get a TV deal for *The Women in His Life*, which is my own favourite novel among those I have written. He's got a script that's fantastic, and they say "No", and so he doesn't even bother to show it any more. "Oh, but it's not going to work, it's a little boy and what actor wants only part of a role," etc., etc.'

Following the original deal with Doubleday for *A Woman of Substance* and shortly afterwards for *Voice of the Heart*, and their subsidiary paperback deals with Avon, a contract was drawn up in April 1983 for $8 million with Barbara's three English-language publishers – Doubleday, Avon and William Collins (UK) – for three new books, which would be *Hold the Dream*, *Act of Will* and *To Be the Best*.

Three years later, with *To Be the Best* not yet published under this contract, another three-book deal with leading US publisher Random House was signed for £6 million, which Bob recalls was a deal Mort Janklow (at that time the world's most successful agent and an influential part of the team) put together. This covered US rights for *The Women in His Life*, *Remember* and *Angel*.

Then came the big one. In 1989 Rupert Murdoch decided to take over Collins in London and publishers Harper & Row in New York, and turned the whole thing into Harper Collins, as already mentioned. An executive called George Craig, who had been William Collins' chief accountant in London, went over to New York to run the new Harper Collins company there as Chairman of the Board. Three years later, in 1992, Barbara made a move from Random House to the US side of Harper Collins, the sister company of her London publisher. The idea was that she would have one English-language publisher with a massive, cohesive, worldwide marketing effort.

The move caused quite a stir for a number of reasons. Ex-*Sunday Times* editor the late Harold Evans, husband of Tina Brown of *Vanity Fair*, was head of Random House when all this was going on, and he was not best pleased. Dialogue reported in the press showed that Evans was having to swallow the bitter pill that his old boss at the *Sunday Times*, Rupert Murdoch, was taking his author. The real story, as far as Barbara was concerned, was never told, however, and makes more fascinating reading. Naturally, Bob was in the middle of it.

'The new contract with George Craig. That was a historic event, that contract,' Bob began. I said I had a report to the effect that in 1992 a contract was drawn for £17 million between Barbara and HarperCollins. I wish you could hear it told by Bob himself, with his twinkling eyes and quietly spoken, highly persuasive German-American accent.

'There was a contract. First of all it wasn't in pounds, it was in dollars, and I will tell you exactly the way this happened; it's a very interesting story. I had made a picture called *Voice of the Heart* and I showed the picture to George Craig. I said, "Look, I want you to see it. I want you to see all the things I'm doing." He'd seen *A Woman of Substance* and *Hold the Dream*. So George said, "Bob, this is a terrific series, really great, looks fabulous."

'I said, "Well, actually I have a favour to ask you," and he said, "Well, what's the favour?'

"The favour is I want to sell this series to Fox Studios [in Los Angeles]."

"What do you want me to do? What exactly are you thinking?"

'I said, "I think this series is going to be terrific for Barbara's books and I want to sell the series to Fox Television because you are both part of [Rupert Murdoch's] News Corp, so it's a natural."

'He said, "What did you have in mind?"

'I said, "If I can be quite honest with you, I would like Rupert Murdoch to see this film …" And he said, "Look, the man is flying all over the world and he never looks at films…"

'Anyway, here's what happened. I got a call two weeks later when we'd just finished editing the film (George had seen the rough cuts). It was just finished. I get a call from George. He says, "What are you doing today? You're not going out of town?" I said, "No, I'm here." He said: "You've got an appointment with Rupert Murdoch at 5 p.m. today. Hire a private studio and get the film over there. He wants to see the film at 5 p.m. sharp."

'I almost fell over. So, I was suddenly scrambling, getting a copy of the film, hiring the studios… At one minute to five, in walks Rupert Murdoch with his wife, Anna. I couldn't believe it. We sit in the theatre and I just explained to him a little bit about the history of how I made the film and he looked at me and said, "Where's Barbara?" I said, "Well, she's home writing, she's working." He said, "I'm not seeing the film unless Barbara comes here, I want her in this room." So I had to call Barbara at home. I spoke to her. I said to her, "I don't give a damn whether you are in blue jeans or a sweater, you must come, we are not running this film until you get here." So Barbara scrambled to get dressed in a hurry and came over. She arrived and we sat in that screening room for three hours. Three hours and thirty minutes – it's a four-hour miniseries with the commercials. I'd made it in thirty-five mm. I wanted the quality of the best motion-picture you can get. So I showed this in thirty-five mm to Rupert Murdoch. It was just unbelievable in this room on the big screen, and he sat there enthralled.

'After we'd finished, he just said, "*Amazing* piece of film, fantastic, I love it." So then he said, "I am taking you to dinner." It's a good thing Barbara had changed. "I'm taking you to Le Cirque." It was unbelievable, we walked in. Champagne. He stayed there till about eleven … eleven thirty, with Anna.

'I didn't discuss the next move with him, I was careful. The next day George called me and said, "We are flying to the west coast, I'm flying with you. I've arranged a meeting, I think you've got two or three days to get it organised and I have the studio organised. A meeting with Fox, with the whole group at Fox. Without Rupert, but with all the heads of departments. George had called the head guy and talked to him and he said, "You want me to look at this film? What do you think, I've got nothing else to do? I don't look at my own films here in the studio. I give them three minutes, ten minutes, and you want me to look at the whole thing with you? You're crazy." George said, "Well the big boss asked me to call and he wants you to look at it because I think it's something we want to talk you about – putting it on the Fox network."

'George wouldn't let me go by myself,' Bob continued. 'We arrived at Fox and there are fifteen, twenty guys in the conference room, every head of department showed up. At the meeting there was a lot of conversation. Yes, we're going to like this, yes we're going to do this. But, to make a long story short, nothing happened. Later, much later, they turned down the film. Finally, they said, "Well, it's a woman's programme, our network is a new network [which it was at the time], and we are looking to attract a young male crowd. Anyway, they didn't turn it down that day and George and I flew back to New York together, and that is where history was made."'

'We were sitting together having drinks. We were friends, we were talking publishing, pictures and publishing – what he was going to do with the company, all his plans. And then George said to me, "What's with our contract with Barbara? Since we're talking business, what's with the contract?" At the time our contract must have been very close to expiration. I said, "Well, George, frankly I haven't figured out all the things but I think Barbara is entitled to get more money. He asked me my opinion on a lot of things. I said, "Primarily I want to make a deal that equals her talent and what she's going to contribute to the company. You know, she wears the uniform of Harper Collins, she's totally Harper Collins, and I think it needs to be given consideration." So he said, "Look ..." He took out his pen and started to write on a paper napkin, and said, "All right, let's work." So, we started doing the figures and he made all kinds of calculations – and George was a good calculator, he's an accountant by trade – we started working figures on a napkin, and we made our contract right there. It was for $24 million, the biggest contract ever written in the history of publishing at that time. The contract was initialled by me. I think Barbara has the napkin. That was our deal. England and America, English-language rights, but not foreign language. Right there on the plane, on the napkin. Mort [Janklow] knew nothing about it, and certainly he was startled when he heard about it.

'From then on there were all kinds of rumours, resentment and jealousy; nothing directed at Barbara, because they all loved Barbara. They said, "this guy Bradford, he's a killer", and the publishers were apprehensive with me. Marketing guys said, "If this guy comes up we are going to be in trouble." Which wasn't the point. My job is only to protect Barbara and to promote her career.'

Clearly, good management and marketing have helped to make her books big bestsellers. Unusually, if not uniquely among novelists, her name is synonymous with the character she created. When she stands up in public she *is* the woman of substance.

Ever since the phenomenal success of her first novel, estimates of Barbara's wealth have been a significant element in Bob's razzmatazz *Woman of Substance* brand strategy, with a warm-hearted acceptance of it by the media. In 2020, the *Sunday Times* Rich List[33] placed her 757th in the world with a worth of £162 million. How accurate the list is there is no easy way of assessing. The question of her wealth is not one I would put to Barbara, and I have never seen her exercised by the validity of estimates bandied about in the press, one way or the other, except to say: 'Money is only important when you're truly poor, when you need it for a roof over your head, for food and clothes. Once you have these essentials taken care of and go beyond them, it is simply a unit, a tool to work with.' Perhaps, then, the true zenith of Bob's strategy was not money at all but

---

[33] Published annually in April.

being summoned to Buckingham Palace by Her Majesty the Queen to receive the OBE for services to literature. Certainly it was a highly appreciated accolade of Barbara's exceptional drive and ambition.

Of the investiture and meeting the Queen, Barbara said: 'She was really rather disarming, warm, sweet and with a lovely smile. She said: "I know you've written a lot of books." I said, "Yes, Your Majesty, mostly about England and British history."

'"Oh well," she said, "you've got a lot of opportunity there."'

CHAPTER THIRTEEN
Hold the Dream

'You will never die, Emma. We are both going to live for ever and ever, here at the Top of the World.'

Edwin Fairley in *A Woman of Substance*

'I'd take a bullet for Bob because I love him more than I love myself,' Barbara reflected a few years ago. Bob, for his part, said simply: 'She's everything... My relationship with her hasn't changed, other than that I now devote all my time to her. I don't like to let her out of my sight. She gives me all I need just by being with me. Her presence is so important to me, I don't think I'd do so good, or feel so well, without her. She's everything. And I pray to God I die first so I don't have to go on living without her."

On July 2, 2019, Bob had his wish. None of us knew his true age. He was active in the office until almost the end. Had it been otherwise, the news of his passing might have been less of a shock. Although looking back, the signs had been there.

On November 7, 2017, Bob and Barbara arrived in London, staying in their suite at the Dorchester Hotel in Park Lane, as they always did. The plan was to rest for several days before beginning a full-on promotional tour. Barbara had written to me about an evening event booked in York, to be held at the famous St Peter's School, founded in the 7th century and numbering Guy Fawkes among its alumni. I suggested I meet her at the station and settle her before the event. But it never happened. Bob had a fall in Knightsbridge and she had to cancel. They made it back to New York eventually. Barbara had been shaken by the episode and possibly by its portent.

Even so, what she had managed to complete of the tour had been successful, particularly in interview with Piers Morgan on ITV's 'Good Morning Britain', where the badinage had been warm after someone mentioned her 1969 trio of books about how to be the perfect wife and Barbara responded that the key to fifty-four years of marriage was her willingness to pick up her husband's socks. Dismayed, Morgan's co-host, Susanna Reid, revealed that a GMB poll showed that seventy-five per cent of their female viewers wouldn't dream of picking up after their partners. Barbara refused to believe it and, much to Susanna's chagrin, Morgan agreed with her. The poll clearly demonstrated, Morgan said, that 'only twenty-five per cent of women know how to behave in a marriage.' It was a fun interview which underlined that there's nothing woke about this writer: 'The novels do not tell women *what* to believe, only to know themselves,' she emphasises. 'Everyone has their own style. Know who and what you are and harness that to your purpose.'

After their return to New York, life settled down once more until at some point in the Spring of 2019 my wife took a phone call from Barbara. Bob had had another accident. In the kitchen of their apartment he had leant across the hob and the sleeve of his dressing gown had caught fire. He had suffered serious burns and been rushed to hospital. Barbara had insisted on staying there with him. Initially the hospital had advised against it and only agreed after she refused to leave. They made up a bed beside him. She remained there for days until he was well enough to go home.

And so we come to one evening in the last week of June. Bob had been complaining of a pain in his hand and had taken to bed early. In the morning Barbara had been unable to wake him. He was rushed to hospital where a stroke was diagnosed. Unable to speak, he remained there for six days, regaining consciousness only briefly once. With his eyes open, he was able to squeeze Barbara's hand to signal that he knew she was there. It was the last communication between them.

Barbara was devastated. They had been together for fifty-seven years and married for fifty-five. Her PR, Maria Boyle, flew to New York to assist as the funeral approached, in particular to manage the press, who besieged her. Barbara would now have to cope with all the things that Bob usually dealt with, including the press: the office had to be closed, employees looked after, publishers, accountants and finance people briefed.

There had been some divesting of material effects even before this upsetting sequence of events. In 2013, forty pieces of jewellery, estimated to be worth £1.5 million, were put up for sale at Bonhams, in New Bond Street, London. Each jewel had been given to Barbara by Bob to commemorate a birthday, an anniversary, a finished novel or simply as a surprise: 'Bob says he doesn't need an occasion to give me a piece of jewellery, only a reason,' she said. Then, in 2014, she and Bob had sold their apartment at River House to the actress Uma Thurman for a reported $10 million, moving to Park Avenue, which was in a way a return home. She and Bob had lived on the Upper East Side when they were first married... Then, in December 2019, there was another sale by Bonhams of more jewellery. Notable pieces from the world's most famous houses, including Verdura, Tiffany and David Morris and watchmakers Rolex, Patek Philippe and Omega.

For the first time she was steering the ship on her own. Throughout it all, she kept her nerve, confiding in a journalist friend what it had taken to do so. A four-page interview with Celia Walden appeared in the *Telegraph Magazine* in November and Barbara made it clear that losing Bob remained 'almost unbearable'.

She knew right at the start there would be only one way out. Even while she was with Bob in hospital she had adjusted her immediate publishing strategy, deciding to delay writing the third book in the Falconer series[34], which would involve her in a great deal of on-the-ground research, and to write instead a prequel to *A Woman of Substance*, which she'd been thinking about for some time. Suddenly, she was back in the time of Edith Walker...

Barbara had so managed her affairs following the death of her husband that this year (2020) she has been able to slip back into the welcome rhythm of a writer's routine, which for her hasn't

---

[34] The House of Falconer Series at this point included *Master of His Fate* (2018) and *In the Lion's Den* (2020).

altered since the first book appeared. There would be no need to travel from home again until the following year, when the new fruits of her labours would be ready to be published. As she said: 'Work is the key, isn't it? That's what gets you through.'

Up to this point in Barbara's life, Freda and Bob had variously inspired and shepherded her talent and drive. Now both had gone, Freda thirty-eight years earlier. I was not surprised to learn that Bob had always been very tender with Freda. On the face of it, they cannot have had a great deal in common, but in their persona both evinced the central theme of lost identity in so many of Barbara's novels. We have seen it as the very drive behind Freda's extraordinary crusade, which set her daughter on the road to success as an author, and we have seen it in Bob, who, as a German Jew, was dispossessed of his identity as a child.

Just as Freda was all the time drawn back to Ripon in search of her lost world, so, in *The Women in His Life*, Barbara makes Maximilian West, the character who comes closest to Bob in the novels, go back to the places of his childhood loss, too: 'The lure of childhood, he thought, how strong it is with me … is it because I lost so much when I was a child … had such irretrievable losses? Do I come back to Paris and Berlin in the hopes of finding something which escaped me long, long ago?' His eternal quest is successfully completed. He comes to articulate the nature of his childhood loss and finds the something he did not know about himself, about his parents, about the love he thought he'd lost.

It is a theme that mirrors universally the sense of loss and alienation which modernity engenders in those who cut themselves off from their roots, the values of home. It is *the* theme of Barbara's own life, her return from Manhattan to her Yorkshire roots in the novels is, as I have shown, an affirmation of her identity. Childhood experience is time and again the key inspiration of writers and artists in general, and it is no different for Barbara.

Another thing that Freda and Bob had in common, of course, was their love for Barbara, and, coming as they did from this similar ground of loss, they surely drew something from her in recompense for it. Barbara, of course, was Freda's saviour.

She does not stint in heaping praise on her mother for the encouragement and love she gave her, but it is also true that she gave Freda a reason for living. Most significantly, Barbara was, in her very personality, an impressive expression of the very identity lost to her mother – her style, as I see it, an amalgam of the sparkle of Edith and the unequivocal self-confidence of a Ripon.

Is it also true to say that Barbara compensated for Bob's childhood loss? Certainly she came to root his work in her own strong Yorkshire culture. She gave him her novels, in which her heroes and heroines call upon her Yorkshire-rooted values to make their decisions and to make their judgements, to make into films. Bob, bereft of family and alienated from his home culture, will surely have benefited from the stability of so certain a cultural influence as this woman of substance.

I imagine the tender relationship between Bob and Freda as an unspoken, subliminal acknowledgement of what, below the line, they shared. In a sense, Freda Walker handed the baton of responsibility for Barbara's work to Robert Bradford. She died after publication of *A Woman of Substance* as if to announce that her job was done.

The midwife's feelings are never thought of in the joy of a mother's first birth, but Freda's part in this was both nurse and mother. The scope of her life took her from the Edwardian era into which she and the idea of the woman of substance were born, right through to the modern world in which people like Maxim West and Robert Bradford operate. Her feelings following her daughter's huge success are unimaginable, but one must believe that she had a few things to say quietly to the spirit of her mother, Edith Walker, the tide of whose ambition lies at the fount of all this.

'My parents died in 1981,' Barbara said. 'They were both alive to see *A Woman of Substance*. I remember after my father died in the October I said to Mummy that I wanted to bring her to New York, but she insisted on staying where she was. I suppose an old person doesn't want to be moved. She said, "Just do me a favour, go back and finish that book [*Voice of the Heart*], I want to read it." But she died before it came out, just five weeks after my father did. I think that she had decided she didn't want to live any more.

'The housekeeper rang me one day and said, "Your mother's really not well," and the doctors came and were going to put her in hospital. I said, "Can she come to the telephone?" And Brenda said, "Let me go and see if Rose and I can help her to come to the telephone." There was another lady there, a neighbour called Rose. I heard the phone go down – of course this is six o'clock in the morning in New York, six thirty because it was about eleven thirty in Yorkshire. They were ages and I'm then saying, "Hello?" and there isn't anybody there – and eventually Brenda came back, about five minutes later. She said, "I don't really know how to tell you this, Barbara, but your mam just died."

'I couldn't believe that she'd just died. I didn't want to believe she was dead at all. Then I thought she must have died earlier and that they had talked it out between themselves because they hadn't known how to tell me. I felt so helpless. Later I found out what they told me was true. Mummy had been sitting in the chair and she had smiled at Rose. Apparently Rose said, "It's me, Mrs Taylor," and my mother didn't answer her, but finally she looked at her and she smiled, and it was a very radiant smile and she had extremely blue eyes. Rose said, "If you could have seen your mother's eyes, they were shining." She told me this when I got to Leeds. Apparently Rose sat and held her hand and talked to her for a few minutes and Mummy looked at her and said, "God help me, please have God help me." Rose said, "He will if you're asking him." She smiled again and Rose said the eyes seemed bluer than ever, and she said, "She smiled at me a third time and her face was so radiant, I don't know what it was that she saw." And Brenda was there – this lady who'd looked after Mummy – and Brenda said, "Well, what she saw was Winston" – my father – "...she was happy when she died."'

Emily stared at Paula. Tremulously she said, 'I've always been afraid of death. But I'll never be afraid of it again. I'll never forget Grandy's face, the way it looked as she was dying. It was filled with such radiance, such luminosity, and her eyes were brimming with happiness. Whatever it was our grandmother saw, it was something beautiful, Paula.'

Hold the Dream

The very paradox of her mother Freda's personality, shy, withdrawn, self-effacing and yet so single-minded and persistent in facilitating her daughter's rise, had been explained and understood now by Barbara. The secrets on which her childhood were constructed, 'layered one on top of the other … hidden so much that it was difficult to unearth it all until now', were out. Now Barbara could clearly define her part in the narrative of her life and the lives of those closest to her, and she told me that after the next novel the stage is set for her autobiography. [29]

Novels by

Barbara Taylor Bradford

The Emma Harte Saga
A Woman of Substance (1979)
Hold the Dream (1985)
To Be the Best (1988)
Emma's Secret (2003)
Unexpected Blessings (2005)
Just Rewards (2005)
Breaking the Rules (2009)

The Ravenscar Trilogy
The Ravenscar Dynasty (2006)
The Heir of Ravenscar (2007)
Being Elizabeth (2008)

The Cavendon Chronicles
Cavendon Hall (2014)
The Cavendon Women (2015)
The Cavendon Luck (2016)
Secrets of Cavendon (2017)

The House of Falconer Series
Master of His Fate (2018)
In the Lion's Den (2020)

Other Fiction
Act of Will (1986)
The Women in His Life (1990)
Remember (1991)
Angel (1993)
Voice of the Heart (1983)
Everything to Gain (1994)
Dangerous to Know (1995)
Love in Another Town (1995)

Her Own Rules (**1996**)
A Secret Affair (**1996**)
Power of a Woman (**1997**)
A Sudden Change of Heart (**1999**)
Where You Belong (**2000**)
The Triumph of Katie Byrne (**2001**)
Three Weeks in Paris (**2002**)
Playing the Game (**2010**)
Letter From a Stranger (**2011**)
Secrets From the Past (**2013**)
Hidden (e-book novella) (**2013**)
Treacherous (e-book novella) (**2014**)
Who Are You? (e-book novella) (**2016**)
Damaged (e-book novella) (**2018**)

Acknowledgements

Principally I would like to thank Barbara Taylor Bradford for her friendship and generous contribution to this book; also Amanda Ridout for commissioning the idea in the first place and Barbara's editor in the UK, the late Patricia Parkin, for performing the requisite balancing act to see it through.

Among those who kindly agreed to be interviewed was of course Robert Bradford, whose warm and charismatic personality I hope comes across in this book. His passing in July 2019 was so very sad for all who knew him. I would also like to acknowledge Billie Figg as a key witness to the era in which Barbara's career as a journalist originally took flight, and to thank her for offering me some of her own early interviews with my subject, as well as many personal memories. My thanks are also due to her husband, Jack, whose gentle humour added a very welcome dimension to the book. I am also indebted to Doreen Armitage, Judy Blanchland, Mark Barty-King, Arthur Brittenden, Bobby Caplin, Margery Clarke, June Kettlelow, Roderick Mann, Shirley Martin, Frederic Mullally, Beryl Thompson, Vera Vaggs, Richard Whiteley and Bob Wyatt.

Once it became clear that the book would require as much detailed archival research as interview I fell into the hands of a number of professionals in institutions and libraries in the North of England, to whom I am very grateful. In particular I would like to thank Doris Johnson, whose scholarship in the science and incisive appraisal of material were not only useful, but taught me a great deal along the way.

I would also like to thank the following: *Architectural Digest*; Lonnie Ostrow; Chapel Allerton Hospital;

Mr B. C. Smith of the de Grey and Ripon Masonic Lodge; Mr P. Allen of the Morpeth Masonic Lodges; Granada Television; Guardian Newspapers; Leeds Library; Mike Yaunge and Ros Norris of the Ripon Local Studies Research Centre; Morpeth Library; Northallerton Library; Northallerton County Archives; Northumberland Record Office; Observer Newspapers; Adrian Munsey and Samanta Elliott of Odyssey Video; Probate Sub-registry: York; Public Record Office: Kew; Registrar: Leeds, York, Harrogate; Christine Holgate of Ripon Library; *Ripon Gazette*; Ripon Workhouse; Scarborough Library; West Yorkshire Archives (Sheepscar and Wakefield); Yorkshire Archaeological Society; Louise Male of the *Yorkshire Evening Post;* David Hartshorn at *Yorkshire Post* Archives; and Doreen Stanbury and Pat Smith for their typing.

There are, in addition, some crucial literary sources, works that I have acknowledged when quoting from them in the text: in particular, by Keith Waterhouse – *City Lights* and *Streets Ahead* (Hodder Headline, 1994 and 1995); Alan Bennett – *Telling Tales* (BBC Worldwide, 2000); Paul Murray Kendall – *Warwick the Kingmaker* (Allen & Unwin, 1957); Jack London – *The People of the Abyss* (Journeyman Press, 1977); Anthony Chadwick and Beryl Thompson – *Life in the Workhouse* series (Ripon Museum Trust, 2003); Jim Gott – *Bits & Blots of T'Owd Spot* (Crakehill Press, 1987); Judith Summers – *Soho* (Bloomsbury, 1989); and Daniel Farson – *Soho in the Fifties* (Pimlico, 1993). Other works which have informed my text include *Lancaster and York: The Wars of the Roses* by Alison Weir (Pimlico, 1998), *Oliver Twist* by Charles Dickens (Penguin Classics, 1966 etc.), *Wuthering Heights* by Emily Bronte (Penguin Classics, 1965 etc.), *Backing Into the Limelight: The Biography of Alan Bennett* by Alexander Games (Headline, 2002), *Empty Cradles* by Margaret Humphreys (Doubleday, 1994) and *Neither Waif Nor Stray: The Search for a Stolen Identity* by Perry Snow (Universal, 2000).

For picture sources I would like to acknowledge the Bradford Photographic Archive, Cris Alexander, Ralph Crocker, Ripon Library, Ripon Workhouse, Dorothy Thelwall,

Leeds Library, Yorkshire Tourist Board, Skyscan Balloon Photography, English Heritage, Lord Lichfield, the *Yorkshire Post*, Columbia Pictures and Odyssey Video.

While every effort has been made to trace copyright sources, the author would be grateful to hear from any unacknowledged ones.

Photographs

Above: St Mary's Hospital where Barbara was born. Below: Armley's rows of terraced housing, where her father's family lived.

Left: Barbara, 'ironed from top to toe' at 3. Above: Her parents Winston and Freda.

Tower Lane, where as a little girl her imagination took flight.

*Barbara's school
and Christ Church
opposite.*

The Towers seemed, to a child's eye, to reach to the sky.

No. 38, the end house of three, the humble home where Barbara first lived.

Above: Barbara's moorland playground and, below, her father Winston's local.

Top Withens, Barbara's introduction to the Brontës.

Ripon Minster and, below, the ancient Market Place.

The roofless halls and ghostly chambers of Middleham Castle.

Water Skellgate as Edith knew it in 1904. Below, Studley Royal Hall, where she dreamt her destiny lay.

Edith with the Diamond Star at her throat, and as detailed below.

Freda's birthplace, that court of dwellings off Water Skellgate.

The Marquess who, by all accounts, pursued his pleasures above his duties.

The forbidding gates of the Grubber, through which seven of Barbara's family passed.

No. 5 Greenock Terrace (far right), to which Barbara moved during the War.

The Yorkshire Post offices where Barbara worked from 15. Below: Willis Hall and Keith Waterhouse, who became her 'hand-holder-in-chief'.

Bob and Barbara were married in London on Christmas Eve, 1963.

Robert Bradford was a tough negotiator, but what he wanted was now what Barbara wanted.

With publication of The Woman of Substance, Barbara's personal wealth soared beyond her wildest dreams.

Jenny Seagrove playing Emma Harte, the woman of substance that Barbara became.

Liam Neeson playing Blackie O'Neill, whose back-story is the subject of Barbara's next novel.

Made in the USA
Middletown, DE
13 October 2021

50227562R00156